MAKING A MARINE
In the 21st Century

MAKING A MARINE
In the 21st Century

Published in collaboration with
Fortitude Graphic Design and Printing and Season Press
Cover and book design by Sean Hollins

For information regarding this book, bulk discounts or speaking engagements please contact Matthew R. Cooper at mattcooper@scsck.com or visit: www.scrafoundation.org

Making a Marine in the 21st Century
is the true letter-writing journey of a father's commitment to help his son stay strong and keep the faith through training at Marine Corps Recruit Depot San Diego, California (MCRD SD)/

Cooper, Drew and Cooper, Matthew- Non-fiction
p.cm

1. Marines-San Diego 2. Recruit-training
3. Memoir-letters

Library of Congress Control Number:
2017945955
ISBN 978-0-9991334-2-2

Printed in the United States of America
FIRST EDITION
10 9 8 7 6 5 4 3 2 1

*To the United States Marine Corps
and all of our Marines.
Semper Fi*

"Old Breed? New Breed? There's not a damn bit of difference so long as it's the Marine Breed."

*Most decorated Marine in American History:
Lt. Gen. Lewis Burwell "Chesty" Puller*

Table of Contents

FOREWORD

I was very honored when Matt asked me to write a few words about his new book. The book is about a family and their son's time as he goes through Marine Boot Camp at Marine Recruit Depot San Diego.

About fifty years ago I was at that same point in my life. I graduated from high school and was about to start college. My high school experience was not good as I changed schools four times in three years. My stepfather was in the space industry and moved with the Apollo Project many times. I was not a very good student and as I started college I knew it wasn't for me. Things in my life were not going well. Vietnam was starting to escalate and I thought about joining the Military Service. I wanted the best so I enlisted in the US Marine Corps without talking to my parents first. When I finally approached them, my mother was beside herself and I could tell that my stepfather was kind of proud that I made this decision. He was a Captain in the Army Tank Corp in WWII.

As time quickly approached, when I was to report for duty, I really had no idea what was ahead of me. At that time all of the services were gearing up for Vietnam. The draft was in effect and lots of young men were being forced to join. I didn't have as much bond with my recruiter as Drew did.

The day I reported to the bus terminal in Los Angeles, California, my stepdad took me. My mother was still having a lot of problems with my enlistment and chose to stay home.

My ride to MCRD San Diego was a short ride down the coast passing many of the beaches I surfed at just months before. When we arrived at MCRD my drill instructor greeted us yelling and putting the fear of God into me. What had I gotten into? Matt's book brought back many memories of boot camp that I locked away many years ago. Fifty years before Drew's experience, I was there. And his experiences were just like mine. The technology has changed, but the training and structure were the same.

I started boot camp not prepared for what was ahead of me. I was not very physically fit. They were about to change that. Not a minute to ourselves and constant yelling and orders. Not until then did I realize what they were trying to do. It was the purpose of boot camp to break you down and build you into a person that could take orders and fear nothing. Some had a lot of problems with that, I didn't. I focused on learning all I could and staying out of trouble. As you read this book, all the things that Drew went through, so did I. Fifty years and things were much the same. I made it through boot camp and it really changed me. I was pretty smart at getting by and ended up doing office work in the platoon office. I sometimes saw a different side of my drill instructors that others didn't. When it was over, and it was time for graduation, I was in the Honor Platoon and named Honorman of the platoon. I had a chance to ask my DI (drill instructor), why me? He told me that with all the extra work helping other recruits pass exams and coming to boot camp only able to do two chin-ups, and leaving doing five, he said I was the obvious choice. This made me feel proud and I knew that I was becoming a Marine.

Graduation day came and my parents and brother were there without knowing I had been honored with the Honorman award. My stepdad was pretty proud, my mother was still pretty apprehensive and my brother just couldn't believe it. It was a proud day.

After boot camp things went by pretty fast and before I knew it I was in Vietnam. I thought back about MCRD and how that training helped me for what was to come in my two tours in combat. War is not the place for a 19-year-old with no real life experiences. My training and learning of how to exist in a war situation got me through a difficult time. I honored myself with a few awards, but none as precious as my Purple Hearts. Wounded in action and recovering made me feel that I truly had become a Marine.

I would like to thank Matt and Drew for this wonderful account of the full experience of Marine Boot Camp. It is great reading for Marines, recruits, families and anyone who wants to experience Marine Recruit Training.

Becoming a Marine changed my life forever. To this day I am proud to call myself a Marine and to know that I share my times with other members of the finest organization in the US Military Services. Semper Fi

Steve Haddad
Cpl Charlie Co.
1st Battalion 9th Marines
3rd Marine Division

PREFACE

When my boy, Drew, was 3 years old, he wanted to be just like me. He loved to wear a button up shirt and a fancy tie. Every day when I would come home from work, he would greet me at the door by jumping up into my arms with the nicest bear hug ever. He was my little bear cub. We lived Semper Fidelis–Latin for "Always Faithful."

He looks just like me. He has the same colic on the back of his head, the same teeth down to the exact tooth that is a baby tooth, never having an adult replacement. We have the same eye color and hooded eye-lids. He truly has become a very handsome specimen of a man. *OORAH!* The Marine Corps motivational statement in acknowledgment or agreement.

When he was 5 years old, the shirt and tie was replaced by camo. He would work days on end developing a series of fox holes down at our campsite. From the age of 5 to 10, his courage was undaunting. From jumping off the dock and snatching a swimming water snake, that all the while he was swimming back to shore, was wrapping its body around his arm and biting his thumb - to making incredibly accurate shots on whitetail deer that I would not even venture to attempt to shoot.

My baby boy was joining the United States Marine Corps. I just quite simply did not know what to do.

Drew has an older sister, Anella and a younger brother, Bennett. His mother, Laurie and I, have been married since 1987 and the two of us set out to have a happy family. We bought a small farm in Southwest Michigan in a town called Paw Paw. It is the ideal setting of vineyards and apple trees. Our property has a hidden pond out back. We were constantly hiking, exploring and hunting everything from deer, ducks, rabbit, geese, turkey and grouse. Drew's mother, Laurie, for the most part, was a stay at home mom, keeping her nursing license active working on some nights and weekends as a registered nurse.

When Drew joined the Marine Corps, I had been a practicing attorney for twenty-seven years. Both Laurie and I were of the mind set that our children should grow up happy and become productive adults doing whatever vocation they found interesting and was something that they wanted to do through their adult lives. We have seen many parents push their children to follow in their footsteps. Be a nurse. Be an attorney. These are great vocations. However, we just were of the mind set that we wanted them to do what made them happy.

When Drew graduated from high school, his sister was in her third year at Western Michigan University. Anella was on track to working in higher education. After graduating high school, Drew enrolled and attended Western Michigan University for an entire academic year.

From all appearances, Drew seemed to be okay at WMU. He lived in dorms for the first academic year and had a job at the University Library and Building and Grounds Department. During home football games, he was able to perform various tasks such as lowering and raising the netting for field goals, or cleaning luxury suites after the game.

After living in the dorms for the first year, Drew decided to share an apartment in downtown Kalamazoo with a friend for the summer. Drew anticipated going back to WMU in the fall.

For whatever reason, that summer, Drew felt as though he was being an unproductive, floundering kid. Was he being mature beyond his years, wanting to be his own man, or was he being impatient with just knuckle down collegiate studies and knowing that it takes time to get an education. For whatever reason, Drew made the decision that he wanted to enter the military service.

Neither his mother nor I had the honor or privilege of serving our country through military service. Not serving, has always been a regret for me. I wish I would have had the opportunity to serve and am always jealous being around those that have served time in the military.

For whatever reason, the reason does not matter, Drew was going to join the service. He was determined to join the Marine Corps. He felt that if he was going to take that leap, he wanted to be part of the most highly esteemed branch of service–The Marines. I really do not understand and only later have been told that a Marine is at the level of the other branches elite groups–an Army Ranger or a Navy Seal, whether true or false, that too really does not matter.

Between working several odd jobs that summer, Drew moved back home with the determination that he was going to get into shape and join the Marine Corps. Throughout high school, Drew was always in good, physical condition. He regularly lifted weights and had no problem running. The year at college set him back a little and it wasn't until Christmas, 2015 that he moved back home and was determined to get back into shape and go to Marine Corps Recruit Training, the USMC version of boot camp. After signing papers, it was determined that Drew would leave 13 March 2016.

I can vividly remember and relive the sensation of my stomach dropping when Drew told me that he had signed papers and joined the Marines. As much as I admired him for making this decision, I could not help but be scared given the current status of world affairs.

I thoroughly enjoyed having Drew back home for Christmas and the following three months. I felt good knowing that he was safe. However, I knew that he needed to do what he wanted to do and that was to be his own man and ship out with the Marines.

In preparation for Drew's departure I read many books and researched the internet about what is required to become a Marine. I particularly enjoyed *Making The Corps* by Thomas E. Rix and *Keeping The Faith* by John and Frank Schaeffer. Both of these books reflect training at Parris Island, South Carolina.

The destination for Marine Recruit Training follows the

simple rule that if men live East of the Mississippi River they go to Parris Island, South Carolina (PI or MCRD PI). Those men living West of the Mississippi River go to the Marine Corps Recruit Depot in San Diego, California. (SD or MCRD SD). However, there is a little nuance to this basic rule that those in Southwest Michigan, Indiana and Illinois, which are East of the Mississippi, are included with those West of the Mississippi going to San Diego, California. Women recruits from anywhere in the country all go to Parris Island.

Most books are about Parris Island. I could not find any books specifically relating to what happens in San Diego. I was able to draw upon numerous friends relating the San Diego experience. A friend of mine dating back to my college days and working at Wickes Lumber Company was Matt Fasbender. Matt is a United States Marine. There is the saying that "once a Marine, always a Marine." Matt was active duty in the 1980's.

Just before Drew departed for San Diego, Matt's son, Alex, graduated from the Marine Corps program in San Diego. In addition, a friend of mine in Paw Paw, Michigan, Patrick Bauschke completed his service as a United States Marine around 10 years ago. He too graduated in San Diego, California. Another friend, Chuck Duncan, was a graduate of the Marine Corps Recruit Training in San Diego and also served for 16 years in the United States Army. Chuck, without hesitation declares that the proudest moment of his life was graduation day at MCRD.

Matt, Chuck and Patrick were very helpful. Chuck and Patrick met with Drew on several occasions before his departure. Chuck even came out to the farm, bringing his M-16 and allowed Drew to fire off several dozen rounds. This was a very exciting period for all of us. Chuck wished that he could go with Drew and work his way through recruit training once again.

Throughout December, January and February, Drew worked out regularly on his own, as well as in organized group activities with his recruiter, Sgt. John D. Butler in Kalamazoo, Michigan. He was prepared both physically and mentally to leave. Before his departure, he could physically pass the specific physical tests of strength that are necessary to pass recruit training.

13 March 2016 came too quickly for me. I was enjoying having Drew home. While I missed him while he was at WMU, I really did not think about it so much because I felt he was doing what he was supposed to be doing and could be reached at a moment's notice. It was a whole different feeling for me thinking that Drew was going to school, living in the dorms versus saying goodbye to him as he was off training with the Marine Corps.

His departure day fell on a Sunday. The day before we had a number of family members over for a brief visit and a pizza dinner. Sunday morning we slept in and had a casual morning visit. A few days before that, Drew, Bennett and I transported Anella to the Detroit airport for her long awaited travels around Europe. Anella was scheduled to travel through London, Scottland, Paris, Brussels and the Netherlands. On departure day that Sunday morning, it was just Laurie, Drew, Bennett and I. We had a laid back and leisurely morning. We planned to take Drew to the recruiters office in Kalamazoo by 11:30 a.m. that day.

It was a cold, rainy and dreary morning. I did not want to just get to the recruiter station and give Drew a big bear hug and start crying. It was my intention for the previous two weeks to some time grab a moment with him and give him a big long hug, a kiss on the cheek and, at that time, verbalize my emotions of how much he means to me and how much I love him.

A few days prior, when Drew, Bennett and I took Anella to Detroit, the four of us stopped for lunch before taking her to the airport. After our meal, and in the parking lot, I told the boys that we needed to say goodbye to Anella there as the curbside drop off at the Detroit Airport would be very hectic and busy. In the parking lot, we all gave Anella a big hug and a kiss and told her how much we loved her. When we got to the airport, and found ourselves triple-parked, I helped Anella with her bag to the curb-side check in.

Prior to getting her luggage out of the car, Anella was standing glued to my side and gave me a big hug and kiss. After delivering her luggage to the curb-side check in and while the car was still triple-parked, I was anxious to get back to the car and get out of the way. Turning to say my last goodbye's, I saw the fear and sadness in her eyes and facial expression that our departure was going to cause in her. She quickly came running back to me at the car to give me another goodbye hug.

The fear, love and apprehension in her eyes will forever strike a cord deep in my core. A few days later, I did not want to relive the look in those eyes with my son, Drew, at the recruiter's office in Kalamazoo.

Two days prior to having some family over to say goodbye to Drew, I had the opportunity to catch him on our back deck. I just told him that I wanted a moment to give him a nice hug, a kiss and to tell him how proud I was and how much he meant to me. I thoroughly enjoyed the opportunity to share this expression of love and admiration with him and to this day, I still do not understand why I was so choked up over the situation or how I was able to express myself over the overwhelming desire to cry. I had to give him some semblance of his father being a man and not a blubbering noodle.

While I was able to contain myself emotionally, I did give Drew one last hug and kiss at the recruiter's office and expressed how much I love and respect him. His mother and brother and I said our final goodbyes and left him in the hands of Marine Recruiter Sgt. John D. Butler. Was it just me, or did I just see the same look in his eyes as I saw in Anella's just a few days before at the Detroit airport? There was not a look of panic, but affection and love.

The ride home was very interesting for Laurie, Bennett and I. It was obviously a situation and circumstance that we had never lived through before. We did not have an understanding about what we were supposed to do.

When the kids were little, it was common practice for us on a

Saturday to take the farm truck down to the gas station and get some candy, pop and maybe some beer. On the way home, we would drive home through the Muvrin Orchard and go to the "Serengeti" (a place of wilderness by our farm) where we would look for ancient sea coral, Petosky stones and ancient sea shell fossils.

When we arrived home after leaving Drew in the care of the Marine Corps, I made Bennett get in our old Ford Explorer, that was now Drew's car, and we traversed the route that he was quite accustomed to as a child. We bought some pop for Bennett, beer for myself and he and I went out looking for ancient sea coral, Petosky stones and ancient sea shell fossils.

We came across a boulder that was much too large for the two of us to lift. In honor of Drew, we forced ourselves to leverage it into the back of the Explorer and delivered it to our "beach house" where we christened it as Drew's Marine Rock. Bennett and I then thoroughly cleaned out Drew's mess in the Explorer. I thought the most appropriate thing to do next on such a wet, rainy, cold and dreary day was to take a nap and sleep off the numerous beers I had just consumed.

Typically, I have a yearly cycle that through January, February and March, I recover from deer hunting season of October and November and the holidays in December by not having any alcoholic beverages, running two miles every day and weight-training every day. I try to lose weight and get physically fit for the summer. Undoubtedly come fall, I will be back to drinking beer, deer hunting and eating in a manner that is only commensurate with an appropriate deer camp. Given it was March, I was due some beers and what more of an appropriate occasion to have a few.

After waking from my nap at about 6 p.m., I was interrupted by a phone call from Drew's recruiter. The recruiter informed me that Drew had been moved to Lansing in preparation for his departure the next morning. In finalizing some medical forms, the recruiter wanted to know if Drew had been diagnosed and suffered from tendinitis while he was in the fourth grade. My initial response was to find the question ridiculous and if he wanted to know how Drew fell in the shower and broke his nose when he was a year and a half old.

Clearly, Drew was thinking about some incident when he was in the fourth grade and a doctor diagnosed a muscle strain. Drew did not have, nor has he ever suffered from conditions relating to tendinitis. In the morning we had delivered Drew to the recruiter. The recruiter was now at our home requesting that we sign a statement indicating that Drew was never diagnosed or has ever suffered from tendinitis. I was quite impressed when the recruiter declared that the Marine Corps, is only interested in securing assets and not taking on liabilities. Recruiter Butler said that they are very selective in who they allow to attend Recruit Training. We had quite a nice visit with Recruiter Butler, he is obviously a very nice young man. His father was a Marine. He is a Marine.

The family is obviously living with great honor and tradition. As we escorted the Recruiter from our kitchen through our dining room and then to the front door, he noticed Drew's high school graduation photograph on the buffet near the front door. He turned and smiled as he pointed to the large photo and said Drew really did not cause him any problems and that he is a well equipped young man. The only problem he had with him was that on a few occasions, he had to scold Drew for urinating outdoors. How could I tell this recruiter at that moment, that it was my fault?

As Drew grew up we enjoyed living outdoors. I taught Drew that outside was the preferred place to urinate. We have complete privacy to do so where we live. Laurie just gave me a look when Sgt. Butler finished speaking, knowing that Drew clearly got that habit from me. Yes, the last words that I would have with Drew's recruiter was a discussion relating to the bad practice my son got from me – urinating outdoors.

Some people spend an entire lifetime wondering
if they made a difference in the world. But, the Marines
don't have that problem.
- Ronald Reagan

In this world we are sheep.
Roaming our planet are bad people – wolves
– looking to devour the sheep.
The sheep dogs, protecting us – the sheep – from the wolves
are the men and women in the United States Military.
– Howard Stern

The fastest way out of MCRD San Diego
is through graduation.
- Recruit Mantra

PHASE 1 – SEMPER FIDELIS

*"Drill, PT, Drill and Classes...
and more Drill"*

The first five weeks of the rest of your life.

The Marine Corps Recruit Depot in San Diego has a thirteen week schedule for recruit training. These thirteen weeks are divided into three phases.

Phase 1 includes Pick-Up Week, which is known as "Receiving Week." The following week of training (while actually the second week that the recruit is there), is labeled Training Week 1. Weeks two, three and four are within Phase 1. Phase II includes training weeks five, six and seven. Phase III includes training weeks eight, nine, ten, eleven and twelve.

Each day is labeled. Training Day One, commencing on the Tuesday of Training Week One. The recruit is typically dropped off or picked up by his recruiter on Sunday. Monday, the recruit travels to San Diego and has the initial time being receiving week the Monday, Tuesday, Wednesday and Thursday of pick up week.

Friday (declared as F-1), Saturday (declared as F-2), Sunday (declared as F-3) and the Monday of training week one (declared as F-4). Training Day One (declared as T-1) commences on Tuesday of Training Week 1. Thereafter, the days are labeled as T-2, T-3, T-4, etc and continue sequentially through T-63.

Sundays are not training days. Sundays are known as S-1, S-2, S-3, and continue through S-11. Following training day 63 (T-63), which is the Thursday of training week 11, the days transition to Marine day 1 (M-1). From there, the days are labeled as M-2, M-3, M-4, etc., and continue through M-7, which is graduation day.

Regardless if it's a F, T, M or even an S, it is characterized by yelling, drill, discipline, drill, obedience, IT and more drill.

Family Day is the Thursday before Friday Graduation Day. Week after week, MCRD San Diego has the routine of Family

Day and Graduation during Week 13 (if the recruit does not sustain a drop). Forty-two weeks a year, the cycle plays itself out week after week. While the Marine Corps is 240 years old, since its inception in Tun Tavern Brewery, the making of new Marines at MCRD SD has been taking place for the last 93 years. The only thing that has changed around the parade deck (the Grinder), in the past 60 years is the addition of solar panels on the roof over the spectator stands.

After meeting with Drew's recruiter the Sunday evening, my next concern was when I would next hear from my son. I was told I would receive a letter after a week or two. This letter would provide me with information with his contact information.

When Drew left on Sunday, he left with only the clothes on his back and $50 cash. He did not have a phone. Even to this day, I still get choked up when I think about how he was wearing a button-up shirt that belonged to me in high school and college. My son, Drew, my little bear cub, was wearing my shirt as he headed for California to the Marine Corps Recruit Depot.

The Matrix. Drew is in the center (full beard and bandana).
A Poole, whose worm is about to turn.

CHAPTER 1
PICK UP / RECEIVING WEEK

"Chill and Nice to Black Friday"

**"A lot of standing and waiting.
During receiving week the DI's
are pretty nice and chill." - Drew**

Monday, I could not stop thinking about Drew flying from Lansing to California and what a sentimental young man he has become.

Unexpectedly, Monday afternoon, I received a telephone call from Drew. He informed me that he was at the airport in Grand Rapids, Michigan. He told me that they were transported by van from Lansing to Grand Rapids, and that they would be flying out of Grand Rapids to Chicago O'Hare and then onto California.   Drew and I had a very nice telephone conversation.

I told him on numerous occasions how proud I was of him. For whatever reason, based on what I was hearing from him during this conversation, I was compelled to tell him how special of a relationship the two of us share and that we would be thinking of one another while he is gone.

Pick Up Week. Black Friday.
What the...?
DREW

Pick up and receiving week involves a lot of standing around and waiting. The first few days, the drill instructors are real chill and nice. T-1 really sucks, because the DI's have been pretty chill and you are believing this is the way it will be. You can deal with a drill instructor like that.

However, then you are hit with your real drill instructors on Black Friday. On T-1, you realize the drill instructors from the previous week are not going to be around any more. How disturbing is it that the most disturbing week isn't even counted as Week 1?

Pick up week is when the recruit's lives are turned upside down and some of the most harsh treatment is experienced. Apparently, this isn't even deserving enough to have the ability to take up space and have a number assigned to it.

Recruits from all over the country west of the Mississippi and parts of Michigan converge at the San Diego airport. Upon enough recruits arriving and the sun having set for enough hours to where darkness is complete, they will be corralled into a bus and brought to the famous yellow footsteps.

DREW

After my mom and dad dropped me off at the recruiter's office in Kalamazoo, Michigan and they said their goodbyes, I really wasn't feeling any different than I was earlier that day, or the day before. I made the decision and this was just the beginning of the journey.

Before the recruiter drove me to Lansing, Michigan, he took me to a barber shop and gave me a new haircut. While during my year in college, my hair was long, quite long, I did get a haircut in preparation for my departure to MCRD San Diego. My recruiter though, felt that it was not quite good enough for my initial presentation, so we went to the barber shop. After the barber shop, we proceeded to the State Capitol in Michigan to MEPS, the Military Entrance Processing Station.

Once my recruiter, Sgt. Butler reels in a poolee and has him secured in the boat, he was more demanding than what we were going to see in San Diego. For example, the strength test at San Diego requires the recruit to run one-and-a-half miles in thirteen minutes, thirty seconds.

Sgt. Butler demanded twelve minutes, thirty seconds. The IT in San Diego requires forty-four crunches, where Sgt. Butler requires 60; SDIT of pull ups is two. Sgt. Butler required us to do 5.

At MEPS, we reviewed the materials that I had already been provided and went through some additional physical testing. We were put into the Comfort Inn, where I shared a room with another recruit. The next morning, we were transported to the Grand Rapids airport, about an hour and a half away from Lansing. We all just assumed that I would be flying out of Lansing.

From the Grand Rapids airport, we were flown to the O'Hare Airport in Chicago, Illinois. There was a lot of time to kill at the Grand Rapids airport before leaving for O'Hare. I was able to take the opportunity to call my dad. It was nice to hear his voice one last time. I know he felt great hearing from me and to learn where I was on my journey.

After getting to the San Diego airport, we sat around waiting until midnight. On the Marine bus, I was surprised to see how the Marine Corps had their own buses. I was expecting a school bus, Travel Coach or a Greyhound-type bus. Obviously the feelings of anticipation and anxiety filled my body and mind.

Throughout the experience, I noticed how very nice the facilities are between the bus, the meeting rooms, the buildings and the barracks. It was much nicer than what I expected as far as bricks and mortar. However, I guess that was what one should expect coming from the most elite fighting force on this planet.

The United States of America provides well for its servicemembers. Between the bricks and mortar and the food, it would have been a nice get away it if weren't for the drill instructors being constantly on us. Constantly.

After a few seconds on the yellow footsteps, we were brought into a meeting room. Keep in mind there are over 100 young men that they are processing. How do you get 100 young men stripped of all of their belongings and clothing, assign them new gear, give them a hair cut and have them call home – all within a couple of hours.

It may seem nuts how the drill instructors are yelling at the recruits, but how else do you get this accomplished in a disciplined and orderly fashion? They have to stow away our wallets, identification and all of our clothing and give us all new stuff, a hair cut and allow us to call home.

We stood in front of cubbies, where we were directed to store our materials. They then moved us into a room where there are ten phones on the wall. Ten lines of ten young men each, all calling home. Pasted on the wall in front of us is what we are allowed to say. The sign reads as follows:

INITIAL PHONE CALL HOME
HELLO, THIS IS RECRUIT (LAST NAME)...
I HAVE ARRIVED SAFELY AT MCRD SAN DIEGO.
THE NEXT TIME I CONTACT YOU WILL BE BY
POSTAL MAIL SO EXPECT A LETTER IN
TWO TO THREE WEEKS...
I LOVE YOU. GOODBYE!!!!!!

It was so chaotic and noisy in the room, I really couldn't hear anything my dad said. I did hear him say "I love you, I'm so proud."

After the phone call home, we were led into a room to get our haircut. It was a large line of recruits just standing there. We were not permitted to speak to one another. We just watched each other get a haircut. There were three barbers working in the room where I was standing in line. Each recruit haircut took about 20-30 seconds.

We were then assigned a bag with our initial equipment and eventually made it to our barracks where we were assigned a rack – either upper rack or lower rack.

* * * * *

The United States Marine Corps has quite an informative website. The Marine Corps Recruit Depot in San Diego has its own detailed link. The website and Matrix that was put together, gives you insight as to what the recruit is going through on a daily basis.

Through reviewing the Matrix and the website, I knew that it would be quite hectic when Drew arrived and was stripped of his personal identity. I imagine the first week would be a hurry up and wait type thing where they are trying to process so many new recruits. Through conversations with Patrick and Chuck, I was expecting a telephone call in the early morning hours of the second day of the receiving week.

Tuesday morning at 2:32 a.m. I received a telephone call from Recruit Cooper informing me that he had safely arrived at the Marine Corps. Recruit Depot in San Diego and that I would be hearing from him next within a week or two via letter. The letter would provide me with his contact information. The phone then went silent.

Both Drew and I were aware that this event would take place (that he would be reading from a script; that he was not permitted to say anything other than what was contained within the script), that after he was done reading the script, the conversation would be cut off.

I told Drew that when he was making this call, I would be telling him how much I loved him, how proud I was of him and that I wished him luck. I simply said to Drew, while he was reading, that "I love you." "I am proud of you." "Good luck, Drew."

That first week, without being able to write to him, I was curious as to whether he would go to the Sunday church service. Drew was raised a Christian and baptized through the Presbyterian church. We were not regular church-goers, but I believe he is a person of faith. Both Chuck and Patrick told Drew that he will want to go to Sunday services, if for any other reason than to get away from the training days and to get a taste of something different.

That first Sunday of receiving week, I was curious if he went to church. On Sundays, Bennett and I typically have the routine of going to the American Legion Hall in Paw Paw, Michigan for Sunday breakfast. We were visiting with a friend, Archie Davies, and informed him that my son is at Marine Corps Recruit Training.

I asked Archie, "What am I going to do with this one?" as I pointed to Bennett. I further indicated that, "Bennett is allergic to eggs and from my reading, there are a lot of eggs eaten during recruit training."

Archie responded, "Bennett, you're joining the Coast Guard. In the Coast Guard, we do the Lord's work. We do not take lives, we save them."

Archie served over forty years in the Coast Guard. Twenty of those years, he also served as a Michigan State Trooper. Through many Sunday breakfasts, Archie has given numerous compelling reasons to Bennett on why he should join the Coast Guard after high school graduation.

We endured Receiving Week without receiving a letter from Drew. We knew this would be the case. I thought about him almost constantly throughout every day. Obviously, one gets busy with tasks at hand; however, he was never far from the front burner. I was simply amazed at how overwhelmed I was with pride, that he was off doing what he was doing, yet that was short-tempered with fear and anxiety over how he was doing. Even though I did not have an address for Drew, I still wrote quite a lengthy letter. I was anticipating the day I could send it. That Friday, I started on a letter and thought I would continue writing it during Training Week 1, during that Monday or Tuesday, hoping that some time that week I would receive Drew's letter, have his address and I would be able to send mine by priority mail.

CHAPTER 2
TRAINING WEEK 1:
GETTING TO T-1 AND S-2

"This Sucks"

"Training Week One on the Matrix is Red Cross and Marine Corps History. Training week one seems so bad because you go from pretty chill and nice drill instructors, hoping that is what it is going to be like and then you get hit with your real drill instructors. Black Friday is when you first meet your DI's."
-Drew

As Monday, Tuesday, Wednesday, and Thursday passed, it came to me that we live the furthest away from the San Diego Recruit Depot than any of the other recruits. Is it possible that a recruit in close proximity to San Diego may have their outgoing mail delivered and a home letter returned before Drew's mail to us ever arrived to us in Michigan?

My heart sank thinking that Drew's fellow recruits might be getting mail for several days, or even a week, before he ever gets anything from us. My heart sank even further, when on Thursday night, the evening of T-3, we received a letter from Drew that he had signed and dated seven days earlier. Clearly there was quite a lag between California and Michigan. The letter that I had been working on for the past several days was sent by priority mail.

* * * * *

18 March, 2016

Dear Mom, Dad, Anella and Bennett,

I have arrived at MCRD San Diego and have been placed in my training platoon. I am fine and in good health. While here at recruit training I am not allowed to receive certain items such as vitamins, alcohol, pornographic material, gambling devices, tobacco products and combustibles. Please do not send any packages (i.e., cookies, candy, socks, underwear, etc.).

Also prescription medication cannot be sent under any circumstance. A medical officer authorized to treat recruits will provide all medication to me. While here at Recruit Training I will not need you to send any money, I earn enough to cover all expenses that will occur while going through day to day training here at MCRD San Diego. I apologize that this letter is short but in the beginning we are somewhat pressed for time. I promise to write later.

Today it took 20 minutes for us to put on our socks another 20 minutes to put on pants.

I miss you guys a lot. I miss Buck too. It sucks here. My feet hurt really bad. Going to sleep is the only good part so far. Chow time is one of the most stressful times of day. Drill Instructors go crazy during chow time.

Everyone always talked about the yellow footprints, but we only were on them for like half a second. Sorry about bad penmanship, I'm using a canteen as a hard writing surface. I passed my IST so I shouldn't be held back. I really want a cigarette though.

Recruit Last Name, First Name, M I
This is where you mail shit to me at.
3rd Bn Lima Co. Platoon 3241
38001 Midway Ave.
San Diego, CA 92140-3241

Sincerely, Drew

Also included with Drew's letter were two other letters that read as follows:

United States Marine Corps
Company L
Third Recruit Training Battalion
Marine Corps Recruit Depot
San Diego, CA 92140-3241

March 18, 2016

To Whom It May Concern:

My name is Staff Sergeant Magallanes. I am the Senior Drill Instructor for your son's Platoon. I have been assigned to care for and train your young man for the next three months. I am responsible for leading and guiding this future Marine through the many challenging and demanding stages of training. I will ensure that he puts forth his maximum effort. Through concerned and positive leadership I will help him develop a strong sense of pride, self-respect, confidence, and a greater level of physical and mental endurance.

He is about to undergo a rigorous training cycle that will test him both physically and mentally. The first phase of training will take place at Marine Corps Recruit Depot (MCRD), San Diego, California. Training consists of physical training, close order drill, water survival qualification, and an introduction to military life. Extensive classes on Marine Corps history, first aid, military customs, and courtesies and military law will be taught.

The second phase of training takes place at Camp Pendleton, California and consists of rifle marksmanship and field skills training. Field week will be a defining moment in your young man's life and the completion of the second phase of recruit training.

For the third phase of training he will return to MCRD and begin his final transition from recruit to Marine. This phase will consist of his final physical fitness test, final examination that covers all subjects taught such as history, customs and courtesies, first aid, and final administrative procedures and preparation for duty in the Fleet Marine Force. The third phase of training is culminated with the completion of the Crucible Event. Finally, your recruit will be graduating on June 10, 2016.

Your young man will be facing many obstacles and may experience periods of frustration, especially during the first phase. Positive and encouraging letters from relatives and friends will greatly contribute to his morale and attitude. This is necessary so that your son can make his proper travel arrangements. High morale and a positive outlook are assets for a solid foundation and attributes to successful training. Your role in maintaining his morale and motivation that can benefit his positive development is vital and encouraged.

Again, I assure you that your young man is in good hands. My team of Drill Instructors and I will always use positive and concerned leadership in the course of training and the development of your future Marine. Your role in helping to encourage and motivate him through letters is greatly appreciated. There is also a web site that may answer some of your questions. www.recruitparents. com

I would highly encourage you to contact me directly via e-mail if you have any concerns at paul.magallanes@usmc.mil, or write at the following address:

SDI Sgt Magallanes, Paul C
3rd Bn Lima Co., Plt. 3241
38001 Midway Ave
San Diego, CA 92140-3241
paul.magallanes@usmc.mil

I am always pleased to receive correspondence from the families of my recruits. I look forward to hearing from you.

Paul C. Magallanes
Staff Sergeant, United States Marine Corps
Senior Drill Instructor
Platoon 3241 / Company L

* * * * *

United States Marine Corps
Company L
3rd Recruit Training Battalion
Recruit Training Regiment
Marine Corps Recruit Depot
3802 Hochmuth Avenue
San Diego, CA 92140-5187

Dear Parent or Guardian:

My name is Captain Bloom, the Company Commander of Company L. My mission is to care for and train your recruit over the next three months. The Marine directly responsible for your recruit's training and welfare is Staff Sergeant Magallanes, the Senior Drill Instructor for Platoon 3241. He is responsible for leading and guiding your future Marine through the many challenging and demanding stages of training. He will ensure that your recruit puts forth maximum effort and, through concerned leadership, will help your recruit develop a strong sense of pride, self-respect, confidence and a greater level of physical and mental endurance.

Your recruit is about to undergo rigorous training that will test him both physically and mentally. He will be instilled with a sense of discipline that will develop his character and transform him into a more confident and stronger person. The first phase of training will take place here at the Marine Corps Recruit Depot (MCRD) San Diego and consists of a rigorous schedule of physical training, close order drill, water survival qualification, an introduction to military life and numerous classes on Marine Corps history, first aid, military customs and courtesies and military law.

The second phase of training will take place at Camp Pendleton, California and will consist of marksmanship training and rifle firing qualification. Your recruit will also conduct field skills training consisting of overnight bivouacs, weapons training and over 25 kilometers of hiking and forced marches. During this period, your recruit and his platoon will develop a higher level of teamwork and espirit de corps through shared hardship.

The third phase of training will take place at MCRD. These last three weeks will consist of final evaluation and testing in close order drill, the Battalion Commander's inspection, the physical fitness test and a practical examination of general military knowledge.

The culminating event of your son's training, the Crucible, will take place at Camp Pendleton. The Crucible is a three day event where your son will be tested physically and mentally, executing numerous field events, obstacle courses and marching over 55 kilometers. At the conclusion of this event he will finally be called a Marine and be awarded the Eagle, Globe and Anchor our most cherished emblem.

Following his training your son will move into Marine week which includes Family Day and the Recruit Training Graduation Ceremony. Your recruit's Family Day is 9 June 2016 and his graduation date is 10 June 2016 at 10:00 a.m. I invite you to review the enclosed material from Marine Corps Community Services (MCCS) on key events for Family Day and Graduation Day. You may find supplemental information on recruit training and graduation from MCCS on the internet at http://www.mccsmcrd.com/Graduation/index.html

Additionally, there are several hotels in the vicinity of MCRD that offer discount rates as well as transportation to MCRD to facilitate your attendance at Marine Week events. I encourage you to review these establishments and options on the internet at http://www.cwtsatotravel.com so you may make an informed decision on your stay while in San Diego.

Your recruit will be faced with many obstacles and may experience periods of frustration, especially during the first phase. I encourage you to write to your recruit during this time. Positive, encouraging letters from relatives and friends will greatly contribute to your recruit's morale and will increase his chances of success. Please be mindful of your recruit's goals in his endeavors at boot camp and avoid distractions that may cloud his focus in achieving the title of U.S. Marine. By maintaining your recruit's motivation, you can assist in his positive development and help him achieve his goals while here at MCRD.

Please be aware that initially your mail may take a little longer than the normal 2-3 days to reach your recruit, and that you may not receive many letters from him during the first week of training as he will be very busy.

Should you have any emergency situations that may arise, your recruit can be contacted quickly through the American Red Cross. Upon furnishing basic information about your recruit, the Red Cross will generate an emergency contact message which can be quickly delivered. The Red Cross can be reached at (877) 272-7337. If you have any non-emergency questions or issues, please feel free to contact your son's recruiter. The recruiter will be able to provide you with information on where your son is in training as well as basic information on recruit training.

I assure you that your young man is in good hands. My Drill Instructors will train your recruit to the best of their ability through concerned, firm and fair leadership. Your son has taken on a difficult and demanding challenge, and through his hard work and dedication, as well as your continued support, he will succeed and become part of one of the premier military organizations in history when he earns the title United States Marine.

J. Bloom

DREW

*The first week was frustrating with the standing and waiting. It was a matter of being processed. It was okay and quite chill. However, training week one was really bad. Black Friday introduced us to our new drill instructors. (**The Marines coincidentally just started putting videos on YouTube. The most watched video of Marine Drill Instructors going nuts is Drew's Black Friday. We were able to see our Drew. But, yikes − if you see that video)*.

It was disappointing to realize that the training weeks were like the first week. We were off and running. Literally 24/7, our every act is directed. Literally we eat, sleep, urinate and defecate when we are told we are allowed to. There is constant yelling and we are on the move every moment. Never are we allowed to sit for any extended period of time.

After every meal, whether breakfast, lunch and dinner, right outside the chow hall we are doing chin-ups and push-ups−everyday−seven days a week. Immediately after chow, pull-ups and push-ups. There seems to never be a break. There is never words exchanged in a conversational tone. Yelling, yelling at the top of your lungs, is a constant. Everyone will lose their voices and become ill with the Marine Corps crud.

* * * * *

[NOTE: this letter was written before receiving a letter from Drew and we therefore, did not have an address to send it yet.]

March 23, 2016

Drew, or as I am sure you are getting used to, Recruit Cooper:

The first three weeks are the worst. You will have fun shooting, swimming and doing obstacle course and pugil sticks. Things will settle down in Phase 2. Final Phase – Phase 3 you will be ready to be a MARINE. Very proud of you. Hang tough. Hang in there.

We are all so proud of you. We all miss you very much and think of you every day. Hardly a moment goes by during the day that we are not wondering what you are doing. Every evening, Buck sits by the patio door watching for you and waiting for you to pull in by the barn. We all miss you very much and cannot wait until we are able to see you again.

Anella has been doing well in Europe. It is very interesting how we are able to communicate with her so easily given how far away she is. We sent text messages easily, exchanging photographs. As you well know, having Face Time with her is easy and clear as well. She will probably be home by the time you get this letter. As you well know, time does not stand still and when you are busy or having fun, it sure does fly by.

Please keep in mind that before you know it, the time will have flown by for you with your recruit training and more importantly, you will be able to look back with great pride on what you have accomplished and you will be a Marine. Being a Marine is something that no one will ever be able to take from you. You will be in a very select few and proud and will have something that you can wear as a badge of honor for the rest of your life. Please know that it will be over before you know it and I am sure you will have moments where you will be entertained and have great rewards and satisfaction in what you are accomplishing.

Remember that a journey of a thousand miles begins with one step. Please just focus on each step and before you know it, it will be over. Remember how we were always the captains of one-liners and while the journey of a thousand miles begins with one step, please remember that it is not about the destination, but the journey itself.

Please take moments each day and be entertained and enjoy what you are dealing with. Remember, Chuck and Patrick both said to keep your sense of humor. You are physically and mentally fit and strong and no doubt will excel at what you are doing.

I am following the weather in San Diego and it looks like you are enjoying a nice summer-time climate. It looks like it cools in the evening and warms well during the day, but is not too hot. It is still rather chilly here and we still get a good frost in the evening and snow later in the week.

Recently, there were United States Congressional Hearings on the Flint Water Crisis. Congressman Elijah Cummings is the ranking member of the Committee that held the hearings. Congressman Cummings was the person that had invited me to testify to Congress on Hurley. I have always loved Congressman Cummings since that time and my admiration for him only grew stronger as he questioned Snyder. It was wonderful watching Snyder sit there and take the verbal assault that he has due and coming to him by Congressman Cummings.

A different Congressman had said to Snyder that plausible deniability is only acceptable if it is plausible. Snyder has no way of asserting plausible deniability as far as the decision to make the poison water and the subsequent cover-up. Congressman Cummings closed his remarks, as did a number of Congressmen, by asking Snyder to resign. At the close of the hearings, the Congressman and witnesses were standing up to leave, it was entertaining to hear the Flint residents in the gallery cat-calling and yelling at Snyder to resign.

That evening, Rachel Maddau discussed on her MSNBC News Program that the water in Flint is still toxic. Snyder not only will not resign, but for months he has done nothing to cure the problem. There are different chemicals in the measurements taken of water that 5,000 parts per billion amount to toxic waste. The water coming from the Flint faucets is still over 11,000 parts. Snyder clearly put dollars ahead of people and still has not taken accountability for what he has done.

You have the bravery, strength, endurance and honor to do this! Something that will be your badge of honor for the rest of your life. You will get this letter some time in week 2 or 3. End of March – beginning of April week 4 is Swim Week. I think you will have fun in Phase 2 and 3. Just get through Phase 1 and you will settle in.

When we dropped you off at the recruiter's office on the Sunday that you left, Bennett took a photograph of the recruit training matrix for the Marine Corps Recruit Depot in San Diego. This is a large chart that lays out what you will be doing from day to day and week to week. Each week ends with the Sunday of having an opportunity for religious services.

Please remember what Chuck and Patrick said about taking advantage of the opportunity to go do something different and to be able to see some time of normalcy. Go to the religious services as an opportunity to experience something fresh and different. It looks like they are available every Sunday. The first week that you were there is referred to as "Receiving" week on the matrix. It is called the "Pick Up and Receiving Week." The following week is referred to as week one.

In my correspondence I will begin discussing with you week one, which will begin on Monday, March 21st. The Receiving Week was probably the most difficult because they were turning your life upside down when you were given your initial strength tests and had in-house procedures explained to you. During week one, after March 21st, you had introduction to core values, instructions relating to interior guard and introduction into ethics and Marine Corps History. I am sure that you had a million other things. I am simply following through with what I see on the Matrix.

Week two, commencing on March 28, you will have running sprints, Pugil Sticks, Circuit Course Basics, the Obstacle Course and lower body strikes, including a two and a half mile course.

Week three, April 4th, you will have the confidence course, log drills, combat conditioning exercise and Marine Corps Mission and Organization. I am sure throughout you will have drills, drills and more drills.

Week four, commencing on April 10, is entitled "Swim Week." I imagine this is when you will learn how to swim with full gear and backpacks and try not to sink. There will be a confidence course, more Pugil Sticks and may take a bus ride to the other location for weeks five and six, April 18 and 25 where you have grass week and work on the rifle range.

Once I get your letter, I will break the weeks down as we proceed through your recruit training, but it looks like week four is Swim Week, week five is Grass Week and week six you will have qualification day on the rifle range. Week seven will be the Field Week. The end of week seven (on that Sunday), you will take a bus back to the Marine Corps Recruit Depot in San Diego. So it looks like you leave San Diego the end of week four and come back at the end of week seven.

I think through week four (Swim Week) and week five (Grass Week) and week six (Shooting and Qualifying) and week seven (Field Week), you will be having a ball throughout that time period. I think by the time you get this letter, the worse will be over.

Love you Drew. I am so very Proud!!!

Just remember when you get into close combat drills to stick with jabs and always striking first. Try to get in the first three to four punches before the other person knows that it is time to throw a punch.

Buck has his final visit with the vet this week and hopefully he should be just fine. He has, on a couple occasions, been running full speed and looks as he did in the past. I do not plan on taking him on my daily runs any longer though and probably will just take him on a run once a week. I don't think it has anything to do with his condition, except for just trying to save his other knees and hips from wearing out.

Bennett and I did a thorough job of cleaning out the Explorer. When we were at his school conferences, his Health Teacher asked if Bennett had approached either one of us to talk about sexual education. I told the health teacher that Bennett did not ask about sexual education. However, while we were cleaning out the Explorer we came across several packages of your condoms and I gave those to Bennett and told him he could keep them for future use. It was interesting watching Bennett look at the boxes to figure out what they were.

I hope all is well with you and that you are feeling mentally and physically fit. Enjoy each day and before you know it, you will be at week nine and ten and feeling like you do not want graduation to come and for the recruit training to end. Find humor in each day knowing that as each day passes you are closer to being a Marine. Focus on each step and do not worry about later today, tomorrow or next week. Enjoy the moment and the journey and just take it all in and excel as I know you will.

I am writing this letter, having not received anything from you yet. I am anxious to get your address and start sending letters. Please let me know if there is anything that you want and we will try to send it as we can. I will send cough drops and Vitamin C lozenges to see if they make it through. Please do not hesitate to ask for whatever it is you may want and we will get it to you. I am sure Grandma will try to sneak her Gingersnap cookies through and hopefully it will not get you into too much trouble on your end.

I love you so much Drew and I am so proud of you.

Love, Dad

* * * * *

I fretted over things such as whether or not I could send it via overnight, Federal Express. Would that draw too much attention to him and cause a punishment of push-ups and sit-ups. I then came to the conclusion that priority mail would not draw too much attention, but would get the letter to Drew in a short period of time.

In addition to the letter I sent by priority mail, I also sent another priority mail envelope containing a letter from Laurie and one from Anella, which she wrote before she left for Europe.

I also sent a letter via First Class Mail. I hoped that the letter sent by First Class mail would arrive shortly after the priority mail. I was drawn to Drew saying how he passed the initial strength test "and would be graduating on time." Love the positive attitude and optimism. While I see at the same time he is saying he hates it, and misses us; his mind is towards graduation.

My anxiety over Drew seeing other recruits receive correspondence was heightened the following Monday when we received his second letter. He closed the letter by expressing how much he cannot wait to receive a letter from us. It was sad to see that he had, what I thought was the appearance of feeling sad that no one was sending him anything.

* * * * *

Dear Mom, Dad, Bennett & Anella:

I got through receiving week and it was real boring. We got to San Diego around 10 and we were the last recruits to arrive. From there we didn't go to sleep until 9 pm on Tuesday. I was so tired I was hallucinating.

We are right next to the airport, like Patrick said, so I always watch jets take off and wish I was on one headed back to Michigan. I can hear them when I'm laying on my rack trying to sleep. There is also a mountain range you can see if its clear out, and its right to the left of the San Diego City skyline.

I don't know when this is going to get to you, but while I'm writing this its Wednesday of the second week, T2, or training Day two. I've been sick as a dog for about three days with a stuffy nose and cough. My throat is also extremely sore from all the screaming they make us do, so it hurts really bad when I cough. It also hurts when I swallow. I haven't coughed up blood yet though, so that's good, but I'm basically in pain everywhere.

My feet are destroyed from how shitty our running shoes are, and I haven't been able to feel my left big toe for a few days. Its hard to fall asleep because of the aching in my feet and knees. Every single day I wish I was back at home and not here. Also, with my shaved head it looks like my hair is thinning out. What if I start balding? I don't look good with a shaved head and there is no way I can rock a hair style like George Castanza.

Anyways, I love you all and I can't wait until I can see you again. Looking forward to receiving your letters.

* * * * *

At the end of training week one, T-4, I sent letters by priority mail and also sent a package of 60 cough drops. I had read that the Recruits at Pariss Island were allowed to have cough drops.

Therefore, I figured this would be something that Drew would enjoy. Prior to his departure, I told him that I thought he could receive cough drops and power bars. We had discussed that I would try to send those to him and he should write about what he was able to receive and I would send him as much as he needed was allowed.

* * * * *

Dear Drew,

Today is Friday, March 25th. Yesterday was a very exciting day for us as we received your letter. Your letter to us was dated 18 March 2016. We received that letter on 24 March. This morning, Friday, 25 March, I went to the Post office and sent three different letters to you, one from me, one from your mother, and one from Anella. I am so sorry if receiving these letters will cause you to have to do additional push-ups.

Today is Good Friday and we are preparing for the Easter holiday this Sunday. This should be a joyous occasion given that Uncle Mike and Aunt Sara had their baby girl Wednesday of this week, 23 March. Mom and baby are doing fine.

Anella is doing wonderful and returned from Europe feeling well and in good spirits. I know you are not able to receive news, but I am sure you would be interested to know that there was a terrorist attack in the City of Brussels that is located in Belgium. There were coordinated attacks at both the Brussels airport and the metro station in Brussels.

How incredible of a coincidence that you are off preparing to be a Marine and help secure the defensive needs of our nation and be a part of the strongest and most elite fighting force on this planet, United States Marine Corps, and fight against such types of terrorist activity to have your sister, while traveling from Paris to Amsterdam, sat in the metro station in Brussels for close to thirty minutes, hours before the terrorist attack.

Obviously Anella was well away from Brussels when the attack occurred and it is incredible to think that she was sitting at the metro station where these mother fuckers killed innocent people. You have the honor and privilege of preparing yourself to be a part of something that can do something about these pieces of shit.

Keep the faith and keep taking one step at a time knowing that you have a future for the rest of your life being a part of something that is bigger than all of us. U.S.M.C.

So Anella is home and will be with us for Easter as well as your new cousin with Uncle Mike and Aunt Sara. All of us will be talking about you and missing you dearly. Please gain strength that you are on our constant minds and we are frequently thinking about you and keeping you in our prayers.

Both Patrick and Chuck are being very supportive and interested in what you are going through. They both say that Phase 1, which is the first few weeks, is the toughest. Chuck has said that Phase 2 will be challenging and Phase 3 you will be feeling like you are ready to be a Marine. Hopefully you will receive our first mailings and this letter will come to you towards the end of week two.

From here on out I will refer to the weeks as marked on the matrix but always know, for example, when I say week 2 is really the end of week 3 because they are not counting the receiving week and the pickup week in the matrix. That is the week that is included in the 13 weeks. Like we discussed, that first week, the receiving week, and the last week come right off the top of the 13 week period basically leaving 11 weeks so that at the end of week two you are almost completing Phase 1.

If you get this letter in week three, you will be looking at the Confidence Course, Combat Conditioning Exercises and Log Exercises. Week three includes the Marine Corps Mission and Organization and you will be getting the initial drill. I am anxious to hear from you when we next see each other and have some time to hear what you have learned from the Marine Corps history, first aid, and the Marine Corps mission and organization. I think it is in week 7 that you learn how to choke another person out in seconds. I'm anxious to have you show me that move. I'm really excited to learn how you do in the rifle work. I still can't get over how many times you have killed game at shots that I would never venture to take. You have a natural ability with a rifle but be sure to listen to what their instruction is as you will be shooting at greater distances than we have done in the past.

Depending on how often they give you mail. This week you will do the obstacle course and 2.5 mile course at end of the week.

Our first three letters were hand-delivered to the post office Friday morning and mailed "priority mail" for Monday delivery. I am dropping this letter in regular mail delivery Friday afternoon.

I think it is funny when I saw week 2, when that is really after you have been there for 3 weeks. Reminds me of that summer we watched the Star Wars movies and always had to note whether we were saying its position being made and coming out in the theaters or its spot in the sequence of the story or its time in history.

Please remember to indicate in your letters home if there is anything I can send to you. Next week I will try to send some cough drops and throat lozenges.

Please know that we all love you and miss you. Just keep taking one step at a time and remember in close-combat drills that you want to have quick jabs and get off the first punch.

Have fun my little buddy.
Love, Dad

* * * * *

Saturday was 26 March, T-5. The following Sunday was S-1 and also, Easter Sunday. I was hoping that he would go to the service to at least explore what was going on and I imagined it was a particularly festive event given that it was Easter Sunday. That weekend, Matt Fasbender, my friend from Colorado, sent an email that Drew would be most likely experiencing Pugil sticks for the first time next week.

Matthew and Drew at age 5.

CHAPTER 3
THREE WEEKS IN BUT ONLY
TRAINING WEEK 2
"Obstacle Course?"

"Training week two on the Matrix has obstacle course, pugil sticks, circuit course, sprints...Obstacle courses you don't really think of doing actual obstacle courses. You think of the DI yelling in place double time, and then you scream back, in place double time, aye aye sir. Ooh Rah Marine Corps, then two claps and kill. We just do that the whole time we are waiting to do the actual obstacle course.

The obstacle course really sucked because some guys did not get to do any of the obstacles in the obstacle course, I got to do two or three each time I did it.

The Matrix may indicate that there is an obstacle course. However, I do not feel that we really got a good chance to run the course. Most of the time was spent standing in line with the drill instructors yelling at us, "in place – double time".

The recruits would then yell back, "in place, double time, aye aye, sir, oorah Marine Corps." We would then clap twice and yell "kill." I would have loved to have played around and exerted myself on the obstacle course rather than continuously yell, yell, yell, "in place, double time, aye aye, sir, (oorah) Marine Corps." *clap* *clap* "kill". It was seeming like this was quite bullshit."

Drew

*We received two letters from Drew this week – one on T-6 and the next on T-9.

* * * * *

I'm having the shittiest time of my life. I can't even enjoy eating because my throat hurts so bad when I swallow my chow. I don't even know if being a Marine is right for me anymore. The only reason I am still doing this is because if I wasn't here I would probably be working a job where I don't make enough money to buy food or go anywhere.

I feel like I'm in prison right now, and I feel like I've been here for so long already. And I still have so much more to go through, and after this I have four years of being a low pay grunt. I can't wait for it all to be over so I can just go be me and do what makes me happy. There isn't much to be happy about here.

The only thing that makes me happy right now is when I get to go to sleep. I've been sweating really bad when I sleep and I don't know why. That has not happened for a while. Every night I have lucid dreams, and in all of them I'm either with you guys and the rest of our family or my friends.

I wonder if I talk at all in my sleep. Sometimes when I'm on fire watch I can hear other guys saying "Aye-Aye Sir" in their sleep.

Could you please write out what my schedule is and send it to me? It would be nice to know what's coming. Thank you.

* * * * *

EVERYBODY HERE IS SICK. They call it the boot camp crud. Coughing, sore throat, an I'm hacking up nasty hard phlegm like I have never had before. It sucks, plus I can barely talk right now because my voice is so gone.

I'm in platoon Lima Company 3rd Battalion. There is a saying that 1st Battalion makes men, 2nd Battalion makes Marines, and 3rd Battalion makes machines. So I think that means I'm in one of the hardest ones you can be in.

My Senior drill instructor is pretty cool. Sometimes he gets mad at the other DI's and makes them leave because they are being too hard on us. The games they are playing got old real fast. It's a little bit more frustrating when you know its just something they do to fuck with us.

There is only a couple things we are allowed to have mailed to us. It's powdered Gatorade and protein bars. I don't care so much about the Gatorade, but protein bars would kick ass. Try to find some that are as close to a candy bar as possible. I remember once Mom bought some called Whenever Bars or something like that. I really liked those, they were kind of like banana bread.

Send some of those if they count as protein bars. Just no Cliff Bars. I don't like those. Send me some pictures of the family and of Buck too please.

At some point I will have to know if after graduation you want to fly back together or if I should get my own flight, because they set up our flights for us, but if you wanted me to I could tell them I don't need that.

Also, we will shoot with scopes, not iron sights, they changed the rules. I love all of you. I can't wait to see you again. Miss you all.

Drew

* * * * *

According to the Matrix, Monday, T-6, would be filled with running sprints. Tuesday, T-7, would consist of pugil sticks. Last week's letter, sent by priority mail, included information about what Drew could expect for training week two and three. I thought it would be nice for him to have a head's up as to what was taking place. This was Fasbender's point.

A month before Drew left, I donned boxing gloves with Drew and showed him some close-quarters combat exercises. The tricks of close-quarters combat are to strike first—quick jabs, striking, striking, striking before the opponent gets off his first swing. In close quarters, quick vicious jabs always beat out slow roundhouses. I was hoping these types of thoughts, relating to striking first and quick, would work as well with the pugil stick combat situation.

I was feeling good for Drew as he is tall, brave and physically fit. His first letter indicated that he had passed all of the initial strength tests. Hopefully that also gave him a mental boost.

Training week two included Circuit Courses, Obstacle Courses and Lower Body Strikes, as well as a two-and-a-half mile running course. Drew's first letter indicated that the chaos involved with the drill instructors yelling, screaming and trying to turn their lives upside down. He indicated that he hated the place.

After getting his second letter, I was so happy that I had sent some more throat lozenges. He discussed how much his throat hurt and I knew that his fellow recruits must have been hurting as well. I sent out over 500 cough drops / throat lozenges hoping that if I had sent enough for everyone that the drill instructors may allow Drew to have at least 2-3, as well as everyone else.

At the end of Training Week 2, I was left very concerned over his third letter. He was struggling. I shared with his mother, who was even more concerned about whether or not he was going to make it. I reminded her that he was simply using us as someone to talk to and vent. Of course it was going to include his most negative feelings.

However, we needed to focus on the positive in his letters, and there were very positive issues to extract. Specifically, he talked about coordinating his flight back after graduation. He stated the things that he would like to receive. To me, Drew was dug in for the long haul.

Responding to his letter, I wrote:

* * * * *

Dear Drew:

Today is Monday, 28 March 2016.
This week is your beginning of training week 2. You will have been there three weeks. It looks like this week you will be working with Pugil Sticks and getting to know the obstacle course. There is no reason for me to tell you what you have done this week as you probably will not get this letter until the week is

almost over and you are enjoying your two-and-a-half mile run.

Next week, Sunday 3 April will be the beginning of your training week three and you will be looking forward to log drills and combat conditioning exercises. The following week, training week four, will begin swim week and will end with getting on a bus and going to a different location. I imagine it will be Camp Pendleton. That will be the end of phase I.

Chuck and Patrick both say Phase I is the longest and most difficult phase. You will have put a lot behind you and I really think that you will enjoy Phase II, which is training weeks 5, 6 and 7. You will get in a lot of field work and shooting. By the time you get to phase III, you are going to be home free and feeling good about everything and will be having a ball. Easier said than done, I imagine. Very easy for me to say, sitting here trying to recover from the Easter holiday.

It was pretty quiet around the house without you being home. We all missed you greatly. Anella was home and she brought her boyfriend, Teja and grandma and grandpa were here. Uncle Mike and Aunt Sara did not come out as they have their new baby. Uncle Dan and Aunt Mindy did not come as their little girl was not feeling well so they just stayed in Detroit. It was relatively low key for us with just grandma and grandpa.

I have been doing a lot of work down at the Cabin. I pulled the old orchard sprayer beneath it up into the antique corner in the barn and I wrapped a chain around the stump by the steps and pulled the stump out. The large pine tree that had fallen, I hauled over to the beach house, where I thought it would be fun to cut up the limbs, strip the pine log and make a new totem pole.

Remember how the day before you left, we were noticing that our told totem pole is about ready to fall over? I thought it might be fun to strip the pine log and do some carvings and do something in commeration of your becoming a Marine. We can varnish it and plant it as a new totem pole at the beach house.

The day you left, Bennett and I, while out looking for rocks, came across a rather large bolder that we relocated down by your cedar log bench by the fire pit and said it is your Marine rock. It is quite a large stone and an interesting color. It has some fossilization on one side.

Under separate letter, I am just going to send some cough drops and throat lozenges. I apologize in advance if it causes any problems for you. I suggest that you recommend to the drill instructor that he punish me at your graduation for sending you something that may present a problem. I just figure with all the heavy breathing and yelling, your throat may enjoy a lozenge. Please tell me if there are things that I can send.

Keep up the good work. Take it day by day and break that day apart into moments that you can garner some success, accomplishment or joy. I imagine everything you do there makes you bigger, faster, stronger and better.

Love you,

Dad

P.S. I mailed cough drops today under separate mailing.

Love you Drew!!! Miss you very much.
Very proud of you.

Buck's rehab is going great. He runs well and is doing a lot of swimming.

* * * * *

Dear Drew,

We received a letter yesterday from you. You indicate that you wrote on Wednesday of the second week or training day 2, which would be 23 March. I have realized that you may have been one of the last ones to get a letter in your platoon given that your home is the greatest distance from San Diego. I feel really bad that you have gone without any correspondence. Hopefully by the time you receive this, you will have received many pieces of mail.

Please realize that immediately upon getting your first letter with your address, I sent by priority mail, three day delivery on a Friday, hoping you would get it on Monday.

Today is 29 March. Your training day number T-7 within week 2. According to the Matrix, today you are doing the pugil sticks. A week from today, training day T-13, you will be involved with log drills. Later in that week, T-14 Combat Conditioning, T-15 Marine Corps Mission and Organization, T-16 Inspection and T-17 Initial Drill. Then like I said, the following week, week 4 is swim week and you leave to a different location by the end of the week and that will be the end of Phase I.

You have to hang in there. You know that other people have gone through this and look at your fellow recruits. You are all in a mess that you can endure and get through. I really hope that once you get through Phase I, Phase II will be full of different types of challenges that you will find some enjoyment in.

In your letter, you discuss being stuffy and coughing. I imagine that a lot of that has to do with the change of climate. Back here it is still quite cold during the evenings. Your mother is using my car as she is getting a tire fixed on her car. I drove the Explorer this morning and had quite a lot of frost to scrape from the windows. Yesterday, Bennett had a golf scrimmage and today is his first golf match. We talk about you every day and you can tell that Bennett is concerned and is thinking about you.

In an earlier package I sent to you some cough drops and lozenges. However, after the lozenges were sent, I received your letter. In your first mailing of cough drops, I only had 60 drops. After seeing your letter, I would imagine that your fellow recruits are suffering as well. I am going to send a package with enough cough drops so that you can share with everyone in your Platoon. Hopefully if there is enough for everyone your Drill Sgt.

will allow the drops to get through.

Please let me know the types of things that make it through as I would be happy to send enough granola bars, fruit bars, or whatever to everyone. Please let me know if I should send the package to the Platoon and not specifically to you.

Before you know it, we will be down at the beach house enjoying a cold beer and putting the finishing touches on your Marine Corps Totem Pole. You cannot stop time. Endure and before you know it, goals and accomplishments will be met. Think big picture and realize that we will all be proud of you for the rest of our lives. By the time you get this letter, Phase I will be almost over and you will have gotten through the worse. Hang in there and know that those like Patrick and Chuck have nothing over you and they were able to get through.

Not much to report on the Presidential Race. I just realized from a news program this weekend that there are more days left in the race than what have passed. This will still all be going on when we come to your graduation in June. Trump and Cruz are still going back and forth as well as Bernie and Hillary.

The Flint water crisis has been relatively quiet as things seem to be in an extended holding pattern. There have been enough calls for Snyder's resignation that people now realize it is falling on deaf ears. It is interesting that Snyder is the Governor that signed into law the current recall legislation that makes it more difficult than ever to recall a governor. However, the petition asking that he be recalled has been put into the system such that this past Sunday is the beginning of the 60-day period within which over 700,000 signatures need to be obtained to put the recall on a state-wide ballot. I am hopeful enough signatures will be obtained and we can get rid of the rat-bastard.

Buck continues to do well and his fur is almost back to the way it was before he was shaved. You can tell that he is feeling better because he regularly climbs the stairs and will sleep upstairs in our room or in your bed.

I feel really bad that you may have had a delay in your mail given the distances involved. Know that we miss you greatly and we have been mailing materials immediately upon learning of your address.

Yesterday I had to send some money to your relatives in the Netherlands. Given the terrorist attack in Brussels, Anella was with your relatives in the Northern part of the Netherlands and we had to make different travel arrangements for her to get home. Your kin in Groningen helped with her flight from Amsterdam to London since the rail system through Brussels is shut down. Yesterday I sent to them reimbursement for the air fair as well as their time and expense of driving her to the airport.

Hang in there and just recall when you are at your low points that you are working on a very noble, honorable and incredible endeavor.

Please indicate in your letters what I can send to you and the rest of your fellow recruits. I am more than happy to send a package to the Platoon if you think it is acceptable.

Love you and miss you dearly,

Dad
Very proud of you Mister!!! Love, Dad

* * * * *

29 March 2016
Dear Drew,

I am sending this brief note as merely another attempt of trying to get some cough drops to you. In the Marine Corps books I have read in preparation for your Recruit training the materials indicate cough drops are allowed.

This is my third attempt at delivery. The first was yesterday where I sent an envelope with 60 drops. Today I sent a package with enough for everyone in 3241 Platoon.

If you are not getting the drops let me know if there is a way for me to get them to you. For example, a package with enough drops and granola bars for everyone and addressed to Platoon 3241.

Please let me know what you want me to send, how many items and how I should address the package. Keep your head up. One moment at a time.

Love you. Miss you greatly.

Love, Dad

* * * * *

I also sent out by express, Priority Mail, a package with eight different protein bars. Then, in another package sent via First Class Mail, I sent three protein bars. My thought was the first package contained some he could share and then within a day or two he would be receiving another package for himself. I also made five separate packages containing three protein bars in each that I could drop in the mail each day the next week. I also sent a package with more cough drops. I am on a mission to send something every day.

From his letters and my own thoughts, I am left with many questions. On four occasions, I sent simple questionnaires that he could easily circle answers or fill in blanks and he could easily return using an enclosed, self-addressed and postage paid envelope.

I was left with sometimes the most silly concerns. Was he able to get letters that I had typed? Why wouldn't he get letters typed, as opposed to ones that were in written form? Why would I think such a silly thing; because he said in his letter to write to him about his schedule. I felt that I had sent to him some letters with his schedule, so I wondered if he had seen the letters because they were typed instead of hand-written.

Then I thought how ridiculous for me to say that and that maybe he had yet to receive them. He would not have known that I had typed letters that he didn't receive. It is amazing how much panic there is over a situation that you have no control over.

When Drew was at University, I had a lot of control over what was going on in his life; but, I pretty much had cut him loose when he was gone. For crying out loud, I don't even know what his grades were at school. His mother and I were the farthest things away from a hover parent, but talk about the other end of the spectrum is that of having a child in the service and not even being able to have any communication with them.

I learned a long time ago to only worry about those things that I have control over and to hang loose on those things where I have none. This is clearly a situation where I have no control, but I could at least send letters, packages and determine at a later date what effect or receipt they may have had. The end of training week two, brought S-2 and my curiosity of what Drew was doing on his Sundays.

* * * * *

Dear Drew, Hope all is well.

Today is 30 March 2016, your T-8. Hump day for middle of training week 2. I am anxious to hear from you and have you get through Phase I. Once you get through Phase I you will know the worst is behind you. Phase II will still be tough but you will see the light at the end of the tunnel. Hang tough!!!!

I am also anxious to hear from you relating to whether you received the cough drops and anything else I can send to you. Enclosed in this envelope is a self-addressed, postage paid envelope with a questionnaire for you to quickly fill out, put back in the envelope and send back to me.

Each evening between 10-11 in Michigan, as you know, I go out on the deck and take Buck out before bedtime. I always like to look up at the stars and think about what is going on with you in San Diego. What are you doing between 7-8 at night? While I am out looking at the stars and letting Buck out, what are you doing.

Keep plugging along Drew, and you will be fine. You have the constitutional fortitude to do well with this recruit training program. Yes, it is going to be very difficult. However, keep in mind that the more difficult it is, the better the reward will be once you have accomplished the training and get to call yourself a Marine.

Miss you greatly!!! Can't wait to see you again. I cannot wait to give you a big hug and call you a Marine. You will be the first in the Cooper family to be a Marine.

Love, Dad...I have sent 3 separate cough drop mailings. Are you getting any??

QUESTIONNAIRE

1. How are you feeling?

    _____ Good; _____ Bad; _____ Horrible; _____ Very Bad, but I will survive;

    _____ I think I will make it   _____ I am not sure can do this.

2. Your favorite thing to eat for breakfast?

    _____Toast; _____Eggs; _____Pancakes; _____ Oatmeal; _____ Cold Cereal.

3. I enjoy drinking a lot of the following throughout the day?

    _____ Water; _____ Milk; _____ Tea; _____ Coffee.

4. The best thing I have had for lunch is _____
   _____.

5. The best thing I have had for dinner is
   _____.

6. I am sleeping on the _____ top _____ bottom bunk.

7. I have _____ (how many) drill instructors.

8. Do you feel that you are building a good relationship with
   them?
   _____ Yes _____ No.

9. Are you looking forward to going to Camp Pendleton to
   learn how to shoot?
   _____ Yes _____ No.

10. How did you do with the Pugil Sticks?
    _____

11. How many letters have you received from us?
    _____

    (Your mother and I are sending mail every day. Do you
    get to receive letters every day or is it once or twice
    a week?)

    _____ (How often)

12. On three different occasions, I have sent cough drops.
    Have you been able to get any?
    _____ Yes _____ No.

13. What else can I send to you?

    _____ 100 granola bars   _____ 20 granola bars

    _____ 100 cough drops   _____ 20 cough drops

    _____ <u>500 cough drops</u>

14. Please send me _____ and send me _____(number) of them.

15. Have you gone to Sunday Services? _____. If no - what do you do?

16. Have you been on night watch? How long is that?

17. Is there anything I can do for you?

*   *   *   *   *

31 March 2016

Dear Drew,

Can you read my writing? I have been having letters typed for you to be able to read more easily; but, no assistants today. Sorry you are left with my writing.

Hope all is well. Next week is training week 3. You will probably get this letter around T14 or T15. Combat conditioning and Marine Corps Mission and Organizations Training week 4 and end of Phase 1 is just around the corner. Training week 4 is swim week. Pugil sticks that week 4 at T21. Bus trip on T23.

3 months. Piece of cake. Today marks the end of my 3 months since Christmas. 2 miles a day and weights everyday.

No beer. 3 months and its over. I am going to continue this regiment until I see you. My 6 pack is tight. Can't wait to compare musculature and 6 packs. I told Bennett that when we next see you the 3 of us need to compare body fat content. Obviously what you are going through is no comparison to my leisurely workouts; but, you get my point of just bearing down and recruit training will be over before you know it! You are paying a high price now because your reward is the highest possible reward - - you will be a Marine!!! Keep your head up. One step at a time. You have to get some enjoyment out of Phase 2. Guns!! Obstacle courses. Running. Kick ass stuff.

I hope you are getting our letters. I feel bad if there was an initial delay for you compared to the other recruits. Your family is probably the furthest away and so it took longer for us to get your first letter and longer to get ours back. I have been mailing a letter every day to you from me and also every day one from your mother! I am curious if they give you mail every day.

Yesterday I mailed you my questionnaire with a postage paid return envelope. Let me know if that helps - I will include one with this too.

I think about you every day - all day. I am anxious to hear how you are doing.

Watching Google Earth a lot. Are your barracks closer to the airport or the marching deck or (where graduations are held)?

Have you seen any Friday graduations going on?

Have you been near their football field?

Run the obstacle course?

Love you!!! Hang tough.

Love, Dad

CHAPTER 4
LETTERS
"Yelling, Yelling and More Yelling"

Training week three is Marine Corps Mission and Organization. That was just a class we had.

Training week three. The light at the end of the Phase 1 tunnel begins to glimmer.

In my letters to Drew, I expressed how exciting training weeks three and four would become. I was anxious to know whether he received my letters on the anticipated receipt date. It would be helpful for him to receive them when I was hoping he would and that he would be able to see what he would be doing during those weeks. The following week, which was training week four, started with swim week. That would bring the end to Phase 1.

I seem to always be thinking ahead, as I was not living through what Drew was doing and I was already jumping from training week three to four and the end of Phase 1. However, T-12, the beginning of training week three is the Confidence Course, followed by T-13 and Log Drills. These seem like more productive days as you get deeper into the Phase and the chaos of the receiving week should be close to forgotten by this week. I have no idea, but I can hope.

DREW

Drill, Drill, and we had some classes. I thought the course could be fun, but we would not get a full opportunity to participate. I doubt some of the guys even had the opportunity to run the course. Sometimes it seemed like more standing in line and yelling and more yelling. Really not a very good week.

Your feet are killing you from the shock of constantly being on them and standing, walking, running, jumping and exercising. Your voice is gone. Your throat is killing you. You are run down because while they provide you with great food, rarely do you get a chance to eat it. Enough time to eat is not allowed. You are run down and are in pain or are experiencing discomfort and continue to suffer from the Marine Corps crud. It is a constant battle – feeling like you have to urinate or defecate and not being allowed the opportunity to go to the restroom when you feel you can no longer not.

Everything, everything is taken from your control. The only thing you have control over is not going to medical and facing the potential of being dropped. We quickly learn that the fastest way out of here is through graduation. Going to medical is only going to present the opportunity for you to be dropped and pushed further back in the graduation sequence. We quickly learn that those that quit, fail or who were unable to continue forward do not just go home.

There is a special platoon, called the Holding Platoon. We did not know what it stood for, except we knew that it was the platoon for those who were not heading to graduation, but who were not going home for months after we left. Our platoon started out with fifty-four recruits. Only fifty made it to graduation. Generally, there is an 11% fail rate. One person was sent home immediately with a heart defect that caused him serious medical problems. Obviously if you do not have the constitutional fortitude to endure fearlessly, you tread into the Marine Corps recruit training blindly as to some of your underlying physical conditions.

* * * * *

It is just so hard having become so accustomed to instant gratification relating to telephone communications, Facetime, or even email and texting. He would get the letter this week that I sent last week. Did he get the cough drops? Is he able to have the cough drops? I know from the last letter he said that his throat was killing him. Wouldn't it have been perfect timing if the day he wrote that letter he received the package of cough drops.

* * * * *

Dear Aunt Mindy,

Thank you very much for the letter and Easter egg/ bunny. Mail call is one of the only things I have to look forward to. That and the hour we get to write letters and stuff. Nobody looks forward to chow time because that is one of the most stressful times of the day. The drill instructors like to go crazy and get in your face a lot in the chow hall. Its basically prime time for them fucking with us.

So I've got mail call, writing letters, and going to bed. Also church on Sundays. I go to the Catholic service because it's the longest and the drill instructors cannot go to church with us.

That Easter egg/bunny really lightened up the mood for me and a couple other guys and gave us some Easter spirit. I wish there was someplace I could hang it up, but there isn't. So I just take it out and look at it when I have a chance.

That is all for now. Give my love to James, Evelyn and Uncle Dan. I love you all.

Drew

* * * * *

1 April 2016

Dear Drew,

Sending Bennett's drawing of the beach house. I never noticed before your shovel and fox hole in his sketch. I remember you would dig all day long.

Mom sent you some photos. We will send a steady stream.

We are both getting protein bars today and shipping them out today as well!

You may be having doubts about being a Marine - Do Not have these doubts. It will be something you carry as a point of pride forever. A Marine is bigger and better than any military position on this earth. Kicks Army Ranger or Navy Seals ass. Marines are the top of the top. That's why it is so tough. They don't make pussys. Hang in there. You can do this.

Today is Friday April 1st. T10. End of training week 2. Two more weeks and you are done with the worst of it. By the time you get this there will be just one week left of Phase 1. At the end of Phase 1 you go to another location. Maybe Camp Pendleton. The last week of Phase 1, which is week 4, is swim week. Phase 1 is the real shitty stuff. Phase 2 is where you are doing more constructive type stuff. The last phase - Phase 3 will be rewarding. Hard - but you will be feeling like a Marine and graduation is right around the corner.

Just take each day, each moment one at a time.

Very proud of you. MISS you - but can't wait to see my son - a Marine.

Love, Dad

QUESTIONNAIRE

1. Have you received all of my letters - particularly the typed ones -

    Have you received letters from me that are typed?
    Yes_____ No_____

(I realize you won't know this. Just curious if you get typed materials)

2. Did you get a short letter from me that included the actual Matrix calender - schedule for 13 weeks?
    Yes_____ No_____

3. Have you received any cough drops?
    Yes_____ No_____

4. Have you received packages by mail only?
    Yes_____ No_____

    I see people getting things from:
    UPS _____
    FedEx _____
    No - just US Mail _____

5. Please send:_____

* * * * *

April 1
Friday

Hey Drew,

Hope everything is going great. Stuff at home is just fine except we miss you a lot, Buck especially. All I can think about is how proud I am of you. This entire deal is changing all of our lives such a freaking huge amount in an amazing way. In 4 years you will be a Marine Veteran, I will be a veteran from some form of military. Dad will hopefully have a few books, and mom and Anella will still be smelly...Can't wait to see you again. Until then just hang in there and think of Buck and the beach house or whatever is your happy land like from Happy Gilmore. Good Luck!

Love, Bennett

* * * * *

Friday a.m.
April 1
(no joke)

Dearest Drew-

Getting your letters.
It sounds very difficult. I am sad reading them and then Dad gives me a pep talk.
This is all so difficult because you are being trained as a Marine. At least all those other guys you are with are in the same boat as you.

I hope you find comfort thinking about your family and the adventures you've had with us. You have a lot of support and people who love you. I like that you grew up in the same house your whole life in this beautiful area. When you think of home its this house, this land. I hope that's comforting.

Long work day yesterday. I have a dentist appointment this morning and then my tire appointment at noon. Need to clean and do laundry. I am going to Chicago with Dawn tomorrow.

I will go pick up those protein bars today.

They have torn down the old Shopping Center building. Going to put up senior apartments. The Marathon by Dad's office is getting torn down along with that little building next to it. They are building a newer bigger Marathon like the one on the way to school.

Bennett's spring break starts today. He was golfing with friends last night. Suppose to snow this weekend. Tired of reading the posts from everyone going somewhere warm. I hope you enjoy photos. Will send a little each time.

Love you bigger than space. Proud of you - YOU GOT THIS!

Love, Mom

*   *   *   *   *

Today is Monday, April 4th and it is the beginning of Training Week 3. There is only this week and next and it will be the end of Phase 1. I am so full of anxiety I am just busting. Patrick and Chuck have both told me how Phase 1 is the toughest. Therefore, I am excited to find out that Drew is doing okay and that he will make it through Phase 1.

Phase 1 is my biggest concern for Drew – not physically or mentally but psychologically. Drew may say, "the heck with this, I don't need this in my life." It is not a matter of whether or not he can or could do it, but whether or not he has decided it is something he wants to do. I really need to find out that he successfully completed Phase 1.

I believe he will flourish in Phase 2. This type of thought process reminds me of my favorite spring vacation. Ironically, today is the day that many people, who have school-aged children, will be off on a scheduled spring break vacation. Drew's mother is always one that wants to go away for spring break and is always aware of someone going somewhere.

It always amazes me that she does not understand that with all of the people that she knows, that, "yes, someone is going off to some wonderful tropical paradise somewhere." While she has always wanted to go to the Cayman Islands or South Florida, my favorite vacation is spent right here at home in Paw Paw, Michigan.

Well off the roadway behind the back of our property and hidden from the road through a change in elevation, rolling hills and woods is a secluded pond. On one side of it, we built a structure that we refer to as the beach house. There are four beds, a couch, a refrigerator and a television. One year, we ran a 3,000 foot long cable under ground to bring power to the beach house.

My favorite spring vacation included myself, Drew, his brother, Bennett and Drew's friend, Connor Anderson. Drew and Connor were in middle school while Bennett was in elementary school. What more do four guys need than a beach house with four beds, a couch and a television. We spent the entire week at the beach house without ever coming home. The beach house grounds has a outhouse and a very large fire pit.

For an entire week, we had a continuous campfire, even during a heavy rain. Sometimes our campfire more resembled a bon fire and burned through an eight hour rain storm. We ate everything from pancakes and popcorn, to hamburgers, fried eggs and steak over the open fire on a tri-pod. Some meals consisted of MRE's that I purchased from a military surplus store in Kalamazoo. We would go on day long hikes where we would bring the necessary rations to be gone for hours from camp.

A couple days, we transplanted cedar trees that we found deep in the woods, up towards the open field by the barn and roadway. Over the years, we have been able to watch the cedar trees grow. We never lost a single tree from our spring break tree transplant operation.

Since Drew was five years old, he has been digging trenches down at the beach house and going on camping expeditions eating MRE's with canteens, ruck sacks and other equipment from the military surplus store. What else would I have ever envisioned Drew doing, than to join the military service.

* * * * *

April 4, 2016

Dear Drew,

When you get this letter it will be the last week of Phase 1. Your mother and I each send separate letters every day Monday through Friday, not Sunday or Saturday. I have sent numerous packages of protein bars and cough drops. Hope you are getting everything. Thus far we have received 3 letters from you. Very nice to hear from you; but, don't let that be an added strain. We love you and know you love us. We are fine. You let us know you are ok. Keep humping forward. When you get this letter the worst is behind you. Keep moving forward.

Today is 4 April 2016, it is the beginning of your week 3 in Phase 1. By the time you get this letter, you will be probably in your last week of Phase 1. Today April 4 is T-12, on T-23, which will be the Saturday of Week 4, which is next week, you will be getting on a bus and heading to Camp Pendleton for the commencement of Phase 2. Stick with it, Drew, you're almost there, Phase 1 is the worst. Phase 2 will be a lot of fun, shooting the gun, having exercises that have you out all night and doing a lot of the things that we used to do out camping.

Today is the first day of Spring Break, and please recall that my favorite Spring Break was when you, Bennett and Connor and I spent the week at the beach house. Remember how we cooked pancakes, popcorn, and hamburgers all on the open fire with the tripod. I bought some MRE's for you and we just had a week camping out. I always remember how we moved the cedar trees from in the woods up towards the open field by the barn and the road so we could watch them grow over the years. It's interesting how we didn't lose a tree!

Probably when you are getting this letter, next week begins with swim week on Monday, April 11, T-18, and ends with you going to Camp Pendleton. I just cannot say it enough, that that is the end of Phase 1. You will have gone through 5 weeks, Phase 2 is only 3 weeks.

Patrick and Chuck say that once you get through Phase 1 the Drill Instructors start to ease up a bit and start treating you like a man other than someone who needs to be taught to brush their teeth or take a shower. Phase 2 is just a few weeks. In your letter you said that you get to use a scope on your gun, I'm curious if through the tests it's with a scope or still with the iron sights. You get to use a scope for scoping distances and shots, but I have to believe the test is still with open sights.

I'm anxious to know if the actual test can be done with the scope. You're a natural marksman, but like I said in a previous letter, see what you can learn from them. At the end of Phase 2 you come back to San Diego and begin Phase 3. Once you get to Phase 3 you're there...you'll get fitted for your graduation uniform and we'll make flight arrangements. I want to fly back with you, so as that time approaches we'll coordinate how that is done. The big question will be, how long you want to stay in San Diego after graduation or how soon you just want to come home.

Your mother, sister, brother and I will probably be in San

Diego that entire week of graduation, and then we will just stay however long you want to stay.

I saw Jim Klett the other day and he was asking how you were doing, and I shared a few of the high points of your letters with him. Please recall how Jim wanted both of his boys to join the service and he is just so happy for me and the pride that I feel that my son is going to be a Marine. Please continue to bear down and do what you need to do to graduate. You are becoming a Marine, which is an enormous accomplishment and something that all of us will all be proud of for the rest of our lives. You have the physical and mental ability and certainly the determination. Please just keep taking one step at a time and before you know it, this will all be over.

I spoke with Patrick today as I was curious about how you receive mail and what the evenings were like for you. Patrick's big advice is to study your Handbook, whatever down time you have, study your Handbook. I think a helpful study technique is just to go over things in your own head. So if you're laying in bed or doing something that allows you the opportunity to escape mentally, think of whatever you can in a reciting fashion.

If there are 7 elements to something or 10 factors to something, recite those 7 elements or 10 factors in your head mentally. You know the tricks to memorization, it's mental memory and mental repetition. Again, Patrick said study your Handbook. You don't want to get through all this bullshit and be hung up on passing some stupid test. Study your Handbook.

This past weekend we had a snowstorm. April 3rd and I'm driving the snowmobile! It really came at a good time, because I had neglected in moving the snowmobile from the old barn to the new barn. We received quite a lot of snow and I was able to easily drive the snowmobile from the old barn to the new barn. Bennet and I have been doing a lot of work down at the cabin. This weekend we were hauling logs and cutting the logs out between the pond and the cabin. Now it's completely clear between the cabin and pond, and I'm going to plant clover and alfalfa so that we'll have an annual food source between the water and the cabin.

Down at the beach house Bennett and I started working on your new totem pole. We cleared the branches from the pine log and stripped all the bark. We'll have it set before your return. I think I told you how, when we came home from dropping you off on that Sunday Bennett and I went for a drive and we found a tremendous boulder and moved it down to the beach house and christened it "Drew's Marine Boulder." The boulder will look nice under this new totem pole.

We think of you daily and miss you tremendously. We are so very proud. Keep humping your way through this.

Love you bigger than the sky, and I am so very proud,

Love, Dad

* * * * *

Monday a.m.
April 4

Dearest Drew-

Oh how I hope you are hanging in there! You are almost done with your phase 1. The hardest challenge to you physically and mentally ever. I'm so proud of you. You are made of all the right stuff.

Of course the mom in me wants to hug you and care for you like no other after reading your letters and knowing you are suffering. Oh Drew! You are somethin'! I love you!

I last wrote Friday morning. Took the weekend off - was away. Dad and I are wondering about your mail. I wonder what days of the week you are without mail because we don't mail anything on Saturdays and Sundays. We both mail to you Mon - Fri everyday. I hope getting our mail is comforting to you and lifts your spirits.

I went to Chicago with Dawn this weekend. She got tickets to a concert at the Chicago Theater downtown. The concert is the 2 cellos. It is two men who play their cellos on stage, nothing else. They have rearranged music and play ac/dc, U2, Nirvana, etc. on their cellos. Dawn is a huge fan. We first saw them a few years ago when we went to see Elton John. They opened for him. She's been following them since. She drove her dad's Tahoe and we went to some friends who live in the city, but not downtown. They drove us to our hotel so we didn't have to park.

The friends are a husband and wife in their late 40s, both police sergeants for City of Chicago. They have different areas, but work same hours. He works in the area of Chicago that has more murders per square mile than anywhere else in the country. Yikes. They have a house next to Dawn's Dad on the lake in Lawton. They go on days off and vacations. They plan to retire there.

So we stayed at hotel downtown overlooking the river. We were just around the corner from the theater. We did a lot of walking. Did some shopping. Had a great dinner, wine. Show was great. Noticed so many foreigners downtown. The couple said all tourists, Chicago is hotspot for tourism. There really is so much to see and do. Have a client from Detroit and she was wondering what I would do in Chicago and what's the difference between Chicago and Detroit. Geez-where to start!

I really enjoyed our breakfast at little café on river.

Right now the news is full of anything and everything about Presidential candidates, especially Trump who is way ahead and the established Republicans are freaking out. Anyway, right across the River from our hotel room, was a Trump building with the name in huge letters, all lit up at eye level view with our 16th floor room. Can't get away from it all anywhere!

Dad and Bennett survived without me. Bennett went to concert last night with Anella and Teja. It was Eddie Money at the State Theater. He spent the night at the condo. Hope they had fun. Anella said Teja has never been to a concert in the USA.

Anella is very happy with him. I hope it continues.
Well my darling, gotta get ready for work.
 Love you bigger than space!
Mom

* * * * *

Through this process, I have been reaching out to a lot of gentlemen that have served in the Marine Corps. Patrick and Chuck have been invaluable. Today I called Patrick to ask him about the method within which the recruits receive their mail. I was trying to envision whether or not they had their own little cubbies and would find mail deposited or was it like you would sometimes see in the movies with a mail-call.

Patrick explained that it is all part of a process and part of a design of allowing their bodies to recover and recuperate. Keep in mind that these recruits do not have an opportunity to lay on the couch and have down time. Mail-call is a situation where they are called out in front of the barracks and are all seated on the ground. It is a time consuming process but it is a down-time and period of recuperation utilized in a productive manner.

At this point, I am curious as to how many letters Drew has actually received from us and whether he has been able to receive any power bars, protein bars and cough drops. In one of his letters to me, he mentioned how he wants me to continue to give him information about their schedule. Therefore, I mailed a copy of the recruit training matrix that I have been following. I am curious as to whether he has been allowed to have the materials.

My concern with him having the matrix is whether it would be too overwhelming. However, I believe that with the timing that I have given it to him, he will almost be through Phase 1 so that he will be able to see how the remaining time left is broken apart into a very doable situation.

I had mentioned to Patrick that today, T-12, Monday of week three was the confidence course. Patrick said it is a very large obstacle course and that he should have a lot of fun at that. I just continuously tell myself that he has gotten through the hardest part the last few weeks. In his last letter, he mentioned coordinating flights back after graduation. That is what I keep hanging onto - the fact that he still has in his mind, graduation.

* * * * *

Tuesday
April 5

Dearest Drew-

Just getting ready to head for work for the day. Beautiful sunshine, but COLD. It snowed on Saturday (right?!) and snowed again last night, April 4. Cold enough for it to stick.

I have some flowers popping up around the yard. Poor things.

Feel bad for Bennett. He would like to be playing golf, but the weather not cooperating.

My brother Mark is back in the States. He took his boys to Tennessee for Spring Break. I really enjoyed our trip there. We did some fun things - white water rafting, zip line, caves, shopping and tram.

I think of you often throughout the day. Little things will remind me of you and I'll either feel like crying or smiling. Oh, its hard to be a mom.

You are awesome! I love you very much.

Mom

* * * * *

5 April 2016

Dear Drew,

Hope you are feeling a sense of accomplishment and settling in a bit. If not - do, please. By the time you get this Phase 1 will be almost over. The worst is over - let the fun begin.

During Phase 2 and particularly Phase 3 DI treatment will be better and you are well on your way to becoming a Marine. WOW. What an awesome accomplishment. I am quite jealous. Just keep your focus and stay healthy and one step at a time.

I have been doing extra ab workouts for our June ab contest. My prediction is you may get a very close 1st, me 2nd, and Bennett 3rd, Anella 4th, then your mother. It will be here before you know it, so enjoy each moment at MCRD because that will all be over so quickly and you will some day miss it. Ha Ha Ha. Its tough, BUT so are you.!!!!!!!

Just keep your eye on the prize. I am so very proud of you.

Buck is doing well. I do not think I will take him on daily runs, but I do take him for a walk every other day, and he still just bounds around like a puppy. He is the greatest dog ever. He still watches for you in the evenings.

I have been talking with Patrick a lot. It helps to get a sense of your day and makes me feel closer to you knowing about some of the little details. It is also nice for him - a reminder of what he did and accomplished. He said he enjoys discussing it all with me.

Hope you are getting protein bars (sending some every day) and cough drops. I will send more - so far I have sent around 600.

Let us know if we can send anything else.

Take Care. Love you. Miss you.

Love, Dad

* * * * *

6 April 2016 - hump day – week three, T-14. Today the Matrix calls for combat conditioning exercise. Next week is the last week of Phase 1. Therefore, I imagine that in the middle of week three, combat conditioning exercises will be quite an exhausting and stressful situation. I am so excited for Drew to get to Swim Week and through Phase 1.

Swim Week starts week four, the final week of Phase 1. At the end of Phase 1, on T-23, they move to Camp Pendleton. Phase 2, looks like the entire three week period is held at Camp Pendleton.

Yesterday I spoke with Patrick. He indicated that much of the time at Camp Pendleton is spent outdoors. In particular, there are several excursions that keep the recruits out throughout the evening. In my mind, this is what Drew is made for and will have such an exciting time. My reservation relates to his feelings and commitment on wanting to continue down the path that he has chosen. I can only keep faith and believe that his stubbornness will carry him through.

Yesterday I discovered a very exciting aspect of the Marine Corps Recruit Depot in San Diego and its website. The website for MCRD San Diego has quite an extensive array of photographs of recruits in action. In addition, they have a Facebook page. Reviewing this, I noticed that many of the photos are identified as being during active recruit training time periods of recruits that have yet to graduate. The recruit is identified by his battalion and company and his position in the training period.

Some of the recruits in Phase 3 are from last week and identify them by name. Obviously we have to check this daily to see whether we can catch a photograph of Drew. Drew's mother is on Facebook, joined the link and received a post just this morning. This is very exciting news to us. I even called Patrick this morning to tell him about this aspect about the MCRD San Diego website and Facebook link. These obviously did not exist when he was there.

I am very anxious just to receive from Drew the self-addressed and postage paid return envelopes with the completed questionnaires. Things seem to be moving along smoothly and I need to receive confirmation from him that he is doing well on his end also. Looking at the photographs both yesterday and today, are just so compelling when you see a mother or father hugging their graduate after the ceremonies. I get so choked up looking at the photographs, I do not know how I will get through the actual event without breaking down numerous times.

Something noted in the news yesterday was that the United States Military Naval Investigative Services (NCIS) declared the recent death of a Marine recruit at Parris Island was not a homicide. A young man from Taylor, Michigan died 18 March at the Marine Corps Recruit Depot in Parris Island, South Carolina. This honorable young man lost his life five days after Drew had left for San Diego. I just cannot imagine what this young man's family is going through.

In a letter to the military, U.S. Representative Debbie Dingell, a democrat from Dearborn, asked for a prompt and unbiased inquiry into the circumstances surrounding recruit Raheel Siddiqul's death. Representative Dingle added that answers will help comfort Siddiqul's family and will provide Congress with oversight. Representative Dingle's letter is as follows:

* * * * *

April 4, 2016

General Robert B. Neller, Commandant
U.S. Marine Corps
3000 Marine Corps, Pentagon, Washington, DC 20350-3000

Dear General Neller:

This letter is in regards to the tragic death of U.S. Marine Corps recruit Private Raheel Siddiqui of Taylor, Michigan. Private Siddiqui died on March 18, 2016 after arriving at Parris Island for boot camp. He was a young man of the Muslim faith who loved his country and wanted to serve it and protect the freedoms for which it stands. My thoughts and prayers go out to his family and friends during this difficult time.

It is our shared responsibility to ensure there is a prompt and unbiased inquiry into the circumstances surrounding his death. Therefore, I respectfully request answers to the following questions to help ensure Congress and the family have a full accounting of the circumstances surrounding this tragedy.

1. What is the timeline for when the Navy Criminal Investigative Service is expected to complete their inquiry into the death of Private Siddiqui? It is critical that this thorough and comprehensive inquiry be completed as soon as possible.

2. Will the Marine Corps commit to preserving all relevant records relating to Private Siddiqui's death, including medical and autopsy records, and share them with Congress and the family at an appropriate time?

3. It is my understanding that Lt. Col. Joshua Kissoon, a recuit battalion commander at Parris Island, was relieved of his command one day prior to Private Siddiqui's death. Why was Lt. Col. Kissoon relieved of his duties? Was there any indication of his not being sensitive enough to the needs of recruits? Did Lt. Col. Kissoon ever interact with Private Siddiqui? Please provide a detailed response.

4. Some are concerned that hazing may have been involved in the death of Private Siddiqui. Has the Marine Corps received any indication that any hazing occurred in this instance? Does the Marine Corps have any policies in place to prevent and deter hazing from happening at basic training? Please provide a detailed response.

Answers to these questions will give the family comfort during these difficult times and will help Congress conduct oversight of this incident. Given the importance of this request, I ask that you respond to this letter no later than the close of business Monday, April 18, 2016. Please do not hesitate to contact me directly if you have any questions or need any more information.

Sincerely,
Debbie Dingell
Member of Congress

* * * * *

Wednesday a.m.
April 6

Dearest Drew-Drew-
Love you.
Looking at weather in San Diego this week, looks cooler with rain in forecast daily. Dad said you will be doing obstacle course this week. That's going to be difficult in the wet weather. We had a thunderstorm overnight with freezing rain. It's cold. Have the fire going.

Bennett spent the entire day yesterday putting the rocker panels on his truck that he got for Christmas. He put a few space heaters in the barn and pulled his truck in. Dad told him to leave it in the barn overnight so the sticker wouldn't come undone. It looks really nice. Can't see any of the rust along the bottom. Good thing it was in the barn because of all the cold rain overnight.

Dad was looking at the recruit website yesterday and saw a Facebook page dedicated to the San Diego Recruits. There are a lot of pictures of all the different companies. There were several pictures of yours when you guys first arrived and during receiving week. We looked and looked, but did not see you :(I will keep looking. How cool would it be to see my Drew Drew?

Dad can't take Buck running. So sad because he sits at patio door and when he sees the top of Dad's hat at sledding hill he starts crying. We've been walking him every day, which, of course, he loves!

Day off today. Cleaning and then doing some errands with Bennett later. His expensive driver has water in it. I have saved receipt. We'll see what happens. He does have golf today if the ground dries out.

Love you bigger than space! So proud of you!

Mom

* * * * *

THE WORST IS OVER

06 April, 2016

Dear Drew,

Here we are at Hump Day of week 3, T14. You will have been gone 5 weeks when you get this letter, and you will be finishing week 4 and the last week of Phase I. On T23, the Saturday at the end of week 4 of Phase I the Matrix says you are leaving for Camp Pendleton. I hope you are feeling good and strong, the worst is behind you.

Phase II is only three weeks long and it looks like a very productive and exciting time. Please remember the drill instructors will ease up just a tad and start treating you more like a man than a raw recruit during the five weeks of Phase I. Phase I was five weeks, Phase II is three, then you are on to Phase III and graduation.

Please continue to buckle down and do your best. I know you have the constitutional fortitude to be successful with this. I know its hard but I know you have the ability to succeed. Please just keep moving forward knowing that this is something you will wear as a badge of honor for the rest of your life.

I frequently look at the Marine Corps Recruit Depot San Diego website. I discovered they have a Facebook page. Your mother has joined the Facebook page. It is very exciting because they post photographs of the last five weeks. It is our hope to catch a photograph of you. The website and Facebook identifies the battalion and company. Even later into Phase III sometimes they identify the recruit by name. We will keep watching for you.

I noticed in one of the photographs an obstacle course including parallel bars and the recruits would do dips as they work their way down the length of the bars. I hope you are telling everyone that your dad can do more dips than anyone on base. You may win the ab contest but let me know whenever you are up for a dip contest.

Patrick says you will still get mail when you are at Camp Pendleton so we will continue to send letters. I am anxious to get your letters back that I included with an addressed, postage paid envelope with the questionnaire.

I will continue to send power bars and throat lozenges until directed otherwise. Buck is doing well. His new knee joint is functioning very well. Bennett speaks of you everyday. You have set yourself out as an exceptional role model for him. You should be very proud of the love and admiration you are achieving from all of your family, particularly your siblings and of course your mom and dad.

Take care and have fun at Camp Pendleton. By the time you get this letter, you will be finishing up week 4 and heading out to Camp Pendleton. It looks like Phase II commences on T24 with grass week. Patrick says Phase II is a lot of overnights out in the wilderness. A lot of shooting and a lot of maneuvering. Stay healthy.

I hope you are able to keep the Matrix I sent you. At first I thought it may seem overwhelming to you, but I figured by the time you recieved it, Phase 1 would almost be over and it would be helpful for you to see what was scheduled. Just take it a day at a time.

I will be curious to see how much of the time you spent there matches up to the Matrix. In case it was taken from you; around the time you get this letter it will be training week 4 - swim week. Mon, Tues, Wed - swimming. Thursday T21 Pugil sticks. Friday T22 Initial PFT - looks like a physical fitness test. Saturday T23 - Leave for Camp Pendleton and Phase 1 is over. 1st week at Camp Pendleton is Grass week.

Love you. Very proud. Love, Dad

* * * * *

Today is Thursday 7 April 2016 or T-15. It looks like an instruction day of Marine Corps mission and organization.

I mailed an envelope today containing three protein bars. Every day, for the past five days, I have sent an envelope containing three protein bars. Under separate mailings, I sent both my letter and Laurie's letter. Last week I sent numerous protein bars. There was about fifteen in one package and several packages of three.

It is my hope that by spreading this out, he may get to enjoy one or two of them. Under separate mailing, I am also sending a package with thirty vitamin C throat lozenges. My method has been to spread things out and send in various packages.

Today I am sending from Bennett, a flip comic that he created. It is perfectly sized for a smaller envelope wrapped in paper. On each side of the flip comic, I put four lozenges. This perhaps may make it directly into his hands as it is simply a small envelope of 2½" x 5" containing a yellow sticky note pad, which is 2 x 2 that Bennett utilized for his comic.

I think this may be the most ingenious manner to get him a throat lozenge. Some days, I honestly believe this is harder on his mother and I than him. Some times I feel there has been such a role reversal that it is ridiculous.

*　*　*　*　*

Thursday a.m.
April 7

Dearest Drew-

Are you getting tired of my letters? I still write every day. Hoping you feel like you know what's going on here.

Rained again all night. Cold and yucky! Bennett spent the day again yesterday in the barn working on his truck. That kid loves all things with a motor!

Did not walk Buck yesterday because of all the rain. I know - I'm a wimp.

I sewed Buck's blue ball together. He is on the couch with it right now. Dumb dog.

I've been working on stitching new stockings for Christmas. Don't worry, I won't throw away the old ones.

I almost took picture of the fruit stickers in the kitchen. I shake my head every time I look up there.

Going to repaint the hallway upstairs this weekend, some light color, haven't decided.

Still need to organize the basement. Last summer you made a mess down there! I've been trying to muster up the energy to deal with it, thinking should be a weekend when we can open the doors and air out.

Dad and I dieting. Of course he is dropping weight like crazy. He is stubborn like you and once he decides to do something he is all focused. He bought Bennett a bunch of Easter Sunday candy all marked down. He bought a bunch for the ladies at the office too. I hate that stuff around the house. During moments of weakness I always crave sugar. Taking a lot of resolve to leave that stuff alone. I AM DOING IT!

I've been making some kind of meat and then a vegetable for dinner. Bennett wants to lose body fat so his muscles are more pronounced. You can imagine him as the food police. He drives me nuts. You have been gone over three weeks. I am so proud you have been hanging in there - this is the most difficult you been challenged and you are doing it!

Have you connected with any of the guys in your company? Be sure to let them know its still snowing back home in Michigan.

Going to get ready for work. Love you so much! Think of you all the time. I'm wearing a charm Dad bought at Christmas, says "MOM", not taking it off.

You are so awesome! Love you bigger than space!
Mom

* * * * *

7 April 2016

Dear Drew,

Hope all is well. Quite a snowstorm here this morning. There are still several feet of snow up by Aunt Elaine.

I really hope you are doing OK. I am so jealous and envious of you. Suck it up for just what are some more weeks and you are a Marine. A badge of honor you will wear for the rest of your life. The worst part is almost over. Clearly you can see the light at the end of the tunnel. Keep humping. Study your handbook. Keep your head above water. Shoot straight. Study your handbook.

I have sent numerous separate packages of protein bars. Hope you get to eat some. Hope you got some cough drops. Mailed some this week. I also included a few in a little envelope from Bennett with the flip comic he made for you. Buck is doing great. He runs and walks normal.

Snyder has been sued with a RICO action. As nice as it is to see him getting what he has coming it is really sad that all of Michigan will be paying for his greed and dereliction for generations. His legacy is that of being the worst Governor in the history of all the States of the United States. Last week Fortune Magazine listed him as #1 - the worst leader in the world.

Anxious to hear how swim week goes for you. Probably over by the time you get this letter. While reading this your next week is Phase 2 and shooting it up at Camp Pendleton. Good Luck. You will do great.

Love you, Dad

* * * * *

I remember when Drew was three and wanted to be me. Every day, I am finding myself wishing to be Drew. I am jealous and envious of what he will be able to wear as a badge of honor for the rest of his life.

The Friday ending training week three, T-17, lists the day as Unit Drill. Yesterday was a very exciting day to hear from my little sister, Mindy. She told about the letter she received from Drew.

* * * * *

Dear Aunt Mindy,

The drill instructors like to mess with us a lot, and they always say that they are messing with us because we are worthless and we have no discipline, but we all caught on to the real reason a long time ago. When they mess with us or trash our house, its literally because we don't have anything else to do. They just make up excuses to punish us so they can kill some time before chow.

That kind of stuff has been toned down a little bit though. Instead they will have us clean the house, which is good because we get points towards honor platoon for having the cleanest house. Right now my pla-

toon is in the lead for honor platoon. We have a problem though, and its that we don't work as a team and we bicker like highschool girls.

I think the problem stems from all the 18 year olds who are fresh out of high school and have never lived outside their parents house before. I mean, I didn't live away from home for very long, but it was probably a little over a year. I think that's long enough to know what its like. A lot of the guys just act like they are still in high school. They are immature, but they think they are more mature than everyone else, and our leaders suck. They don't know how to lead.

That is all for now. Give my love to everyone else. Love, Drew

* * * * *

The exciting and settling part that I take from the letter is just how wonderful a young man Drew is. He expresses appreciation and a conveyance of concern, well-being and love for his aunt, uncle and young cousins. James is now 5 and Evelyn just 2. What I found comforting from the letter is that Drew is adapting and overcoming. I do not believe that he has ever been to a Catholic service before, other than his Aunt Pat's funeral service. I just love how he determined that the Catholic service was the right fit because it was longer and the Drill Instructors were not permitted into the service.

My Marine friend, Chuck had talked about how during church services, the DI's would walk the isles and openly yell and scream during the service if the recruit was doing something that the DI did not feel was appropriate. This could have been reading a letter or dozing off.

Today I went to the post office and mailed by priority mail a package of envelopes, blank paper and a book of stamps, along with today's letter. I did not address the envelopes so that he could send correspondence to whomever he chooses. The receipt indicated that the large envelope would be delivered in San Diego on Monday, 11 April. Surely he has received my letters with the self-addressed, postage paid envelopes and question-naires. I am anxious to go home this evening to check the mail.

* * * * *

8 April 2016

Dear Drew -

Today is Friday, T17. I do not know if you received the Ma-trix I sent so I will continue to identify the days. I am anxious to see if you have been receiving my letters.

When you get this letter Phase 1 will be in its last week and coming to an end. On T23 you bus to Camp Pendleton.

You wrote a wonderful letter to Aunt Mindy. You are such a nice young man. I love how you learn and adapt. Going to the Catholic Services because they are longer and DIs cannot go in. Brilliant.

I am sitting at my desk at Law office looking outside watch-ing it snow. SNOW!!! I can't believe it is still snowing. I want to go turkey hunting next week, not in cold wet snow.

I am going home for lunch today. Anella is home. She dropped Blazer off at Chris' for an oil change.

Bennett was jealous you sent Aunt Mindy a note. Try and send Bennett at least one quick note if you can.

I wish I knew what I could do to help you or send. Please let us know and it will get out to you.

I watched Pugil Stick fights on MCRD San Diego website and Facebook. Looks very violent. Hope you get mean - strike first - use great force - move forward with extreme violence! Get mean and aggressive! Move with an intent to kick ass. Get mean with that fucker, damn it !!!!! Knock that fucker's head off. Drive that Pugil stick through his chest.

No big plans for the weekend. Too cold to plant seeds down at cabin. May work some on your totem pole. Friday night - hip hip hurrah 5 hours of Modern Family.

Hang tough. You are the one that can do anything you set your mind to.

Love you. Very Proud !!!

Love, Dad

Drew at age 3

CHAPTER 5
SWIM WEEK /
TRAINING WEEK 4
"POWER BREATHING"

Training week four is swim week. Yeah, we swam the first day, and then the second day the people who failed the basic swim had to retake it. Then Wednesday, we did intermediate swim. So intermediate swim qualification, and I think maybe only one person passed.

They would pull people out of the pool and tell them they failed and they did not do anything wrong. Because they pulled me out of the pool and I did not do anything wrong, and I was mad. I got back to the locker room where we put all of our stuff on, and I was changing back into my stuff, and I said man that sucks, they failed me for bullshit, and then everybody else said yeah, I did not do anything wrong either and they pulled me out of the pool and that is what everybody said.

But that was for the higher certification. We would have to swim down the pool and back five times, and that would have been easy to do. I definately could have passed intermediate. But they just wanted you to pass the basic requirement. They just pulled us all from the pool because they did not want to take the time to put everyone through everything.

The end of phase I is move to WFTBN, for Phase 2. That is when we moved to camp Pendelton.

Today is 11 April, 2016, T-18, Monday of training week four. Drew has now been gone for four weeks going on five weeks. This is the beginning of the fifth week since he left.

Looking at the Matrix, it appears that it is the beginning of swim week. His mother and I discussed on Sunday how much he loved swimming and being in the water. Surely he will do well this week. Drew was one to jump into a patch of lily pads or swim into the depths of dark water. He is truly fearless around the water. How could one be afraid of something they love so much?

My anxiety today is wondering when I will receive a letter from Drew, returning my questionnaires. Under separate cover, I sent two separate mailings with postage paid envelopes. I have yet to receive one back. My thoughts have been questioning whether or not he has been able to receive any of the cough drops I have sent and how his throat is feeling. He has always had nasal and congestive type allergies.

I am further concerned with the change of environment that he could be having allergy-type symptoms with congestion and sore throats. His previous letters indicated throat pain from all the yelling. Both Patrick and Chuck have said everyone gets Marine Corps crud the first few weeks. It is miserable.

* * * * *

11 April 2016
T18 Monday
Training Week 4
Gone 5 weeks
End of Phase 1

Dear Drew,

You leave for Camp Pendleton and the beginning of Phase 2 at the end of this week. Phase 1 is over!!

By the time you read this swimming is over.

Phase 2 is 3 weeks at Camp Pendleton. After 3 weeks you return to MCRD San Diego and Phase 2 is over.

When you return to MCRD you get fitted for your graduation uniform. Light at the end of the tunnel is shining bright.

The week after you get this is Training Week 5, April 18, Monday, Grass week, Shooting. Phase 2, week 6 Table 1 - More shooting. Week 7, Table 2 - Field week. A lot of long hikes and runs.

Keep studying your handbook.

The weather is bad here. Snow and cold all weekend. Coldest opening day in Detroit Tiger history of past 116 years.

This weekend I found a ton of ancient sea corral and sea shells. Photo attached. Incredible shell cluster. All of my finds were in our vineyard!!! Our vineyard is a major ancient sea corral, sea shell fossil and shell cluster deposit. I am finding tons and tons. No Petoskey stones yet.

We have never found a cluster of shells like the attached photo before. I am also finding a lot of ancient sea shell fossils.

Buck is just swell. Doing great. I do not take him on runs, but take him for a walk every day.

Miss you greatly. Can't wait to see you and share some time.

Hang tough. Kick ass.
Very proud. Love you.
Dad

DREW

Basic swim qualification. For those of us who were able to swim on the first day and those that failed the basic swim qualifications were allowed to try again to push it through. On the third day of swimming, intermediate swim qualification, was the frustrating part of swim week. The instructors would pull you out of the pool even though you didn't do anything wrong. No one in the entire company was allowed to pass the intermediate certification. Something was up.

To me, it was very easy to accomplish, but for some reasons they did not make a declaration that you passed the intermediate qual. We would swim and be pulled out for not doing anything wrong. Back at the locker room, when I was changing my clothes, I was thinking that it was complete bullshit. Everyone in the locker room uttered the same sentiment. Again, for me it was simple. You swam down and back in the pool five times. It was quite easy to do but I think that basically they did not want to take the time to have the entire company go through everything because we had all passed the basic requirement.

The intermediate was not necessary and it would have taken a lot of time to have the entire company do it. Essentially they started pulling people out of the pool to be done.

* * * * *

Throughout the weekend, we rejoiced with him attending religious services on Sunday. Generally, the Catholics we have known or other Christians have complained about how lengthy Catholic services are and it is fun to see a situation where one relishes in the longevity of a Catholic service. He is adjusting and adapting to his circumstances and I am anxious to see whether there are other tricks and secrets that he has developed.

This is the last week in Phase 1. All of the Marines that we have consulted with, including Patrick, Chuck and Matt, have indicated that Phase 1 is the most difficult. At the end of Phase 1 on Saturday, T-23, the Matrix indicates that they will be moved to Camp Pendleton for the commencement of Phase 2. I am sure that he will be looking forward to moving onto the next Phase. I am anxious to hear from him.

Hooray! Hooray! This afternoon's mail (12 April) brought a postage paid, self-addressed envelope back that I had sent to Drew. The postmark is 8 April from San Diego, California. I am so excited that he has received some cough drops. I do not like that he is feeling bad and horrible. Interestingly, tea and coffee are not allowed, but he is drinking a lot of water, chocolate milk and Powerade. His responses to the Questionnaire are as follows, together with the letter that came with it:

* * * * *

Dear Family,

Week two went by fast. The days drag on forever, but the cough drops help to break up the day. Having a cough drop is kind of the same as having a smoke when I was back at home. It's something to do when I am bored or something to keep my mind off what's really going on.

I've grown fond of the coleslaw in the chow hall. I don't even know what it is. Is it lettuce or something? Let me know.

I spend most of the free time we get in the shitter room. Drill instructors like to walk into our squad bay during square away time and fuck our shit up for no reason. A bunch of us think its because they are scared that our platoon will win honor platoon instead of theirs. We have some fuck ups in our platoon, but I think we are the better platoon in the company.

The SDI said no more cough drops, but if I get more the worst he can do is take them away. He said that he will allow us to receive protein bars and powdered Gator-ade. Do not send it to the platoon, just send it to me. I shared a lot of the cough drops, but I have to stop because I don't want to run out before I get over this sickness, and yes I'm sick sick. It sucks ass.

When I run it feels like I'm breathing with one lung because the shit builds up in my throat and I can't get it out. And my nose is always super stuffed up. But anyways those cough drops came in handy. One of the recruits is called the scribe. He writes shit down for the DI. He is the one who makes the firewatch list, so I gave him a handful of cough drops to not write my name down for firewatch. Firewatch sucks.

I love you all, and I think about you every day.

Drew

ANSWERS TO QUESTIONNAIRE # 1

1. How are you feeling?
   _____ Good; _____ Bad; __X__ Horrible; __X__ Very Bad, but I will survive; _____ I think I will make it   _____ I am not sure I can do this.

2. Your favorite thing to eat for breakfast?
   _____Toast; _____Eggs; _____Pancakes; _____ Oatmeal; __X__ Cold Cereal.

3. I enjoy drinking a lot of the following throughout the day?
   _____ Water; __X__ (Chocolate) Milk; _____ Tea; _____ Coffee; __X__ Powerade.
   (Coffee and Tea are not allowed).

4. The best thing I have had for lunch is Chicken, Strawberry Banana Yogurt.

5. The best thing I have had for dinner is Chocolate cake or Apple Crisp. Noodles.

6. I am sleeping on the __X__ top _____ bottom bunk.

7. I have __4__ (how many) drill instructors.

8. Do you feel that you are building a good relationship with them?
   _____ Yes   __X__ No.

9. Are you looking forward to going to Camp Pendleton to learn how to shoot?
   __X___ Yes _____ No.

10. How did you do with the Pugil Sticks? Good.

11. How many letters have you received from us? A lot.
    (Your mother and I are sending mail every day. Do you get to
    receive letters every day or is it once or twice a week?) Every
    week day. I get at least one or two a day (How often)

    People from Michigan were the first ones to get mail.

12. On three different occasions, I have sent cough drops. Have
    you been able to get any?
    __X__ Yes _____ No.

13. What else can I send to you?
    _____ 100 granola bars   _____ 20 granola bars
    _____ 100 cough drops   _____ 20 cough drops
    _____ 500 cough drops

Only send one or two protein bars at a time. Maybe a bag of
drops at a time.

14. Please send me _____ and send me
    _____(number) of them.

15. Have you gone to Sunday Services? _____.
    If no - what do you do?

16. Have you been on night watch? How long is that?

17. Is there anything I can do for you?
    What are you doing each night?

Around 7-8 p.m. what are you doing? Square away time. Getting
things in order, taking a shit, reading/writing letters.
Have you had close quarters combat? Not actual fighting. Just
shadow boxing to learn technique.

I am just so excited about how the cough drops came in so "handy."

His letters indicate that the senior drill instructor does not want me to send any more cough drops. However, I think I will try to devise a method of sneaking a few through here and there.

Part of the excitement that I am feeling upon reading Drew's letter is also that he is requesting that I send powerbars, one or two at a time. Every day last week, I sent a package containing three in each package.

Interestingly, when he wrote this letter asking for Powerbars to be packaged one or two at a time, the very next day he started receiving a series of packages—one each day containing two or three at a time. How cool is it that immediately upon him making a request, it appears that it was met.

I had such a deep fear that he had not returned my letter with postage paid questionnaire, because he was feeling angry towards me for whatever reason, whether or not he was blaming me for him being there or he is feeling like I am trying to control him through my questionnaires and postage. So what a relief to get that back and to have him so appreciative of what I have done.

It has made me excited to think that my anticipation of separate packages of powerbars appears to have worked. Hopefully he received the envelopes, a book of stamps and paper. I am really hoping to just continue to provide him with what he needs. I like having the feeling that he has love and appreciation for me and what I have done and try to do for him.

The letter with the questionnaire, dated from San Diego, 8 April 2016, was sent to my Post Office Box in Paw Paw. That evening upon returning from work, I found in my home mailbox an envelope from Drew that is dated 4 April 2016. That letter is as follows:

* * * * *

Dear Family:

Every day at boot camp gets a little better as time goes on. But each day it gets harder and harder to wake up to a screaming drill instructor and march my aching feet to PT, classes and chow. Chow doesn't even matter much to me anymore. Its just an opportunity to sit down. I can't taste the food and it hurts too much to eat and swallow so I can't enjoy the food at all.

Its so hard to keep going sometimes. I can't think of the beach house to keep me going like dad does because it just makes me want to quit more and go back there. Instead I think about the book, "Night" by Ellie Wiesel that I read a long time ago for high school. It's about the Holocaust and its the author's true autobiography of what happened to him and his father.

Him, his father and all the other Jews with them had to walk something like 40 miles to a concentration camp in the snow with barely any clothing. That probably sucked a lot worse than what I'm doing. I am also grateful that the worst thing they can do to me is stress me or yell or give me two hours of firewatch. In some other places around the world they would just kill you if you weren't working out right for them.

Mom, Dad, Bennett, Anella and Buck:

Its really hard to write letters here. We get an hour of free time a day, called square away time. But it is barely a full hour and there is always something they tell us we have to do during that time. Today we had to mark our uniforms. It is something different every day.

My feet are not hurting because of running or marching, its because of all the standing. Sometimes we have to stand for 45 minutes to an hour without moving. After that walking actually feels good on my feet.

I got the first set of cough drops. We are not allowed to have them so I had to give them to the DI to put on the SDI's desk. Today the SDI got all the stuff from on his desk and decided if people could have it or not. He said I could have the cough drops, but no more cough drops after that. Then I opened up a package and there were a shit ton more cough drops in it, so I raised my hand and said "this recruit just received more cough drops sir", and the SDI said "Fuck it just keep the cough drops".

Thank you so much, these cough drops mean a lot to me. My throat is fucked up beyond all recognition. They probably won't let me keep any more though.

Also, I got a letter from Chuck Duncan. It was very nice. He told me not to write him back and to save the time for writing you guys, so tell him that I got the letter and I appreciate it very much. I will try to write him at some point, but after this I need to work on a letter to Aunt Mindy because I got some very nice things from her.

Every night I dream about being at home with all of you. Miss you all bigger than space.

Drew

* * * * *

It is important to note that this letter was written prior to the other letter. I believe it is important for the process of writing this book that it is interesting that the time sequence of the letter being written was before the letter sequence in the book. However, that is part of the process of mailing and retrieving correspondence. The systemic analysis is not complete until delivery. Further, it is a factual, accurate recreation of the events as they occur. It is interesting that the envelope postmarked 4 April, he is referencing the letter that was received by his Aunt Mindy last week Friday. For some reason, the 4 April letter took a while to get to us.

On T-19, Tuesday, 12 April, I sent a package including a stick of chapstick and an array of different throat lozenges. He has said that I cannot send cough drops. Therefore, I will now send throat lozenges, as well as three power bars.

I would really like to know how they receive their mail. Patrick had mentioned how they would occasionally meet out in front of the barracks. It would be a time consuming event where they are allowing their bodies to recover and having a period of relaxation while mail is being distributed. However, I would like to know whether this happens every day.

Drew's letter indicates that every week day he receives his mail. However, I am not envisioning how it is being distributed. In particular, the packages of whether he is receiving pieces of candy or snicker's bars. It is some how an honor system, which is indicated, given his last letter where he announced that "Recruit Cooper received some more cough drops". Is this mail distribution and package distribution an honor system?

Drew conveyed in his letter, that I received today, not to send any more cough drops. The letter that I sent out today indicated that I will stop sending cough drops and will now only send throat lozenges. How funny is it that the package he received today, 11 April (which was sent by priority mail on the previous Friday) a package containing Vitamin C throat lozenges.

It is very interesting that we are working off the same page, such that when he requested that I send power bars one or two at a time, he would have received packages containing three power bars each.

* * * * *

Today is 12 April 2016, T-19. It is the second day of swimming. Last night on the Marine Corps Recruit Depot San Diego Facebook page, we saw the Third Battalion Lima Company in the pool. These were photographs from this very same day!! We searched and searched looking for our Drew Drew.

* * * * *

Tuesday 12, April
Training week 4
T-19

Dear Drew,

I received two of your letters today. One was postmarked from San Diego on April 8th and was in an envelope that I sent to you with postage paid for your return, along with the questionnaire. It is interesting how the April 4th letter arrived at the house the same day that you had just sent that went to my P.O. Box.

The letter that was at the mailbox at home, I found very interesting relating to your reflection on the book Night by Ellie Wiesel. How heart wrenching it must have been for the people that endured the pain and torture to meet their death. You are fighting your elements, the reward recognizing great achievement. It is nice that you have the perspective and ability to understand the plight with others in comparison with what you are dealing with and trying to cope with. It is a very good, admirable human quality. I can understand your dilemma with trying to remove yourself to the beach house and how it would exacerbate your feelings from your absence from such a paradise. Just know that you soon will be returning to our little slice of utopia and a very nice festive bon fire – and you will be a Marine.

The portion of letter about you having to stand for long periods of time causes me to reflect on my Marine friend, Matt Fasbender. You may recall an exchange of correspondence between him and I where I reflected on that tree-hunting platform he placed on our east line by the pine forest. I could never get over how he would stand there for hours at a time and find that at all relaxing. To a Marine, having the ability to lean against a tree or partially sit, must be a piece of cake after doing the hours of standing like you are doing at recruit training.

You have also given me instruction that I am not to provide you with any more cough drops. From now on, I will be providing you with throat lozenges.

In the letter you sent home, you questioned what is in cole slaw. Typically cole slaw is finely chopped up cabbage, sometimes carrots and typically mayonnaise and sugar. These days, they also make a specific dressing identified as cole slaw dressing that is simply poured over cabbage and carrots.

I find it interesting how you enjoy the catholic services because they are longer and the DI's cannot come in from the perspective that you are adapting, learning and over-coming your obstacles. I think this is true with the little trick you have learned of going in the shitter when there are times when the other DI's come through to mess with the recruits and screw things up in the barracks.

By the time you get this letter, Phase I will be almost over and you will be getting on the bus to head to T-23, April 16, to Camp Pendleton. The first week of Phase II is April 18, T-24 and that is grass week on the Matrix. There is only three weeks in Phase II. Week 5, starting on T-24 is grass week. Week 6, starting on April 25, T-30 is table 1. Week 7, beginning on May 2, T-36 is field week with table 2.

You will then return on Sunday, May 8, S-7, which is after Saturday, T-41. I think that Phase II will be a lot of fun for you. A lot of long hikes and runs and you will be learning to shoot and work in the field. The first week upon returning from Camp Pendleton on May 10, T-43, you get fitted for your graduation uniform. Phase III looks really tough but you will you be almost done. Just keep humping, know that we miss you greatly and think of you often.

Love you, Dad

P.S. MCRD San Diego Facebook had photos of your company in the pool from Monday on Monday! We think we see you!!

Hopefully the pool is cleaning out your nasal passages and you kick the crud you are suffering from. Change in climate - allergies - or Marine Corps Crud, as Patrick would say. When you get this Phase 1 is over!!!

Hope you are getting the protein bars. I sent out at least 5 packages with 3 in each. One larger package and after today I have 8 packages with 2 in each I will send one package every day, and restock when those are gone, the same way or some other fashion if I get a letter from you so indicating. No more cough drops - just lozenges.

Stay strong. Stay committed. Study your classroom materials. Kick Ass.

Take care. Very proud. Love you. See you soon. Dad

* * * * *

Tuesday a.m.
April 12

Dearest Drew-

Got two letters yesterday, woohoo! We eagerly soak up each sentence and then talk about it the rest of the night.

Wondering when your poor throat will feel better. I'm sure hoping that swimming this week will help with your stuffiness. You were always better in the summer when you swim everyday. Good way to clean out your nose.

Coleslaw is shredded cabbage, mayo, little sugar, and sometimes shredded carrot. Dad's grandma Nellie made the best coleslaw. It had cucumber and onion in it too. I regret not learning how she put it all together.

The weather here is on the upswing. Getting warmer as the week goes on. Looking forward to working outside this weekend.

The birds have been so loud in the morning. Do you have any song birds around there?

Bennett was not pleased with how he played yesterday but he did O.K. He said the course was the hardest he has ever played. He enjoyed the group of kids he was placed with.

You still sound like you in your letters. You are clever and you figure it out. Kudos to you and the cough drop bribe as well as avoiding chaos in the evening by going to the toilet. That's my Drew.

Wondering if some of the kids could not swim and really struggled. That would be terrifying. There were seven pictures of your company in the pool area yesterday on Facebook. I follow the San Diego Recruit Page and they post a lot of photos. We think we see you in one but aren't sure as it is slim slice of face in distance.

You're so awesome!

I love you bigger than space!

Mom

* * * * *

In his letters, he complains of congestion and having the

crud. It is my hope that the pool will help cleanse his nasal passages and he will come out of it feeling well. Drew was born and raised in the water and should not have any problem with the swimming certification.

I always hate living by targeting a certain date in the future. Yes, there is the formation of goals and the accomplishment of those goals; however, I have found that life passes you by so quickly when you are always living for the future. It is more important to try to enjoy each day. I am finding it difficult to do that while Drew is at Marine Corps Recruit Training. You know that he is miserable each day and therefore, you too are looking forward to a future date.

Hopefully, getting cleansed through swimming and the completion of Phase 1 will not be such a bad thing of wishing time to pass.

* * * * *

13 April 2016
Training Day 20

Dear Drew,

Today is last day of swimming and hump day for the last week of Phase 1.

Patrick says you will get some mail at Camp Pendleton so hopefully you are reading this in the midst of Grass week and Phase 2.

According to the Matrix you had Pugil sticks the day after swimming. I do not see any more Pugil stick days on the schedule.

The 3 weeks at Camp Pendleton looks like a lot of training outdoors and rifle certification. Good luck. I am anxious to see how great you are at shooting. You are quite deadly here in Michigan. A natural shooter.

There is quite a disagreement as to whether we see you in the pool photos. Some people in the photos are clearly identifiable, but the person some of us believe to be you is a tough shot to make out. Can't really see the person very well so there is disagreement as to whether it is you. I say yes, as well as Grandma. Mom is a probably, Bennett is no, and Aunt Mindy is a maybe. When I show you the photo, my interest other than whether it is you; and I think another photo may have you in it, is a photo of a guy that is quite a tubby. I can't believe this guy is doing any pull ups. He looks happy, but he can't be ripping off a pull up.

You should be getting a package of protein bars every day. I hope you are not running out of drops and lozenges. I am still sending those too. Not every day like the protein bars, but frequently.

My friend Matt said his son Alex had somebody receive a large box of Snickers bars and the DI allowed them to eat them. Alex said it was the best candy bar he ever ate. It was during Phase 3 so DI let it go.

I figure after Phase 2 and the first week of Phase 3 I will try and get some through to you.

The first week of Phase 3 is Team week. Interior guard and then your favorite - blood drive.

I really hope the pool cleaned out your respiratory system and the fresh air of Camp Pendleton has you breathing better.

Stay Strong. Miss you.

Love, Dad

P.S. Watched Napoleon Dynamite yesterday.

* * * * *

Dearest Drew-

May be funny but also entirely possible for me given my tendency towards clumsiness and bad luck.

I remember Aunt Mindy had a story - she and Dan were out to dinner and she was feeling cute in her little dress. She came out of bathroom and didn't know until someone told her at the end of dinner that her dress was tucked in her underwear. Yikes!

Today is your last day in the pool. I sure hope it has helped your nose and throat.

Took Buck for a walk yesterday after work. Laps around the vineyard. He sure enjoyed it. Knee looking good.

If we have some warm weather we should be getting mushrooms soon. Remember the Muvrin Orchard that year they were everywhere! I won't tell you when Dad cooks them. That would be cruel.

Have meeting this morning then coming home to weed the flower bed and sweep garage, pick up sticks. Maybe mow this weekend.

I'm so proud of you Drew. I miss you terribly. Miss the smirk.

Love you bigger than space!

Mom

* * * * *

Having time pass makes me think of other veterans that I have known, such as Andy Myers from World War II and James Klett from the Vietnam era.

Andy was on the Beaches of Normandy, at the Battle of the Bulge, and liberated a number of concentration camps. After returning safely from the war, he lived life with the best attitude ever. All he wanted to do was get married, have children and live on a farm. While living that dream there was a tragic accident. Andy's wife and daughter were killed as a result of a driver running a stop sign. You never would have known the pain and suffering that Andy saw in his life, given the manner in which he lived each day as though it were a blessing. He treated each individual with dignity and honor. Andy Myers was a true American Hero.

James Klett was a recent graduate from University and was looking forward to his future running a business. However, shortly after graduation, he received his draft notice and was driven to the Van Buren County Courthouse by his wife, Andy. A draftee in a war that he knew nothing about. Jim would go on to live his life as a captain of industry. He sold his asphalt road paving business for tens of millions of dollars.

Two men of distinguished lives and honor. I pray each day that my Drew is on the path for such a life.

* * * * *

Today is 14 April, T-21. Swim Week is coming to an end and they get to light things up with more pugil stick combat. In Drew's response to my first questionnaire, he responded that he did "good" at pugil sticks. After seeing the MCRD website and what takes place with pugil sticks, it is quite different than the photograph on the matrix.

It appears to be quite a violent endeavor. It is my hope that the chlorine in the pool cleaned out his nasal passages and he is starting to feel better relating to his respiratory system. My fear is that he could develop a serious lung infection or pneumonia and that could set him back in the process. Hopefully between the pool and going to Camp Pendleton next week, physically relating to his organ functions, he should be feeling well.

* * * * *

14 April 2016
Training Day 21

Dear Drew,

Pugil sticks today. MCRD website makes it look very violent. Hope you get mean and kick ass!!! Phase 1 is over when you get this. You are probably at Camp Pendleton. Google Earth dials it in pretty good. MCRD is in the heart of San Diego. Camp Pendleton is Northeast of San Diego. Looks like it is out in the countryside and mountainous. Mountains and desolate.

I am betting your bus ride was 1-2 hours depending on traffic. You start and end Phase 2 at Camp Pendleton. 3 weeks. It will be a very tough 3 weeks, but, hopefully a different kind of tough situation than the past 5 weeks. After Phase 2 I hope you experience what Patrick and Chuck report about the DI's being better about treating you like a man. It all had its purpose and hopefully you are not sick sick anymore and feeling better, both physically and mentally and done with the bullshit DI games.

I am anxious to hear about the swimming certification, pugil sticks, rifle range, over nights at Camp Pendleton, and a breakdown of each day. You know how I like the little details, like the Babin book - every minute of your day has been kept occupied. I am anxious for you to tell me how, for example: Wake up on T13 at what time jump out of bed to do what? Then what? And then? And then? Compared to T19 - go to the pool - what time? Did what? Etc., etc., etc., etc.

You will get to Camp Pendleton on Saturday T23. On Saturday T29 you have a 5 mile hike. That will be tough - hard etc - but have fun with it. Qualification Day is T34. Friday. (These dates are from Matrix I have - I do not know how accurate it is). I am interested to hear how accurate the Matrix was from what you experienced. I keep it on my office desk and refer to it throughout the day.

I also frequently look at Marine Corps Recruit Depot San

Diego website and their Facebook page. I also like checking things out on Google Earth. Thinking about you everyday - all day.

The first week of Phase 2 is called Grass Week. The 3rd week is called Field week. What is Grass week? What is Field week? And what is the difference between grass week and field week?

I think the crucible is everything you are doing in Phase 2 at Camp Pendleton compacted into a couple of days. Keep that in mind - the crucible will be things you have done already. It is T61 - just days before graduation and that will be here before you know it. I mean - look - Phase 1 is done!!!!

You cannot stop time. A lot of times we wish it away and other times we try and slow it down. Can't - moves at its own pace. We just gotta cope and deal with it on our terms the best we can. That is where counting your blessings and taking stock in yourself comes into big time play. You are brave, fearless, strong, fit, smart, highly intelligent, polite, honorable, fun, funny, and have the constitutional fortitude to be a wonderful man and human being. Just hang on tight and take one day at a time and soon we will be in each others arms and I will be calling you a Marine!!!

When I think of your overnights at Camp Pendleton I think of our camping at the pond, cabin - beach house and that time we pitched a tent at the Pine Forest. I can vividly picture you sitting in a chair in front of the tent with a smile from ear to ear. That was a fun camping experience.

Of course the best Pine Forest story is the time it was raining on me when there was a blue sky and the sun was shining. I will never forget having the thought flash through my mind "how is it raining all over my head when the sun is shining and there is not a cloud in the sky!!!"

When you are reading this you will almost be done with week 6 or maybe even 7 depending how you get mail at Camp Pendleton. You get back to MCRD during training week 8. 9

weeks there. Hang tough. Love you.

Love, Dad

P.S. I just received the questionnaire back from you. We have and will continue sending protein bars and drops. Every day package of 2-3 bars go out. Once a week - bag of drops. More if you want.

I love how you got to keep the Matrix !!! Awesome. Keep track in your notes its accuracy.

We all will fly back when you want, our beach house is paradise in June.

Love you.
Very proud, Dad

* * * * *

Dearest Drew -

A quick note this morning. It's my Thursday morning meeting - run out the door quick morning.

We have a sunny day. Still cool, but it looks beautiful!!

I can't wait to get home today and walk outside. I've been walking Buck every day (or he's been walking me) and he looks good (me, not so much). He's such a happy dog.

Mark is going back to China on Monday until October. I'm now on a mission to find a home for his cat. She is black with a white face and is really sweet. I wish we could take her but Bennett would fuss. He really was snotty and sneezy when Gambit stayed with us.

Anella is now on Facebook. Can you believe it?. Teja is pretty much staying with her. They are talking about the future.

You are almost done with week 4. WOW!! You are amazing! I sure hope you are feeling better.

Love you bigger than space!
Mom

* * * * *

I sent photographs of Drew's company in the pool to Chuck Duncan. Chuck's response was that it brought back such memories, which for Chuck, would have been over 30 years ago. How similar was the pool experience for Drew versus what Chuck went through? Is it the same pool? Is it the same facility? How much has MCRD changed or stayed the same in the past 20, 30, 40 years.

The pool brings Phase 1 to a close. Chuck mentioned that the worst is over and he wishes that he could say that it will get better, as it will, however, it is still extremely tough. Clearly the first few weeks is when the recruit numbers thin down the most.

I just cannot imagine what it would be like to be 18 years old, away from home the first time and put through a meat grinder. Every minute of the day is accounted for and in a manner that sets your normal upside down. Phase 1 is five weeks, where Phase 2 is three weeks. Clearly the purpose for each Phase has its definitive missions.

Phase 1 ends by getting on a bus and heading to Camp Pendleton. Phase 2 ends by getting on a bus and coming back to MCRD San Diego with the return week being Interior Guard and Team Week. The second day into Phase 3, you get fitted for your graduation uniform. The thought process and planning is strategic and is a clearly defined mission of creating and developing a Marine.

The ground is cultivated and the seeds planted. It is not only a test of will, but of one's constitutional fortitude as to the very basic foundation and principles of whether or not the recruit is able to make the cut. It is not simply a matter of wanting to or having the will, one also has to have the guttural ability and the foundational make up, the constitutional fortitude, to be able to succeed through the three Phases.

Interestingly Matt Fasbender recalled his most strenuous and testing time being half way through. He was feeling that he could see the light at the end of the tunnel, but quite frankly, he had enough of the drill instructors who were continuing to ride his ass. He had enough of them and wanted to proceed to the finish line. I am anxious to see what Drew's feelings are relating to Chuck's status, ideas and the training following swim week versus Matt's feelings concerning the most difficult time for him. Matt would have graduated from Marine Recruit Training around 1982. Patrick said everyone gets to their breaking point. You just have to get past it.

* * * * *

Dear Gramma and Grandpa,

Boot camp is going well. I only have one week left in the first phase, so the worst of it is over. I am starting to get used to the routine. My only complaints are that we have to stand from morning to night so my feet always ache and that we only get to brush our teeth once a day. I thought that they would stress the importance of brushing twice a day.

I sleep well every night because of how tiring the days are. I look forward to rack time all day.

I think I have trench foot because my big toe and heel on my left foot have been numb for about three weeks. Its starting to happen to my right foot too. Its weird because they are numb, but they still hurt really bad.

On Sundays they offer about six different religious services. I have been attending the Catholic service, but today is the first Sunday that I haven't gone to church because I wanted to see what we would be doing if we don't go to church. It turns out that we get three hours to do whatever we want. I'm using the time to write letters and study for a test that's coming up. By now it feels unnatural having so much time to myself.

Thank you for the letters and for the pictures. Mail call is one of the few things we have to look forward to here. Its always refreshing when we get mail.

I love you and I look forward to seeing you again.

-DREW

* * * * *

Today is 15 April 2016, T-22. I am very excited as Drew is leaving tomorrow for Camp Pendleton and he has made it through Phase 1. I received a questionnaire back from him yesterday that I had sent on 1 April 2016. He completed the questionnaire, returned it to me and I received it on 14 April.

* * * * *

Dear Dad,

1. Circle one (yes no) *I can read your and moms cur sive writing. "But its tough."*

2. I (**will** will not) beat you in the 6-pack contest.

3. I get mail (*daily - except weekends once a week or twice a week)*

4. I (**did** did not) get any cough drops.

5. I have seen 6 of your letters (**yes** no).

6. Postage paid return envelopes (**are** are not) helpful.

7. Please send **protein bars** and **cough drops**.

Please provide answers - write thoughts that come to mind and return in the postage paid envelope. Just seal and put in the U.S. Mail.

1. Have you received all of my letters — particularly the typed ones. *Yes.*

Have you received letters from me that are typed?
Circle one: (**yes** no)

2. Did you get a short letter from me that included the actual Matrix calender - schedule for 13 weeks? - *No "I got one where you told me a lot about the schedule but not actual Matrix - Yes. Just opened that one up."*

3. Have you received any cough drops? (**yes** no)

4. Can you receive packages by mail only? (**yes** or no)? I see people getting things from: UPS? FedEx? Just US mail?

"I don't know"

5. Please send: Cough drops; Protein bars; *Not a lot at a time anymore.*

As far as coming home, I want to come home as soon as possible. Fuck San Diego, I want to be on a plane to Michigan as soon as possible. I want to spend the whole ten days in Paw Paw and Kalamazoo.

Thank you for the Matrix, it comes in handy.

* * * * *

Reviewing what he says, I can see that he is willing and able to communicate. However, he does not have a lot of time to do so. Therefore, in today's mail I sent to him postage paid envelopes with addresses to his Gramma and Grandpa Barton in Portage, Michigan, his Grandpa Cooper, who is residing in a nursing home in Florida, his Uncle Mark and Aunt Susan in Leslie, Michigan and his Uncle Dick and Aunt Lisa who reside in South Haven, Michigan.

I realize that Uncle Dan and Aunt Mindy have communicated with him and he has corresponded with them, as well as his Uncle Mike and Aunt Sarah have communicated and I am sure he will get something back to them. I believe it is likely that his Uncle Mark and Uncle Dick have not sent him anything.

I thought it may be nice for Drew to send them a little note. I believe just having him have an awareness of others that care for him and him thinking about them and expressing thoughts towards them will give him strength and continued confidence.

Today I am sending him a more detailed questionnaire along with today's letter that lays out the idea that time is getting us closer to the light at the end of the tunnel.

* * * * *

15 April
T-22

Drew,

Hope all is well. According to the Matrix you have finished swim week and are heading to Camp Pendleton tomorrow. I received correspondence from you indicating that you were able to receive the Matrix I sent.

I am surprised they are allowing you to keep it so be careful with how much you expose it to others. I am really curious as to how accurate the Matrix is with your daily events.

I was hoping that being in the swimming pool and having your respiratory system flushed, it may have helped with your Marine Corps crud. However, Patrick tells me that you will be sick throughout most of your stay there just because of the circumstances and exposure to all of the different elements.

I think it is part of whether or not someone can become a Marine as well as whether or not you have the constitutional fortitude to not just physically pass the physical tests of strength, but whether or not you have the body make up to make it through. It is kind of like anything else with people and what they are exposed to and their ability to endure or pass. Obviously with this situation, it is a lot more intense and the test is a lot more difficult.

You are probably getting this letter in the midst of Phase II. Patrick said that you will get mail at Camp Pendleton so I am hoping that this gets to you there and not waiting for you when you get back to MCRD.

I received your letter indicating that you want to leave San Diego as soon as possible. I will make arrangements for us to fly out on Saturday. You graduate on Friday and it would be nice to have a celebration with you, relax and the next morning get up and head home.

Previously in the last week or so I have sent some stamps and envelopes. I hope that you received those and are able to find them useful.

Enclosed is another questionnaire that I hope you can quickly fill out and put in the postage paid, return envelope.

The weather here is finally turning and hopefully we will have some warmth. While this past week we have had blue skies and sunshine, it still has been very cold. I imagine morel mushrooms should start popping. I am going to take a look this weekend. Of course your mother has asked that I get the lawn mower out so that she can continue with her obsession of mowing. My hero is Paul Adams that lives by the golf course and has not mowed his lawn in five years.

Please keep in mind that it is going to continue to get better as you not only get the worse behind you, but the drill instructors will start treating you in a different manner. You will also be feeling better about yourself and your ability to accomplish all that you have.

Yesterday I received the questionnaire that I had sent to you on the first of April. It is interesting that I received it back on the 14th of April. So, if you hold this questionnaire to fill out the rifle range test and then mail it back to me, I will not be getting it until the end of Phase II or the beginning of Phase III. That will mean that you are just weeks away from graduation.

I am making flight arrangements now, but I am insuring the reservation so that I can move things up or push them back. For now, we are figuring that we will leave Saturday after graduation. If things change for your scheduling and desires, we can always push things back.

Love,
Dad

* * * * *

QUESTIONNAIRE

Circle Answers.

1. You went to the swimming pool for three consecutive days. Each day, did you get a set of dry clothes and boots or did you have to wear the same wet stuff each day?

Same Clothes Same Boots Different Clothes Different Boots

2. Did flushing out nasal passages swimming help with your sickness at all?

Yes No Still feeling like shit Feeling a little better

3. The website indicates that you get certified for swimming and that certification lasts for two years. How did you do?

Did very well and passed   Struggled and passed

Had a lot of fun   Hated swimming

4. Are you still going to Catholic Services?

Yes_____ No_____

5. If you are still going to Catholic Services, you should try communion sometime. Have you tried it?
Yes_____ No_____
(I was baptized in the Catholic Church. Aunt Pat and my grandma and grandpa loved being Catholic. The funeral service we had in Three Rivers (that I spoke at) was a Catholic Service).

6. Are you still sure that you want to come back to Michigan as soon as possible?

Yes_____ No_____

7. Graduation is Friday, are you okay with leaving Saturday morning?

    Yes_____ No_____

8. Do you want me to try and send Snicker bars?

    Yes_____ No_____

9. If yes, do you want me to try to send:

    1 or 2   100

10. List for me what you want me to send:

    _____

    _____

    _____

11. Describe for me how you did with the rifle range?

    Passed   Failed   Loved It
    Hated It

    Open sights   Scope

12. Are you able to go to church services at Camp Pendleton?

    Yes_____ No_____

13. If yes, what service are you going to?

14. The bus ride from MCRD from Camp Pendleton took:

1 hour   2 hours   3 hours

15. The bus ride was:

A nice break   A bunch of bullshit
A very scenic tour

*   *   *   *   *

Dearest Drew -

I liked this card because reminded me of you. Whenever you want to tell Dad or me something you start out with, "hey mom". Love that.

Going to be a beautiful day today. I am working extra - bummer! Remember the orange plastic fence we would pull across the driveway when you guys were playing out front. That was a good idea - really. The cars go so fast down our road. The scooters were always fun in the driveway. It was fun taking them to the Celery Flats Trail. You guys were so cute.

I can't tell you how much we are all looking forward to SPRING. You've got some nice weather in San Diego, though probably last thing on your mind. Think carefully about when you want to return home. I don't want you to regret not spending a day at the beach. Don't worry about us - we will go a week early if need be. Dad and Benett going to Ducks Unlimited tonight.

Love you bigger than space!

Mom

*   *   *   *   *

Answers to Questionnaire

Circle / Underline Answers.

1. You went to the swimming pool for three consecutive days.   Each day, did you get a set of dry clothes and boots or did   you have to wear the same wet stuff each day?

Same Clothes   Same Boots   Different Clothes
Different Boots

They had old shitty clothes and boots for us to wear.
We got in our shorts and walked through a hallway to put the shitty stuff on.

2. Did flushing out nasal passages swimming help with your sickness at all?

Yes_____ No_____ Still feeling like shit _____
Feeling a little better_____

3. The website indicates that you get certified for swimming and

that certification lasts for two years. How did you do?

Did very well and passed   Struggled and passed

Had a lot of fun   Hated swimming

Nobody passed intermediate. I could have passed, it was very easy. Everybody got called out for bullshit. I didn't do anything, they just didn't like how I looked or something.

4. Are you still going to Catholic Services?
Yes No. If you don't go to church you get square away time.

5. If you are still going to Catholic Services, you should try communion sometime. Have you tried it?

Yes No. I don't think I'm eligible even though I'm baptized.

(I was baptized in the Catholic Church. Aunt Pat and my grandma and grandpa loved being Catholic. The funeral service we had in Three Rivers for Aunt Pat (that I spoke at)

was a Catholic Service).

6. Are you still sure that you want to come back to Michigan as   soon as possible?

Yes_____ No_____ Fuck Yes_____

7. Graduation is Friday, are you okay with leaving Saturday morning?

Yes_____ No_____

I might hang out with some of the guys from my platoon Friday night.

8. Do you want me to try and send Snicker bars?

Yes_____ No_____

And more Gatorade bars.

9. If yes, do you want me to try to send:

1 or 2   100

10. List for me what you want me to send:
Cough drops, ricolas, protein bars - please send at least 3

at a time. The Gatorade ones are the best. Snickers bars.

11. Describe for me how you did with the rifle range?
Passed   Failed   Loved It
Hated It

Open sights   Scope. I haven't done the rifle range yet.
That's happening this week. I'll let you know.

12. Are you able to go to church services at Camp Pendleton?

Yes_____ No_____

13. If yes, what service are you going to?
I don't go to church anymore. I use the time to read and
write letters.

14. The bus ride from MCRD to Camp Pendleton took:
1 hour - maybe 2   2 hours 3 hours

15. The bus ride was:

A nice break   A bunch of bullshit
A very scenic tour. I saw the Pacific Ocean for the first
time while on the bus.

16. Pugil sticks:

Ok   Fun   Bullshit
I am pugil sticks: Champ Chump I did very well but not
too impressive.

17. Any boxing?   Yes   No. Not until the crucible.

PHASE 2 – OORAH
"CAMP PENDLETON –
DO NOT GO TO MEDICAL"

According to the Matrix, week five is Grass Week. 18 April 2016, T-24 is the first day of Phase 2. Phase 2 takes place at Camp Pendleton in California. On Saturday, the recruits would have left Marine Corps Recruit Depot in San Diego and traveled to Camp Pendleton.

Depending on traffic, this trip takes between 1-2 hours. The Friday before Drew's departure, his Gramma and Grandpa Barton received a letter from him that was very uplifting for all of us. Drew's letter to Gramma and Grandpa indicates that he is doing well and seems to be in good spirits.

Dear Gramma & Grandpa.

As far as the sock situation goes, I could change my socks every day if I wanted to, but then I would have to sacrifice sleep in order to do laundry. I do laundry on Sundays when we get time in the morning, so that allows me to change socks about every two or three days. It gets tricky when we have a hike or something though because I only have a couple pairs of good hiking socks. They are very expensive so I didn't want to buy a lot. The hiking socks help a lot, but the DI's say that infantry guys better get used to numb feet. I meant to buy some powder to put in my boots to absorb the moisture, but I keep forgetting. We always get rushed at the PX. (PX means personal exchange, its just a store).

I'm almost done with phase two. I remember being a brand new recruit and seeing phase three recruits. They looked so much more developed as Marines, and they were always so loud and good at marching. It is weird to think that in a week new recruits will be looking at me and the rest of my platoon, and they will be thinking the same things I thought. I can't wait to graduate and go home to see everyone. I miss Buck a lot too. I can't wait to see him. I'm also looking forward to meeting my new cousin. Whenever we are just standing around I can't help thinking about all the good food I want to eat when I get out. Pizza and burgers are both number one on the list.

I love you very much,
-DREW

*   *   *   *   *

His feet hurt terribly and it is our belief that as long as there is pain, there is still sensation in the feet and he will endure. I am sure from the words expressed in his letter that he will no longer be attending church services. While it was nice that the Catholics did not let the drill instructors come in and their services are longer, as a result of staying in his barracks and seeing what happens if you do not go to church services (being left alone and allowed to do whatever you want for a few hours) had to be quite a culture shock from having every moment of the day accounted for during the week. It will be interesting to see what he does in S-2 and 3 relating to the religious services.

Something that I have always admired about Drew that will bode well for him at MCRD is his natural inclination to be fearless. Being fearless has always allowed him to be an exceptional marksman. This first week of Phase 2, learning to shoot a rifle, should be something in which he excels. I have seen Drew harvest numerous types of wild game with shots that I would hesitate and blow, while he methodically and carefully takes well aim and performs timely. His first buck was at a distance that would have caused me to hesitate and completely blow the opportunity.

I am anxious to know how he is feeling physically. I am sure the Marine training regimen is aimed towards building muscles and endurance. There is no room for body fat for a Marine to endure whatever situation they are put in. Whether it is running, walking, standing or exerting core muscle groups, a United States Marine has to be a lean, mean fighting machine.

Going into MCRD, Drew was able to physically accomplish the minimum requirements for the feats of physical strength. I am interested to see how his musculature has changed and how he is feeling. Attempting to cope with the endeavor ahead, prior to leaving, Drew formed a healthy attitude that he was heading out to 13 weeks with his own personal trainer. I wonder how that plan has worked out for him.

* * * * *

18 April 2016

Dear Drew,

Gramma and Grandpa shared the letter that you sent to them the Sunday before your last week of Phase I. It was a wonderful letter in a number of ways. First, I thought it was very nice that you did not swear to your Gramma and Grandpa. Second, I think that you were pleasantly surprised to learn what happens if you do not go to Sunday services. I imagine that your attendance of services on Sunday has come to an end. It had to be an overwhelming experience having a few hours to yourself when during the week every minute of the day is accounted for.

In your letter you expressed finding it odd that they only allow you to brush your teeth once a day. That is interesting as I too would think that they would have required you to perform better hygiene. I imagine that many people have not been very well instructed in dental care and expressing the need for once a day does not seem very sufficient.

I was very pleased with how you sounded in the letter; such that you were feeling well and in good spirits. I hope you have continued down that path finishing Phase I and by the time you get this letter you're in the middle or toward the end of finishing Phase II.

Today is 18 April, T-24 and the first day of Phase II and the beginning of Grass week. The Matrix shows a Marine firing his rifle. I sure hope this is the beginning of a very exciting week. I see towards the end of the week there is a large hike and I would very much welcome a five-mile hike at this time. You will probably get this letter some time after T-30, which would be week two of Phase II and the whole matrix shows Marines firing guns. You will probably get this letter towards the end of the week or the beginning of next week. Next week, the middle of Phase II,

T-34, is qualification day. I imagine that is when you will have your shooting test. You have always had the ability to shoot well through understanding your breathing and how that plays into when you squeeze, not pull the trigger. I would imagine that once you get the sighting down on your weapon, you will excel at the range.

I am continuing to send two power bars a day and will intermittently include cough drops. Today is Monday, last Friday I sent a questionnaire asking if there are other things that you want me to send. I also sent under a separate package, envelopes addressed to Uncle Mark and Aunt Susan, Uncle Dick and Aunt Lisa, Gramma and Grandpa and Grandpa Cooper in the nursing home in Florida. Please do not feel pressure to send something to them.

I was hoping towards some time during Phase III you could express to them your feelings of pride and satisfaction in what you have accomplished. You have the postage paid addressed envelopes. Just a few sentences will be sufficient. However, I completely understand if you do not have the time or desire to send something to some of these individuals. My dad in Florida has always been very professional and had a great sense of pride for military service. I have written to him and have told him about your joining of the Marines and being in San Diego at the Marine Recruit Depot. He called me with great excitement. I am sure he thinks about you every day. You will be the first in quite an extended Cooper Family Clan to be a Marine.

You have a tremendous amount to be proud of. I think of you every day and cannot express in a letter of this nature how proud I am of you. Please continue to hump and excel.

I have been finding large amounts of ancient sea coral in our vineyard and will soon be finding morel mushrooms. Later in this week we are supposed to get a lot of rain and I imagine I will find an abundance this weekend. We are meeting at Gramma's house on Sunday for a brunch to celebrate Evelyn's birthday. Most of the family will be there and I imagine a large part of the conversation will be about the letters we have received from you. Later that Sunday we are going to the Riveria in Three Rivers as Ronnie Cox is back in town for a concert. This time I am going to bring my childhood guitar and have Ronnie sign it.

Given the misery of Phase I, hopefully with the more substance-type activities you are now engaged in, Phase II will fly into Phase III and before you know it, we will be flying out to see you. I am making arrangements for us to fly out the morning after your graduation. You graduate on Friday and we will be leaving Saturday. Please do not worry if your graduation is pushed back a week or two because we have the flexibility in our schedules to be there. Do not worry about us, just simply continue to take it day by day and moment by moment. Be safe and know that we love and miss you greatly.

Love, Dad

P.S. Today I purchased enough protein bars and cough drops to cover daily mailing for the rest of your training at MCRD San Diego. Every day I will mail 2 bars and will send a package of drops on Monday and Friday. I have a wide variety of bars and drops.

I have been doing a lot of work at the cabin. I am excited to see it this summer. I put a bag of corn between the cabin and pond and it was gone within a week.

I worked on my hides this weekend, giving them some sun and tanning solution. 2 coyotes, 1 rabbit, 1 opossum and 3 squirrels. The opossum is complete - belly, claws, tail - ears, lips, etc. I think I am going to stuff it and eventually put it on your mother's toilet some night.

Love you buddy.
Love, Dad

Monday
April 18

Dearest Drew -

According to Matrix you have moved to Camp Pendleton this weekend. You are done with Phase I!!! I wonder if the change of surroundings will boost your spirits. I love you. I'm proud of you!

We had beautiful weather here all weekend. It was so glorious! Remember just last week - literally- we had snow.

Dad and B went to banquet in Dowagiac. Didn't win any guns. Mark Plewa went with them.

Saturday we worked outside all day. Dad has been doing a lot of work at the cabin. Trimming trees, planting grasses, etc. I mowed the lawn, cleaned up in garage. The yard looks nice. The grass so green. Still no leaves on the trees. Many are starting to bud. Hopefully no more heavy frosts.

Yesterday worked outside. Went to some garage sales in the morning. Saturday late afternoon my brother Mark came over. He came in on Friday evening. He played in a golf tournament with his friend, Smitty, both Saturday and Sunday. We got Mancinos for dinner.

I got the rubber raft boat out and floated around the pond for a few hours yesterday. Looks kind of strange because no leaves on trees yet. I surely didn't swim. Just floated around listening to the frogs. Few trees fell over along edge and the turtles are loving the extra space to sun themselves. There must have been 15 of them on one log alone. There were a lot of frogs swimming around the middle. I don't remember seeing that before.

I got a wicked red face, oh dear. Bennett and I drove over to Uncle Todd's yesterday early evening to see Mark. He was going to spend the night again with Todd and leave for Detroit this morning. He flies to China today, leaving at 1 pm. He does not think he will be back until October.

While he was at our house Saturday night, Dad talked to him about his living arrangements. He is spending $1,300/month on rent. That's about $10,000 until October and he is not going to be there at all. It doesn't make sense for him to live outside of Michigan because when he comes back to the States for a few weeks he wants to see his boys and us (me, Todd, etc). It makes sense for him to have a place on West Lake, so Saturday night he and Todd took fishing boat by a house Todd's aware the guy wants to sell. Mark is thinking he would have Uncle Tim move in with him. Uncle Tim is wanting to sell his house in Kalamazoo. Sounds like a win-win. Hope he makes it happen.

Meg has her license.

Bennett golfed a lot over weekend. He has match today. Friday evening I walked into family room, and as I moved toward my chair my foot brushed against something furry. I gasped, and Dad asked what is wrong, he was on the deck. I said there is a dead squirrel half under the loveseat. Dad was like - I don't think its dead, get away, probably rabid. He goes to the garage and grabs the big fishing net and sneaks up on the rabid squirrel to scoop it up in the fishing net. Once scooped up it was obviously dead. Bennett started laughing. It was the stuffed squirrel from your room. Buck must have brought it down. It was a vision.

Buck got a lot of exercise over the weekend. By later Saturday afternoon he went to rest on the couch instead of following Dad to the pond.

I keep you in my heart always and think of you often.

Love you bigger than space!

Mom

CHAPTER 6
GRASS WEEK /
TRAINING WEEK 5
"Shooting Positions"

Training week 5 Grass week, on the Matrix. Shooting positions.

During week five of recruit training, Marine Corps Marksmanship is taught. A recruit learns the different positions that they will shoot in, arm placements and various issues that will help them when they shoot for qualification the following week. Much of the instruction relates to correcting bad habits that a recruit may have formed from their shooting prior to entering the Marine Corps. Some say a recruit that has never shot a gun before MCRD are the best students.

The Marine Corps Recruit Depot in San Diego has an indoor simulated marksmanship training device - ISMT. The ISMT is located at the weapons and field training battalion in the Marine Corps base located at Camp Pendleton, California. Phase 2 of MCRD San Diego is spent at the Marine Corps base in Camp Pendleton.

Prior to shooting a live weapon, the recruits get to practice their shooting in the ISMT. Interestingly, the regular drill instructors that the recruits have become accustomed to, are not present during classes and shooting instructions as a means to ensure that the recruits are focused and are learning the Marine Corps standards of shooting.

It is important to learn the standards of shooting and to practice the positions that the Marine Corps instills in its marksmen. The fundamentals of marksmanship start at recruit training for Marines and it is important to note that every Marine is a rifleman. The shooting score that the recruit obtains during week five carries over with them into the Marine Corps.

A Marine is well-versed and familiar with their M16-A4 service rifle.

Each Phase includes a build up to the eventual Crucible that every recruit must endure before becoming a Marine. Through Phase 1, there was a three-mile hike. During Phase 2 there will be a six mile hike. During the Crucible, the recruits are required to wear their kevlar helmet, sling their M16-A4 service rifle and carry a 40-pound sack. Before departing Camp Pendleton during Phase 2, the recruits will complete a sustainment hike that is estimated at eight miles at the Edison Range Weapons and Field Training Battalion at the Marine Corps base located at Camp Pendleton.

T-5 brought a two mile hike. On T-11 and T-25 there were three mile hikes. On T-29 the recruits will undergo a five mile hike. By T-35 they will undergo an eight mile hike. Later, at T-47 there is a three mile hike. On T-53 there is a sustainment hike. A recruit may never realize the amount of miles they have traveled and endured to earn the title of United States Marine.

Today, T-25 is a three mile hike at Camp Pendleton. I would imagine that during the hike there is a lot of instruction given through the ingraining into their minds, the different statements, slogans, rules and principles that they recite as they run and hike. I also imagine that there are times of loneliness as they tramp through the forest.

I recall Patrick telling me how he never even learned some of his fellow recruits' first names, the recruits that he became most friendly with, until the end of recruit training and they went out for a cup of coffee. Most recruits go to the depot by themselves. I found it interesting to know that the Marine Corps has a buddy system and allows you to join up and go through recruit training with a close friend.

* * * * *

Yesterday, Drew's grandmother (my mother) called concerned about his last letter relating to trench foot. Gramma has been "googling" trench foot. I am of the opinion that as long as he has pain, as stated in his letter, it is a good thing. Good because there is sensation as opposed to dying flesh.

My mother was born in the 1930's and was an adolescent during World War II. She recalls her father, a polish immigrant, frequently saying that parents worry about their daughters getting pregnant in high school and their sons joining the service. It is nice that Drew has grandparents that care and who are following his progress through the recruit training depot. It is my understanding that gramma and grandpa have agreed to alternate weeks between the two of them writing letters to Drew.

I am interested to see how this three mile hike on T-25 differs from or is similar to the five mile hike this coming Saturday, T-29.

* * * * *

19 April 2016
T-25
Grass Week

Dear Drew,

By the time you get this letter you will be getting ready for next week, which will be Table I on the Matrix. At the end of that week on T-34 is qualification day. It looks like you have quite a lot of hiking at Camp Pendleton. This will include a 3 mile hike on T-25, a 5 mile hike on T-29 and an 8 mile hike on T-35. They sure are keeping you humping. Hopefully not so much just standing still.

After being there for nine weeks during training week 8, that is your team week and interior guard. From what I remember reading, that is an opportunity to where you get a lot of good chow. That is the first week of Phase III and they are introducing you to the final path to being a Marine. Just keep on humping, you are almost there.

You have mentioned that you want to come home right away. That is cool. I think graduation is on Friday and we will fly out Saturday morning. Today I am going to continue my discussions with our travel agent. I have had a few temporary plans in place with Ellen Jones at Sea, Land, Air in Paw Paw with preliminary ideas. I think what I am going to do is check into going from Saturday to Saturday and having a place on the beach. Ellen had initially suggested a place in town. However, I think I would be most happy with a place on the beach so I can lay on the couch and watch T.V. and your mother and brother and sister can walk on the beach without having me take them places.

Last night your mother was talking about the Cooper family tattoo. I think during the week in San Diego, Anella, Bennett, your mother and I should get our tattoos done and have an appointment for you that Friday afternoon or Saturday morning. That way you do not have to wait around while we do ours and we will have a reservation to get you what we have. The sketch of what I am going to have on my shoulder is included in this correspondence.

Love,

Dad

Let me know if you want another plan for the tattoo. For example, doing it in Kalamazoo all together or whatever. I am just along for the ride on this deal. I am thinking I will have it on the side of my left shoulder. I should have my stick figure guy theme continue on through the tattoo. Tat on left shoulder. Side of arm.

What do you think? Facing right or left?

Love you Drew! Very proud!

Shoot straight. Keep humpin'

* * * * *

Dearest Drew-

Hope you're feeling bit better? Gramma is freaking out about your feet. They will be OK. What are the other guys doing about their feet? Long work day Monday and then I went to Meg's soccer game in Mattawan. She is on the JV team for Portage Central. It was a beautiful night to be outside. Bennett didn't get home until 9:30 p.m. He says he did OK. The cherry tree in the front yard looks beautiful!

What would you like to do about Cooper family tattoos? Do you want to get them in Kalamazoo while you are home or do you want to stay in San Diego an extra day. Dad is on board too! Let us know as we will be making travel arrangements.

Love you bigger than space!

Mom

* * * * *

What a very exciting evening for us. Today is 20 April, T-26. While we have been regularly checking the MCRD website and Facebook page, for some reason Drew's mother pulled up Youtube and we found a video and could see clear and concise shots of our Drew.

The video was Lima Company on Black Friday. We are just so very excited to see that he looks well, see his living conditions and what he has been going through. We are just so very proud of him. This will be something that he will be able to live with honor for the rest of his life. I am quite jealous and envious. I imagine that we will be scouring Youtube now, following what Marine recruits go through. The Youtube video of the obstacle course is something that you just know that a young man full of testosterone has to have a certain part of him enjoy.

* * * * *

20 April 2016
T-26

Dear Drew,

Everyone here is all excited. We regularly check Facebook for MCRD, as well the MCRD website. Not only that, but yesterday your mother pulled up YouTube and there was our Drew. It is a scene where you are in your barracks and your barracks is getting worked over pretty good by all the drill instructors. The shots of you look really good. You look really good.

Today I am going to pull the video up, pause it on my office computer and take some photographs. There was a moment where one of the recruits could not find his stamp where you were stamping your names on a white bag. You had to feel sorry for that guy with the drill instructor trying to help him find the stamp.

There is also a long video of recruits going through a large obstacle course. I want to run that course. You cannot tell me that there are not moments where you are feeling like a man and having your testosterone and adrenalin running through your body. Those are the types of things that a young man is made for. You don't ever want to be a Nebuchadnezzar – pot-belly and sunken shoulders is not suitable for your frame or testosterone levels.

I am so excited for you because this will be something that will be an honor for you for the rest of your life. I am so very proud. Keep humping, keep studying and shoot straight.

Love,

Dad

P.S. Just so you know, May 8 is Mother's Day. That is S7 (Sunday 7) Day after T41. Enclosed with this letter is a Mother's Day card. I put postage on it to cover the card and a little paper so don't add any weight to it. Please fill out address information so she sees it came from you. By the time you get this you should just send it back out.

T53 is Friday May 21. That is the end of the 2nd week in Phase III. I think to celebrate Armed Forces Day I will send enough candy bars for everyone. Is that OK with you?

After your 10 days off after you graduate you go back for Infantry Training. I read that that is a lot different pace than your current training. You get daily down time; so I am excited about coming out there and visiting with you during the training.

Try and keep all the photos and letters you are recieving. Please do not worry about it if that is not something you are able to do.

Sooo excited about seeing you on You Tube and sharing it with my friends. So proud!!! One of your Drill Instructors looks quite jacked, BUT - I will out dip anyone in the barracks and you know that Jack!!!

Hopefully you are feeling well. Getting past the half way point and getting more substantial training has to help. You look really cool, calm and collected - moving with deliberation in the video - keep it up. Be proud and happy - you have a lot of each to be so.

Be cautious yet be aggressive and move with a purpose. You have a lot to be proud of. I am so very proud my buddy.

Study study study.

Hump hump hump.

Love you, Drew!

Hang tough. Keep humpin.

April 20
Wednesday

Dearest Drew,

Love you so!
Very interesting thing happened yesterday. I was with a client I've had for a long time. She is actually going to be discharged from Hospice. She is 90. She always wants updates on how you are doing. I wanted to show her the pool pictures that were posted on facebook by the Marines. I didn't have my phone or the tablet, just had my work tablet. So, I looked on you-tube, thinking maybe the pictures were put on you-tube.

There are several videos from "Marine Recruit San Diego". I clicked on the one that was posted 2 weeks ago. It was a video of new recruits just in their barracks, marking equipment and making beds. Four minutes into video, THERE YOU WERE!! We got a good visual of you for a few seconds. You were standing in front of your bed holding out your boot in front of you. I couldn't wait to get home and show Dad. We watched it several times, Bennett too.

It was so emotional seeing you there! The drill instructors, all the yelling and "aye, Sir". Geesh! I can see how your throat is raw. This morning we were talking about it again and Dad, of course, responded to Bennett's comment about the drill instructors looking ripped, by stating he can do more dips and bench more, LOL! I'm sure he's right :)

Wondering how its going for you at Camp Pendleton. Dad is going to get the Cooper tattoo on his shoulder. Bennett gets to miss the school day today. He has a golf jamboree. Kind of cloudy today, a little cool. Wondering what you'll be hungry for when you're home. I can't wait to see you.

Dad and I are so proud of you!

Love you bigger than space!

Mom

* * * * *

21 April is Thursday, T-27. Much of the day was spent wondering and worrying. We have not received a letter from Drew in quite some time. The last we heard from him, was the letter that he sent to my mother. Gaging how well he looked in the Youtube video and how great he sounded in the letter to "Gramma", our spirits are high. However, that does not eliminate the concern and worry from not hearing from him. Hopefully we will hear something from him soon.

* * * * *

21 April 2016
T27

Dear Drew,

1st week of Phase 2 almost over. You are well into 2nd week of Phase 2 when you get this. Heading back to MCRD in a week and Phase 1 and 2 OVER !!!

Keep humping. I am sure some of the bullshit or a lot of the bullshit is getting old - very old. Hang in there. Easier said than done; but, know it will be over soon and it is something you will carry as an honor forever. Think of those that had it worse than you or remove yourself mentally for a break to happier times or moments. Just keep humpin so you can accomplish your goal of completing this training.

Everyone is getting a kick out of the YouTube video. Nice to see you!!! I enjoy seeing the barracks, the DIs, where your rack is and who is sleeping near you. A kid next to you looks like he has not ever shaved before compared to how thick your beard is. Funny how you look at the camera, reminds me of the Tennessee River raft ride and how you always looked at the camera person.

Patrick says they gave his fellow recruits a photo album at the end. Chuck could not believe how cool the video is. He sure loved boot camp. He would go back in a minute.

Be strong. Stay healthy. Be proud of yourself - know we are extremely proud of you.

Keep humpin.

Love you.

* * * * *

April 21
Thursday a.m.

Dearest Drew -

I think I have watched that video 100X. I will be interested to talk to you about all the guys and the drill instructors. I'm sure you will have a lot of stories. What experiences you are having.

Anella messages that she misses her best friend. It is a special relationship you two have. It's always been that way. You two were always the best of friends. If she had a friend over and you felt left out, you would go to great lengths to get their attention.

Remember when Katie was over. You went up to my bathroom and wrapped yourself in toilet paper and baby powder and walked down the stairs with your arms out straight repeating "coin, coin", like the zombie from Scooby Doo? That was pretty funny! You two had a lot of adventures together. Guess what?! Bennett has outgrown his egg allergy. No kidding. He now eats a ton of scrambled eggs - making up for all of the years without.

Breakfast meeting at work today. I'm making a french toast casserole to bring. In the oven now.

Had the honor of attending the death of an amazing woman yesterday. This lady was the kindest, most positive, loving person I had ever met. She's been my client since Christmas. She never complains about anything. She laughs a lot. Has something nice to say always. She was a true role model for good and decent behavior, kindness. What a loss for this family. I am truly humbled by her and plan on honoring her by behaving more like her. No complaining, more positivity. I meet people who humble me!

Still lots of Presidential election news. Trump still way ahead for the Republicans.

Busy work day today.

Your days are full.

I love you bigger than space! You are a special guy.

I'll look at the video today maybe only 50X :) How do you like Dad's stick guys? Funny. Hope today is a good day!

Love you, Mom

* * * * *

Friday am April 22

Dearest Drew -

Writing on Elvis card today as it's appropriate. My all time favorite performer died yesterday, Prince. You can imagine my heavy heart. The news since yesterday is nothing but clips and music from Prince. Being called greatest entertainer ever, as he wrote, arranged, produced, play all instruments, sang, and danced. He was only 57. He was found in his home in Minneapolis. Sounds like he had flu that went into pneumonia. I am so sad. I'm so happy I was able to see him. Saw him twice in concert (Sad & crying Emoji).

Yesterday was Evelyn's 2nd birthday. I called and sang Happy Birthday on voice mail. They are coming to town on Saturday. Zac & Melissa had their baby. A healthy boy, Luca. (Melissa is 100% Italian. Her brother's name is Luciano). So Dan and Mindy are coming to see the baby. We are going to have a brunch at Grandma's on Sunday. I'm excited to hold baby Annabelle. She is so precious! I have to get Evelyn something for her birthday. Thinking a summer outfit and an outside toy. Sunday afternoon is the Ronnie Cox concert in Three Rivers. Remember he is the actor/musician from the movie Deliverance. We will go from brunch there.

I miss talking to you. That is, me talking and you responding with 1 word. LOL.

I love you, Drew, bigger than space!

Mom

* * * * *

22 April 2016

Dear Drew,

Hope all is well. Been thinking about you daily. Been watching a lot of Youtube videos between the first two hours of bootcamp, the obstacle courses, the firing range and it has been really nice to see that. It is a great deal that they share that with us.

Bennett has been struggling with whether or not he wants to play football this next year. He is having such a great time playing golf, I can understand why he would not want to go out for football. Your mother was concerned about how much he enjoyed it, but does not understand how teenage boys are just assholes at that age and it is really not as much fun as what she thinks.

Yeah, he can hang out with the guys and she thinks it is a good time, but it really is not a good time because... you know how it is... how stupid teenagers are, the things they do and the things they say. I think it is a lot of how you see in the Corps, it is a matter of how you are treated. How do you take 100 young men and get them to go from point A to point B. It has to be very organized with discipline. There is no fucking off or screwing off. You have the drill instructors there keeping everyone in line and on task. It reminded me of a friend of mine that talked about how his uncle joined the Marine Corps. He said that if he was going to war, he wanted Marine's around him and not knuckle-fucks from the other branches. I thought it was pretty interesting. Think about it, if you are going to be there, who do you want to your left, right and behind you? You want the best of the best.

I hope you received the Mother's Day card that I sent to you. If it is not too much trouble, please get it addressed, write a few words and get it right back in the mail. It should get here right before Mother's Day.

All I am going on right now is how well you looked in the Youtube video we saw and how well you sounded in the letter that you sent to my mother. The letter that you sent to my mother was written by you on the Sunday before the last week of Phase I. It has been two weeks now and we haven't been able to hear anything from you. We are hoping that everything is okay. By the time you get this letter, you will be at the end of the second week in Phase II. In another week you will be heading back to the Marine Corps Recruit Depot in San Diego.

After recruit training and you go back to Camp Pendleton for your next training, things will be a lot different. So in the long term, always remember that in the future, you will be able to get on the phone and talk with people, you will be able to watch T.V. and have a more normal life. I think it will be very nice to be able to visit you wherever you are.

You are engaged in an awesome endeavor. Just keep taking it one day at a time.

Love,
Dad

I sent the YouTube video to my Marine friend, Matt Fasbender. Remember his son Alex graduated this past year from MCRD San Diego? Matt's reply to the YouTube video was that it "made him hard". That is testosterone my brother!!! Once a Marine always a Marine.

Speaking of boners - I am betting you have not had one since getting to MCRD San Diego, not even a piss hard on. That is a common experience. The legend is the Marine Corps put saltpeter in your food. It has been said forever that the military puts saltpeter in new recruits food to suppress their sexual urges. Young men are always thinking of sex.

I think the reality is that there is not any saltpeter added to your chow. You guys are just too tired and worn out to be thinking about sex or getting stiffys.

Further potassium nitrate - what is in saltpeter does not have any effect on sexual desires or ability to get a woody. Soo - you are just exhausted and not in any place to be getting hard.

Speaking of boners - or bonehead - Buck is doing great. He is such a big teddy bear. This weekend he will get a lot of exercise helping me look for morels.

I have greatly increased my Ab workout - so fear our upcoming Ab contest.

Stay strong. Stay healthy. Study your handbook. Keep humpin. Love you. Very proud.

Matt proudly poses with Drew on Graduation Day.

CHAPTER 7
TABLE 1 AND QUALIFICATION DAY
"Actually Shooting Our Weapon"

Training week 6 table 1. You actually get to shoot your guns.

T-30 marks the first day of Training Week 6. The 7th week at MCRD – second week into Phase 2.

DREW

We never call our gun our gun. It is our weapon. Training week six is when we actually got to shoot out weapon. The previous week was tedious to say the least. Just sitting around and learning to hold our weapon and acting as though we are allowed to shoot.

Since I was about three years old, I have had a gun and have been hunting. At ten years old, I took a hunter's safety course through our local conservation club. I was taught to sight my weapon at the conservation club by focusing on the smallest piece of an identifiable object on the target and where I wanted to hit it. I focused in on a piece of hair and put my sights on the hair and fired.

The big difference I learned through Marine Corps instruction was that you do not focus on the target, you focus on your sights and place your sights over the target. Safety and precaution were of the upmost concern at Camp Pendleton. The rounds of ammo were strictly counted and never was a recruit allowed to leave with live ammo. Keep in mind that we always have our weapons back at the squad bay and you certainly do not want a disgruntled recruit or one in severe despair having live ammo.

While I was able to shoot expert, I know I could have shot much better if I could have gone to medical and had my pink eye treated. However, we learned that at Camp Pendleton and particularly during Phase II, you do not want to go to medical. You cannot miss one day on the range or you will be dropped.

The instructors were pretty chill and cool. They were a wonderful break from our DI's. When we would get back to the squad bay, it seems that the DI's would go nuts, just because they needed to make up for the time they lost while we were at the range. The range instructors were pretty cool and we enjoyed the opportunity to be taught in an environment that was conducive to making us each a marksman. Every Marine is a rifleman.

* * * * *

Honor, courage and commitment. The three key ingredients of the Marine Code. The learning process for a civilian that has never had the honor or privilege of providing service to our country is a continuous experience.

There are over 500,000 members in the United States Army. There are under 200,000 in the United States Marine Corps. Many bar room brawls have started over what branch of the military service has the toughest members.

Senator John McCain, decorated war veteran and POW once declared that after he graduated from the academy, he wanted to join the Marines, but his parents were married. Senator McCain insinuated that Marines are displaced and come from broken homes. Senator McCain's son, who is a Marine, has stated that the Marines are a Department of the Navy, the Men's Department.

Many individuals that have served in both the Marine Corps and the Army have noted that the standards of the two branches are the same. However, while meeting the standard in the Army is the goal, meeting the standards for a Marine is the just the beginning.

I love to think of principles such as honor, courage and commitment and that the standards that my son will soon meet will be the minimum. Further, I relish the readings where I have seen that Marines out of service continue to lead and serve humanity.

We are clearly a war-centric planet. The other day while attending a musical concert by the great Ronny Cox, Ronny shared the story of the final words of the world-renown screenwriter, actor and director, John Huston. Prior to his service in World War II, John Huston was a calvary rider in Mexico. The Mexican Revolution was deeply routed in his heart. On his death bed, his last words involved him asking "do we have enough rifles?" After hearing that they did, his next question was "do we have enough bullets?" After hearing that they did, John Huston stated "then give them hell." Soon after, he passed away.

I do not know how parents send their sons and daughters off to war.

This is the end of training week five. Drew has been at the Marine Corps Recruit Depot for six weeks now. Training week five is actually the sixth week since the first week was entitled receiving week. Phase 1, the first five weeks, is over. Drew has relocated to Camp Pendleton. He has completed the first week of Phase 2, which is entitled Grass Week. We have not heard from him since the letter he sent to my mother, which he wrote on the Sunday before the last week of Phase 1, which was Swim Week.

I am very anxious to hear how he did with the swimming certification. While it was nice to see that he looked well, I am anxious to hear something from him.

My anxiety about hearing from him was relieved in that he

sent a letter to his brother, Bennett. Drew sounds very good in this letter. While I was anxious to hear how he is doing and how swim week went, the issues were not specifically addressed. However, given the tone and nature of his communication, I am elated. I do not get to hear the details of his swimming, but I am able to understand that he is farting a lot and the gaseous odors coming from his body are quite deadly.

His adventurous nature is being satisfied as he points out that he has seen the Pacific Ocean for the first time in his life. Oh how he is going to enjoy hiking in the mountains on the long arduous hikes that are included in Phase 2. Camp Pendleton is located near the Santa Ana Mountain Range and he will have his desires of hiking through the mountains satisfied. When Drew was 17 or 18, he wanted to run off and hike the Appalachian Trail. I am sure his fancy for doing such incredible feats will bode well at Camp Pendleton.

*   *   *   *   *

25 April 2016
Monday T30

Dear Drew,

I am writing this letter to you on Monday, T-30. It is the first day of training week six, which is the beginning of the second week of Phase II. By the time you get this, the second week of Phase II will be over and you will just have one more week in Phase 2 and have been there 8 weeks. Then you will head back to MCRD San Diego for the beginning of Phase III. I am very anxious to hear how you did on the rifle range.

We appreciated the letter that you sent, addressed to Bennett, that we received this weekend. You entitled one of your notes as Swim Week, but did not tell us anything about the swimming certification or whether you enjoyed the swimming. Rather, you

142

spoke of your flatulence and its deadly odor. Very nice !!!

I loved hearing about the can of Pepsi and donuts you found under the bleachers. I am curious to hear what assignments you were on in Phase I to have been able to obtain ice cream, pop and donuts. Very very nice!!!!

I am continuing to send Power bars every day. Twice a week, I am sending cough drops. I hope you are able to enjoy what I am sending. The YouTube videos certainly show why the recruits and drill instructors should be enjoying the cough drops that I am sending.

This past Sunday we went to Gramma and Grandpa's for Evelyn's birthday. Sarah was there will Bella, Anella brought Teja and we all had a very nice brunch. All of us greatly enjoyed talking about you and what you have reported back in your letters. Everyone is so proud of you Drew. You are accomplishing something that no one at this gathering has done. We all are so proud of you !!!!! Before you know it you will be done and home!!

After brunch, we went to Three Rivers to watch Ronny Cox perform at the Riviera. I brought the guitar I received when I was around ten years old and had Mr. Cox sign it. Bennett had Ronny sign the Ukelele that Bennett made. I told Ronny that I am not an autograph collector and that I now have two autographs. His, on my childhood guitar and one from Muhammad Ali.

We are nailing down our travel arrangements. Grandpa has decided to come with his. Gramma is just not up for the journey and has high school graduation obligations to attend to for the both of them. It is looking like we will fly out on June 4, and have you fly home with us on Saturday, June 11th. That Friday we will have a nice graduation, go out for dinner, go to bed, get up and come home. I think we need to relish in your graduation Friday and plan on flying home Saturday morning. I hope that is acceptable to you. There needs to be time to get you your Cooper family tattoo. As well as you will want an opportunity to swim in the Pacific Ocean.

I love how you have been training for the Marine Corps your entire life – wearing the same clothes every day and changing your underwear once a week. Your fox holes and trench system down at the beach house I am sure got the ball rolling.

Miss you!!! I was cuddling with Buck this weekend and told Mom how much I bet you are missing him. Love you.

Love,

Dad

* * * * *

Dear Bennett,

Today is Sunday. Yesterday we got on a bus and went from MCRD San Diego to Camp Pendelton. I saw the Pacific Ocean for the first time in my life. You can see the ocean and mountains from right outside the barracks I'm in.

Tell Dad that at MCRD I'm in building 585 Squad-Bay D1. It is right next to the parade deck. On Fridays we can see and hear graduations. Its really weird to see people dressed in normal clothes, and its painful to see people drinking coffee and smoking cigarettes. I think about cigarettes all the time. I even dream about them when I sleep.

I have a lot of dreams where we are all at home and I'm graduated and everything, and it will make me really happy. Then I wake up and remember where I am and I get sad again. When I get home I want us all to go out for breakfast somewhere, like that Waffle House in Lawrence. I really want a super tall stack of pancakes and they have to be from a waffle house because Mom's pancakes aren't very good and they would probably be made from almond flour.

We had to get a lot of shots when we first got to boot camp. We had to get the same ones yesterday before moving camp. One of the shots has to go in our left ass cheek. That one is called the peanut butter shot because the stuff they inject you with is the same consistency as peanut butter. It literally feels like they are shooting peanut butter into your ass cheek. It hurts so bad and then its sore for three or four days afterwards.

Another thing to tell Mom and Dad:

I think that they can buy my plane ticket home if they want to so we can be on the same flight. I'm not 100% sure though. Also, when you guys come to my graduation bring my phone, my boots, my Batman belt, and my gray sweater. The sweater and belt might be in the trailer. I love you. Tell everyone else I love them too.

Drew

Thursday Week 4- Swim week

The food here gives me really bad farts. They are silent but deadly, and they smell horrible. By far the worst smelling farts that I've ever had in my life.

I think its mostly the peanut butter they have in the chow hall. It comes in little packets and I usually either make a PB&J or put the peanut butter on an apple as I eat the apple.

I stopped eating the peanut butter a few days ago and my farts are still super smelly, but now they are loud sometimes. I think I'll have to keep not eating the peanut butter, which sucks because a lot of the time its one of the only tasty things in the chow hall besides the deserts. The best deserts are the cinnamon rolls they have out at breakfast and the devils food cake. The cookies are pretty good too.

I feel like I've been preparing for this my whole life because I wear the same clothes every day, even the same underwear I'll wear for a whole week.

Friday Week 4

I get about 45 minutes free time a day, and most of that time I have to use to shave, shit and shower. We call bathroom breaks head calls here, and whenever they let us take a head call they normally give us 200 seconds and they count so fast that its more like 60 seconds. That makes it almost impossible to take a shit throughout the day. Our free time isn't until a couple hours after evening chow, so I normally have to hold it from morning to night, unless I'm lucky and get an unsupervised head call. That doesn't happen often though.

Side note: The Marines only make you brush your teeth once a day.

I've been craving ice cream for so long. I was in a working party today. We set stuff up for a graduation and then cleaned up after the graduation. In working parties you eat chow by yourself and its really nice because you can take your time and you don't get yelled at. The chow halls have soft serve machines that we aren't allowed to use, but I filled a cup up with chocolate and vanilla swirl when I had lunch with the working party. It was heavenly. Best thing that happened in boot camp so far.

Also, during the working party we had to clean under the bleachers after graduation and I found a full unopened can of Pepsi and a bag that had two perfectly good donuts in it. One was chocolate and the other one had pink frosting and sprinkles like in the Simpsons. They were delicious.

* * * * *

I remember talking with Patrick about the location of his barracks and whether or not he would see the other graduates. I am glad that Drew addressed something that I had written to him about relating to the proximity of his barracks to the graduation ceremonies. I imagine that it is quite difficult going through what they are going through and seeing the elation from the graduates and their families.

Drew draws upon having a smoke and being relaxed; at least watching others do this at graduation as a Marine Recruit has absolutely no ability to have tobacco of any kind. I love the dreams he is having about his family and enjoy talking about it with his mother during our morning cup of coffee.

It is amusing how he remembers his mother mistakenly making his tree nut allergy suffering brother eat a batch of almond pasted pancakes. Oh boy, how do I break the news that the Waffle House in Lawrence, Michigan has closed?

What I find most refreshing from his letters is that he has graduation on his mind. I think that at Drew's graduation, I will have to mistakenly drop a box of a dozen donuts and a six pack of Pepsi beneath the bleachers. This should become a tradition for family members attending the graduation services at MCRD to pay it forward and drop something beneath the bleachers for a well-deserving young recruit.

I still cannot get over how he captions one of his notes entitled "swim week". He goes on to talk about nothing that occurred during the swimming certification. How could you, when there are gaseous moments to talk about? I see that Drew is keeping his sense of humor. I am curious to find out how he was assigned such privileged duties during Phase 1. I did not think he would have the opportunity for private chow, ice cream and cinnamon rolls until the first week of Phase 3.

* * * * *

Tuesday
April 26

Dearest Drew - As always, hoping this finds you well. You must feel very supported by your family. Dad and I send mail every day. Are you the mail King of your company? I had a long, but good day yesterday. Was parked at the McDonald's in Bangor to do some charting and phone calls after a visit near there. I had the windows and the sun roof open. I was on the phone with a pharmacist and a bird pooped on my shoulder right through the sun roof. Geez, only me.

I went to Meg's soccer game after work. It was at Loy Norrix. She did great. I enjoy watching her. I sit with Paige. She's very 13.

Todd is very excited about Mark moving to the lake. Bennett almost shot his "career" high 42 at match last night, but choked on last hole and got 45. He feels he is fine tuning his game and thinks he will just get better and better. He's not going to play football. He wants to golf/work. He's hoping to get job at Lake Cora. That would be pretty nice. Can you hear birds there in the morning?

I think of you often, I am so proud of you.

Love you bigger than space!

Mom

* * * * *

Tuesday
26 April T31

Dear Drew,

You will get this towards the end of week 3 of Phase 2 training week 7. You have been gone 8 weeks. Just 4-1/2 weeks left. Phase 1 & 2 are almost over. Anxious to hear about swimming and shooting.

Enclosed are some Zip-Lock gallon-sized plastic bags. I read you are allowed to receive these and that they are useful for storing your personal stuff in, like photos and letters you have been getting in the mail.

Life here is same ole, same ole. Working and working out. Mushroom hunting, gathering fresh eggs.

Going to stain beach house and cabin before you come home. I plan on getting a big turkey next week or week after.

Working on final edits of *A Soldier's Home.* It may or may not be out before I see you next. Very close. To close to call today.

I have been trying to share your struggle and feel your pain. I have been losing a lot of weight; but am still hard at work developing musculature. A six pack is made in the kitchen, but one still must work out. With my lower weight, dips are easier so I am now doing 3 sets of 30.

Keep humpin. Try and find some joy in whatever you can. Know time flies and you will be a Marine soon.

Very proud of you.

Love you. Love, Dad.

* * * * *

I recalled the young Marine in a YouTube video discussing his top ten pointers getting ready for Recruit training for the Marine Corps. One of the pointers was learning how to go to the head at appropriate times. Imagine not being able to regularly pee or have a bowel movement when your body is requesting such an occasion.

This past week I spoke regularly with Ellen Jones at Sea Land Air Travel in Paw Paw, Michigan, attempting to narrow down our travel arrangements. It seems pretty well decided that we will leave San Diego the Saturday morning following Friday's graduation. Drew's mother has come to understand that Drew has seen enough of San Diego and just wants to go home. For the time being, it looks like the family will fly out Saturday, June 4th, spending the week there and coming back with Drew on our flight the next day after graduation.

The Marine Corps will be perfect for Drew. He has been training his entire life to not have to change his clothes. He can wear the same clothes every day, the same underwear for a week and only has to brush his teeth once a day. When in elementary and middle school, Drew would shower at night and put on the clothes he was going to wear to school, requiring only a ten minute head start before leaving on school mornings.

27 April 2016 brings us to T-32, hump day of Table 1. The middle of the week in Phase 2. Drew and his fellow recruits are at Camp Pendleton learning how to shoot.

* * * * *

Wednesday a.m.
April 27

Dearest Drew,

Do you enjoy getting daily mail? Dad goes to the post office every day to send you the small envelope with the protein bars. I hope they are helpful and you find them tasty.

Just a regular work day yesterday, it was cool and chilly.

Bennett was home early from practice. He did all the work for a group project. The presentations are scheduled for Thursday and Bennett has an all day golf tournament.

I made pulled pork last night. Bennett golfs in match in South Haven tonight. He will see Jerry Canonie. Dad stopped to the baseball field at the high school last night because South Haven was playing Paw Paw. Both Luke and Casey are playing for South Haven. Luke graduates this spring. Last I knew he was going to live with his grandma Diane in Kalamazoo and go to KVCC. I think they are hoping Casey joins the Navy.

Hoping this rain brings some mushrooms by weekend!

Day off today. Yippee! Going to clean, Not a Yippee!

I hope you have good stuff happen today!

Love you bigger than space!

Mom

* * * * *

27 April 2016
T-32, Wednesday

Dear Drew,

By the time you get this you are more than ½ way. The hardest - worst is over.

On the way home from Court in Kalamazoo today, I stopped by the recruiter's office in Kalamazoo. I had a very nice meeting with Sgt. Butler. He was very happy to hear how well you are doing. I was curious to know if they get reports relating to how their recruits are doing and he indicated only if they have problems. He has not heard of any problems relating to your performance. Quite to the contrary, he indicated that you must be doing rather well for you to have received the ability to work at different dinners and graduations.

He reiterated to me the bet challenge he had with you relating to your shooting score. I am not sure of the numbers, but he said that if you shot a 242, he was going to treat you to dinner.

We are finalizing our travel arrangements and are having you fly back with us Saturday morning. We are arriving on Saturday and are spending the week in San Diego and will be flying out the following Saturday morning after graduation. Obviously if these need to be pushed back, that is fine as I am buying insurance for our travel arrangements. However, if you are wanting to stay longer you need to notify me immediately.

It is my understanding that in the last week or two during your stay at the MCRD, they will discuss travel plans with you. When I have your travel arrangements, I will mail them to you so that you will be able to show them that you have a flight out of there.

I took a picture of the photo that they have of you on the Matrix poster at the recruiter's office. They have a picture of you and it shows where you are on the Matrix. Each day they move it along as you progress through. It looks like there is someone from Kalamazoo exactly one week behind you.

I did not notice anyone ahead of you so it looks to me that it is just the two of you on their Matrix right now. They were very happy that I stopped by and reported how well you sound. I showed them the YouTube video. There were 3 recruiters there. When we froze the pic on you they commented that you look great, cool and calm. Not scared like guy next to you.

Hump Day of Hump week of Hump Phase. The middle of the middle. 6-1/2 weeks of 13 weeks.

Very proud. Keep humping.

Love,
Dad

* * * * *

I stopped by Drew's recruiter's office today to check in and to see whether or not they ever hear anything from MCRD. Sgt. Butler informed me that they hear how things are going, only if there are problems. The recruiter is seen as the mentor and advisor to the recruit and if there are problems at recruit training, they will reach out to the recruiter to have them talk things over with the recruit and see whether they are able to help and get them through whatever issues that may be at play.

It was a very uplifting meeting with Sgt. Butler and the other recruiters today. Discussing what Drew had written about, relating to the dinners, graduations, etc., they indicated it was special treatment that he is getting for behaving well and that he must be doing well to receive those opportunities.

I recently mailed Drew one-gallon Zip- Lock plastic bags that I read they are able to receive. It is my understanding that it is helpful for them to store their personal items in a ziplock bag.

* * * * *

Thursday
April 28

Dearest Drew -

Hope today has been a good day for you! So many things during the day remind me of you.

I miss you and will work on not making a spectacle of myself when I see you in June.

Sleep tight tonight.

Love you bigger than space!

Mom

*   *   *   *   *

T- 33, Thursday
28 April 2016

Dear Drew

Here is your flight information. Saturday June 11, leave San Diego 11:34 in morning. Remember there is a 3 hour time difference that is why we do not get to Detroit until 7:07 at night. Get to Kalamazoo at 9:27.

The Delta flight is 3421 from Detroit to Kalamazoo. Nice numbers. I have been playing 3241, but no winner - yet.

If your plane ticket home is not motivation to keep humpin there is none. This will be here before you know it.

I think in the 2nd to last week in Phase 3 you will need this Itinerary. I think the MCRD meets with you to discuss travel after graduation. So - hold onto this information. It is nice Grandpa is coming to San Diego. Your ticket is with all of us. We all have seats together.

It is still pretty chilly here. When I ran yesterday I wore long underwear and sweat pants, winter jacket and cap. 48 degrees, but with windchill feels below freezing.

For Mother's day - next week, May 8, your mother is getting a blue martin bird house and 12 foot pole and 3 martin decoys. We have always done something for the yard - new trees - bird houses, bird feeders etc. Also we are moving the antique green boat by the barn to the garden area - the garden area I so had to develop that she never gardened.

Very proud of you. I bet you are loving Phase 2. I know it

sucks and is hard, but it has to be better than the first 2 weeks in Phase 1. Keep pushin. Love you!!!

Love,

Dad

* * * * *

We are nailing down the travel arrangements. I am doing what Drew asked from his letters that we leave as soon as possible. He graduates on Friday and we will be flying out Saturday. I am arranging for a one-way ticket for Drew to fly with us. It is my understanding that the Marine Corps provides transportation from where you are currently located to your next assignment. Given that Drew's next assignment is infantry training at Camp Pendleton, he will not be given much of a travel allowance given that he is currently located in San Diego and going from San Diego to San Diego does not provide him with a substantial allowance. Essentially, he is "on vacation" after his graduation.

I guess, or so I am told by Marines back home that it is really very dependent upon the drill instructor whether or not the recruits are able to eat power bars as they come in or whether they are accumulated in a box until enough come in. It seems that it is handled in a unique way, given each individual drill instructor. Some will wait for an accumulation and others will allow the recruits to eat the bars as they come in. Sometimes the recruits on their own will accumulate and share.

Because the packages are sent through the United States Mail, the drill instructors are not allowed to open the recruit's mail. However, the drill instructor will typically watch the recruit open the package. If the contents feel like an obvious letter, they just pass that on to the recruit. However, if there is something within the package, it is something that is required to be opened in front of the drill instructor.

It was very nice meeting with Sgt. Butler today. He seemed very receptive to discussing these issues with me and looking at the YouTube video of Drew's platoon. He again told me that Drew must be doing well to have received the appointment to the projects that he has been permitted to work on which allowed him the private chow and to work at graduations. It was nice to see that the recruiter's office is following Drew's progress and has his photograph placed on whatever training day it is at the time on the poster size Matrix in their office. It was also nice to know that they have not heard anything negative.

* * * * *

Friday a.m.
April 29

Dearest Drew-

I need to get more pictures printed, running out. I hope you enjoy getting one here and there.

Been busy at work, got home late yesterday. Working today : (

Gloomy and cold. Have the heat on.

A boy from PPHS killed last night in car accident. Riley Manning. I don't know anything else about the accident. Makes all parents sick to hear such news. I see motorcycle deaths in the area nearly every day and have the highest hope you change your mind about a motorcycle.

My brother Mark should move in his new place before summer. How exciting for him. My Uncle Tim is super stoked. He's already putting together plans for a dock and a deck. It'll be nice for Mark's cat. She'll have Uncle Tim for company when Mark is gone.

Went to Meg's soccer game Wednesday in St. Joe. They lost but nice to see her. Wore my winter coat. I remember many spring youth baseball games wearing my winter coat. I do enjoy watching sports. Sadly, golf not spectator sport.

Bennett had all day tournament yesterday. He didn't do great. Feel bad for him. His teammate got 1st place out of 13 schools.

Dad is looking so good. He's going to win the ab contest!!
I hope you sleep well.
Love you bigger than space!
Mom

* * * * *

T34-Friday
29 April 2016

Dear Drew

Only one week left in Phase 2. T34 is Qualification Day. The Matrix shows a medal with Rifles and the words Rifle Expert.

I am excited to get the questionnaire back from you that covered swimming certification and how you did on the rifle range. Curious to how you did relating to Sgt. Butler's challenge.

Yesterday I mailed you your flight information from San Diego home. I hope you have received it. We leave - all together Saturday morning after Friday graduation.

I have been helping your Uncle Mark Niedzwiecki with a Power of Attorney so he can purchase a home here while he is in China. He does not come back until October. He is buying a house in Portage on West Lake!!!! The house is just a few doors down from Uncle Todd. The house is set up as a duplex so it will be nice having Uncle Tim in one side and Mark's quarters in the other. A lot of exciting issues all around.

Cold and rainy here. Very cold and it is getting very old. April only saw 3-4 nice nice days. Fortunately they were on weekends. Buck is doing well. I love taking him to the pond and watching how he just goes in on his own volition and swims around and around. I like making eye contact with him when he does that - while he is swimming - he s like saying "I love this swim". The other day we were by the cabin and he went for a swim in the little cove. He just walked in and swam around and around. He is so cool. I think when he sees you we will have to be careful not to send him into cardiac arrest.

Hope to go turkey hunting next week or so. Mushrooms are starting to pop.

Brigadier General McDaniel has agreed to have a few words on my book, *A Soldier's Home* cover. Colonel Odom has agreed to write the foreword, very exciting. Very!!! It should be coming out just before, or after your graduation.

May is your home stretch. The last week of Phase 2 is the first week of May. Phase 3 is the rest of May. You graduate the first week of June—which is Marine week. Home stretch dude, keep humpin. Stay healthy, stay strong, better be workin those abs. You are going to be feeling mighty soft when your old man beats you in an Ab contest. Dang - smoking a Marine I am. My prediction of contest results: Me - you - Bennett - Anella - Mom. Ha Ha. Like Colonel Odom likes to sing: "I will be kicking some ass today."

You will be getting this letter near end or after Phase 2. Congratulations. Great job. You have a lot to be proud of - now finish the job and imagine/know how proud you will be. Forever a Marine. THAT is Awesome. I am jealous - envious and SO proud!!!

Love you Drew, Keep Humpin.

Love, Dad

* * * * *

It is my understanding that recruiters are selected among the finest Marines and it is certainly beneficial to develop a relationship with your son or daughter's recruiter. I appreciate that Sgt. Butler has demonstrated kindness, warmth and support for our son and our family.

Making a Marine in the 21st century is quite an endeavor. Today's Marine parent is not one from the greatest generation. The recruit and his or her parent is from a generation who has had the most given to them and the least expected. Spoiled? Maybe. With all the advances in technology and advances in medical treatment and care, today's society is much better off in many respects. How has anyone sent their child off to war. Making a Marine in the 21st century is a reflection of these times and is of the members of society and the generations of today.

What is it about this generation and making a Marine in the 21st century? Look at the differences among the different generations. Who are the millennials? Who are the baby boomers? Drew's parents fall into that gap between the baby boomers and the millennials. So what are we, Generation X?

I recall the story about when my Great Uncle Ed came back from serving in Europe during World War II. He was delivered to the Kalamazoo train station and made his way home. His mom, dad, brothers and sisters lived on a farm sixty miles away. Uncle Ed, who was part of the Greatest Generation, departed the train and started walking home. In his mind, I am sure he thought that someone would pick him up, but he was not concerned. He would just walk and at night fall when he got tired, he would go to sleep where ever he found himself for the night. He had certainly come from a more dangerous place than walking from Kalamazoo to Leonidas.

Compare that to when veterans came home from Vietnam. Where Uncle Ed was greeted with open arms, hugs and kisses, the Vietnam Vet saw strife, anger and demonstration. What did that mean to the different generations of soldiers, marines and all servicemembers that serve our Nation?

Today we have helicopter parents sending their children off to university and constantly hovering above them. Certainly you cannot have that as a parent sending your son or daughter off to the Corps.

When I dropped Drew off at WMU and helped him move into the dorm, it was the second child that I had moved onto campus. I was not a helicopter parent with my daughter, Anella, and I swore I would not hover over Drew. Anella is now soon to graduate from WMU and Drew attended WMU for a full academic year. I have yet to see any of my childrens' report cards from WMU. I do not think that I went in the other extreme of a helicopter parent hovering, but simply tried to allow my children to become productive adults.

Today's parental generation are those obsessed with travel baseball and having their child be the next professional athlete. Knute Rockne and Little League Baseball are no longer good enough. We have to develop our own travel leagues and travel hundreds of miles on the weekend. We have ODT (Olympic Designated Teams) training.

How are we so much better and greater than those wonderful souls that lived through the greatest generation. This generational distinction clearly has an impact upon who we are and how we are developing our Marines in the 21st century.

Everyone has heard the nightmare stories from Parris Island and San Diego. It is now a failure for a drill instructor to make physical contact with a recruit. A drill instructor cannot open a recruit's mail. That is federal documentation. There is the bone-chilling truthful tale of how recruits were forced to put their penises in their open rifle chambers before slamming shut. Would drill instructor performance in the 30's, 40's, 50's and 60's create a situation for criminal action today?

Making a Marine in the 21st century must take into consideration the generation we are now dealing with. Human kind is always evolving.

Currently, approximately 550 Marines have the responsibility to shape more than 17,000 recruits annually at the Marine Corps Recruit Depot in San Diego. Drill Instructors are those entrusted with continuing the more than 240-year legacy of transforming society's new generation into the next generation of Marines. MCRD not only trains recruits, it is the base training drill instructors and recruiters. It is an incredible facility.

CHAPTER 8
TABLE 2 – FIELD WEEK /
TRAINING WEEK 7
"Pretty Fun. Really. Field Week Is Fun."

Training week 7, field week table 2, you get to shoot your guns for two days out of the week, then the rest of the week was field week. Field week was pretty fun.

So Phase 2 ends with MCMAP review. On the Matrix, that is a guy choking a guy out. That is MCMAP review, Marine Corps Martial Arts Program. So we just did a review of everything we learned.

Then you come back to MCRD for training week 8. Phase 2 is the best phase. A lot of people say the way the phases go is 1, 2 and 3, drill, kill and chill, because the first phase is mostly drills, the second phase they kill you with workouts and stuff, and the third is chill, but I thought the second phase was the chillest, and then the third phase for us was like the first three weeks of Phase 1 all over again.

* * * * *

There are quite a lot of different reasons why someone joins the military. In general, these can be placed in a very few broad categories. For many, it is family tradition. For others, it is primarily about a sense of patriotism. Others feel as though it is simply a matter of getting a job. Some seek the challenge and adventure.

Those that are lost and are trying to find employment or direction, clearly have the available option of different branches of the military that will not be so chaotic and difficult to graduate from their basic training. Joining the Marine Corps just because someone needs a job is not a very well thought out plan.

Clearly, given the difficulty of the Marine Corps Recruit Training, there has to be something more deep within a person who makes the decision to join the Corps. Some purely seek the challenge and being able to accomplish something important and being a part of something big. Once a Marine, always a Marine AND you become part of something bigger than all of us.

Family tradition; because one's father, grandfather, uncles, mothers or aunts may have joined the Corps is an overriding principle for many. Maybe for someone like Recruit Cooper, it is because it has never been done before in his family. What a way to start his own family tradition. Maybe also Recruit Cooper did not have a sense of accomplishment or fulfillment that one receives at University. If he was just simply trying to find himself and seek adventure, other branches of the military service would have provided a much easier avenue.

Clearly, the Marines provides someone with the tests and

challenges they somehow feel the need to fulfill.

The last week of Phase 2, training week 7, commencing on T-36, is Field Week and Table 2. I believe this will be a defining week for Drew. He has become a Rifleman and the field work will give him the sense of adventure and accomplishment that he has been looking for.

* * * * *

Monday a.m.
May 2

Dearest Drew-

Wow the weekend goes fast. I wonder about yours. Church or no church?

I get caught off guard with the mailings. Dad typically sits at his desk to write you. I fall asleep in the evening and then feel I am scrambling in the morning.

We have our plane tickets. I am so excited to see you. I'm sure it will feel good to you to see us too. Nothing like your family. The people who love you most. The woman who carried you for 9 months ...... :)

Had a nice weekend. Saturday Bennett had guitar then a haircut with Alicia. We then went to garage sales in the Winchell area neighborhood. Found a couple treasures. Some really nice flower pots. Bennett found a small portable amp for $30. We visited with my Uncle Todd and family while we waited for pizza to be ready for dad. He wanted Chicago Style.

Yesterday, (Sunday) Todd and the girls came over to look for mushrooms. Bennett and girls went for long ride on quad/motorcycle. We had lunch here. Grandma and Grandpa came over later to drop off some plants and that rain barrel Grandma used to keep at the corner of the garage. She's going to do a rock garden there.

I think a lot about our experiences as you were growing up. You are an interesting kid. You've always preferred the outdoors. Anything outdoors. Remember the summer you slept in barn every night. I think that was 7th grade.

Dad is betting you can't wait to watch TV. You sure love movies, always have.

Bennett and I looked at the outside of the house my brother is buying. Pretty nice.

You are heading towards the home stretch. You knew you had this.

Love you bigger than space!

Mom

* * * * *

2 May 2016
T36, Monday

Dear Drew

By the time you get this letter you will have been away from home for 8 weeks. After 4 more weeks you will be heading into the graduation week. Phase 1 and 2 are over. WOW. What an awesome accomplishment. You must now finish. Study your handbook and blaze through the rest of the testing. You will love how the Crucible tests you and pushes you. Enjoy the burn and exhaustion.

I am excited to hear about your shooting. T36 - Monday of the final week of Phase 2 - called Field Week. Hopefully you are healthy - how are the feet doing? If you are feeling well I hope you are - and are getting some feelings of personal satisfaction, even having moments of fun.

I am curious - guys that did not qualify last week - are they working with them this week - to get them to qualify.

How many over nights in the field and woods have you done? In tents? Pretty mountains and terrain?

Getting mail at Camp Pendleton? I send a letter and protein bars every day. Cough drops twice a week.

I have been trying to feel your pain by depriving myself of a lot and hard work outs, but I get breaks - you recruits do not until graduation. That is tough, very tough to not get a break. Keep humpin. I know it is extremely hard; but you are working for something great and it will be over very soon. Grab the breaks you need in meditation or in your dreams.

We are all set with our travel arrangements and I have sent you your ticket information. If you get pushed back do not worry - the itinerary is insured and we will push things back as well and will be there with you when you are ready.

It has been so cold here. Still cold. When I run today I will be wearing my winter running jacket and hat. You will be coming home at just the perfect time of year. Just think how nice a cooler full of pop, lifewater, Gatorade and Busch Lite, Coors Lite, Miller High Life and Bud Lite will be at the beach house. I have not had a beer since you left, and before that was at Christmas. Chilly ones on ice and a big bonfire for days sounds good.

After recruit training you will get breaks, we can have regular communication etc. Those type of things will be very different. I look forward to visiting you at Camp Pendleton during your training later this year.

I realize you are probably feeling like shit and are just wanting the bull shit to be over, but hang in there. You are almost to Phase 3 and I think the DIs will start treating you different - better and you are so close to accomplishing something very great and something you will wear as a badge of honor for the rest of your life. I am so proud of you. Love and miss you very very much. See you soon. You are on my mind every day - all day.

Love, Dad

* * * * *

Phase 2 is at Camp Pendleton. The first week is the recruit's introduction to their weapon and its use. There are several positions that a Marine is required to be able to perform with their rifle. The second week, the recruit receives an opportunity to hone their skills and finishes the week with a test to become certified as a Rifleman. Throughout this training, there are also extensive hikes. The day after the final test and certification there is an eight mile hike. These hikes are done with full packs and gear and are tremendously strenuous.

The recruits feet have been hurting and aching throughout Phase 1 and while they thought they were going to get a break from the marching on the parade deck to allow their feet and ankles to rest, they are hiking with full packs and gear throughout Phase 2, which prevents good recovery. In the final week of Phase 2, those that were not able to qualify during certification week are allowed another opportunity to become certified? I don't know.

Throughout each week, there have been numerous recruits falling from the ranks. They fell like flies through Swim Certification and Grass Week. Now with the shooting requirements, many recruits are unable to continue forward.

The first week, many left at the end of Pick Up Week and through Training Week 1. Some left during Training Week 2. Some simply could not pass the Swim Certification in week 4. Even more dropped trying to become certified with their rifle. Hopefully as Phase 2 comes to an end and we enter Phase 3, Drew's battalion should be closely defined as to those who will graduate.

HE-MAN.

He-Man was a cartoon character idolized by Drew who was known for his superhuman strength. When Drew was very young, he would refer to me as "He-Man."

Since high school and college, I have always continued to

lift weights and have a cardio work out. All of my children were raised with engaging in some type of physical fitness regimen each week.

Drew was very kind in referring to me as He-Man. I recalled reading in Keeping Faith, the young Marine Recruit having a meeting with a civilian towards the end of his training at Parris Island. The meeting involved the recruit's placement after becoming a Marine. As a result of the constant attention to working out and food, Marines become quite physically fit. In the book, *Keeping Faith*, by John and Frank Schaeffer, seeing a pudgy civilian was grotesque to the recruit. I certainly do not want to be perceived by my son as a morbidly obese or pudgy sloth. He-Man to the Pudge just will not cut it.

One day at the dinner table a very young Drew was expressing excitement about me and He-Man. Drew asked me if our property was our kingdom, and our house my castle. Quite dejected, I lowered my head to my chest and said, "no son, sorry, your mother rules this roost." He could accept failure by He-Man then, but I could not allow him to see me as a fat civilian now.

While I regularly lift weights and run two miles a day, I have come to learn that a six pack is made in the kitchen. Drew's mother is such a good cook that my six pack development has always suffered because of the meals coming out of her kitchen. My yearly cycle involves going through January, February and March without any beer to try to overcome the deer camp eating and drinking in October and November to the Thanksgiving Holiday and through December celebrations and further eating and drinking.

Of course, throughout the summer months, there is nothing like drinking a cold beer while fishing or hanging out at the beach. Throughout this, I regularly lift weights and run two miles a day. However, even with the work out, without proper diet, my weight is like a yo-yo.

When Drew left on 13 March 2016, I had not had a beer or

any type of alcohol since Christmas. However, on the 13th I did drink some beer after dropping Drew off at the recruiter's office. Since that time, however, I have not had any alcohol – beer or otherwise. In the past, while I say I run two miles a day, there are days that I would miss because of meetings or different events.

Literally, during this time of Drew's absence, I have not missed a day since the day after Christmas. On Monday, Wednesday and Friday, I have a strenuous work-out on my biceps and triceps, straight bar curls, dumb bells and bar dips. I also work my abdominals and chest. With my weight loss, I am now doing three sets of thirty-two on the bar dip rack. I used to do three sets of twenty five. However, with the weight loss, it is easier to do a dip and therefore, I have increased the amount.

On Tuesday, Thursday and Saturday, I work out on the bench press and do chin-ups, pull-ups and a wide variety of specific targeted abdominal muscle exercises. On Sunday, after I run my two miles, I do an additional abdominal work out. I am on a mission that allows me to commiserate with the pain and discipline that Drew is undergoing and I am not going to allow him to see me as a fat civilian.

All of the above is something that I have been doing for years. However, when consuming beer and eating on a see-food diet (I see food and I eat it) at Christmas, 2015 before Drew left, I did not think I was in that bad of shape. During the spring and summer of 2015, I had lost weight and felt pretty physically fit. Throughout the last deer season, I did not feel as though I had put on a lot of weight. At Christmas, 2015, I felt pretty fit running two miles a day and lifting weights every day. Given that I am always working out, it has never been more true to me the affect of diet as during this time while Drew has been gone.

Since Christmas, I have lost 40 pounds. I am hoping to lose another ten pounds by the time I see Drew. I simply cannot believe that I have lost that kind of weight. The day after Christmas, I ran two miles and did 75 dips and a work out on a curl bar with more weight than I have ever curled before. Hopefully by the next time I see Drew, I will be more like He-Man than a fat civilian. For sure, Drew will not see me as a dough-boy.

* * * * *

This last week of Phase 2 looks like a lot of field work, hiking and doing obstacle courses in the wilderness. I am starting to feel on the home stretch as well. I will not consume any alcohol until after seeing Drew and will continue to tighten up in preparation for our ab contest. Certainly during T-36 through T-41 Drew will not have the time to do the stomach exercises that I have in mind for myself. He will be doing way too many crunches and other core workouts.

* * * * *

May 3, 2016

Dear Family,

The Gatorade bars are my favorite out of all the protein bars I have received, followed closely by the Luna Protein bars, the coconut and the caramel. I also like the cookie dough one. But the Gatorade one takes the cake. I bought an electric shaver and it saves me a lot of time and effort. Now during our free time I can shave while I take a shit. I got the electric shaver from the Recruit PX for $125. About once a week we go to the PX, which is just a store to buy things we might need. They already gave us our Debit cards that our paychecks go to, so that is what we use to buy stuff.

Right now I have about 15-20 letters that are unopened because I haven't had a chance to read them yet. Like I've said before, our free time is barely FREE. There are always different things they make us do on free time, and we always have to hygiene on free time. And, it is the only time where there is enough time to take a shit.

Being in Pendleton I miss being in MCRD. Its easier for us to win field day at MCRD because there is less dust and I like the MCRD chow hall better.

The amount of mail I get has really put some things into perspective for me. Some people don't get letters very often, and a lot of people have never gotten protein bars. It just makes it easier to see how many people I have that care about me compared to everyone else.

Side note: (The PMI, the guy that teaches us how to shoot MIG's is the same age as Anella. I just thought that was weird). But yeah, it is really nice getting all those letters.

We ate an MRE after the first hike. I got chili and macaroni. It had coffee in it so I got some cold watered down coffee. It sucked, but I still enjoyed having some coffee, and the chili macaroni was real good. Its so nice receiving protein bars. I get really hungry at night.

By the time I hit the rack I can only think about breakfast chow the next day. For breakfast chow there is a rotation where one day they have pancakes, the next day they have waffles, and the next day they have french toast. I like the pancakes the best. I also like the cereal. I normally get Apple Jacks, Fruit Loops or Mini Wheats. I eat the Mini Wheats with chocolate milk. When I was sick though I was staying away from dairy.

I'm almost 100% better. It moved from my throat to my sinus and now its almost clear. I traded some cough drops and a couple of protein bars for a bunch of Mucinex and Sudafed, so that helped a lot and I didn't have to go to medical for it. Being sick sucked mostly because it would feel like I couldn't breathe while run-

ning from all the crud blocking my throat.

Dear Loved Ones,

I just finished grass week. Grass week is basically just a bunch of classes teaching us how to shoot. And, we spent a lot of time sitting in a half circle aiming at a barrel with black circles on it. We would sit there and practice sighting in and pulling the trigger. We have magazines in, but no ammo. We just dry fire. We use ACOG scopes. We call them RCO's though. The positions we shoot in are standing, kneeling, sitting, and prone. Sitting is my favorite. It's the most stable. Standing sucks and prone hurts the elbows and the ribs. We are taught by a PMI, and he is cool. He actually talks to us like people and tells us about what happens in boot camp, and what happens after boot camp in SOI. Our PMI is about the same age as Anella. I thought that was crazy.

We wake up at 0500 and go to sleep at 2100 (except during field week we will wake up at 0400 and hit the rack at 2000). But when we wake up it goes like this:

Somebody, usually a firewatch guy or sometimes a DI will scream "lights lights lights lights lights lights lights". Then the lights will come on and we all have 20-30 seconds to jump out of bed and be on line with our two sheets and two blankets.

Then we put our linen on our footlockers and they tell us to attack the head. Then we get back on line, but before we hit the head we count off to make sure nobody ran off at night. After that we get dressed. It goes one piece of clothing at a time. Starting with the boot socks, then our blouse, then trousers, then boots. There is a time limit for everything and if one person doesn't make it we have to start over.

After dressed we make the racks, one sheet at a time. If someone doesn't make the time or moves after the DI say zero, we start over. When a DI says we have 100 seconds to do something, they count so fast its more like 40 seconds. After the racks are made we go to chow. If we have time to spare before chow then we get fucked with until its time to go to chow. They always just fuck with us to kill time.

Yesterday was Saturday. I think Saturday the 23rd. Yesterday we had nothing to do between evening chow and square away time, so all the DI's switched houses and fucked the houses up, all the mattresses were stacked up, all the racks were disassembled, and there were like 20 ammo cans full of sand that we had to dump out onto the deck. Then we had to clean it all up. Another thing we did was we were outside, it was us, platoon 41, and platoon 42. Our DI said "41 get inside 42's head" and 42's DI told them not to let us in. So we were charging their head and they were trying to keep us out. We ended up getting in so the DI's let us take a piss. It wasn't that bad fucking up the house and cleaning it up. It was kind of hilarious. The DI's left after they told us to clean it up, so we were all laughing over how ridiculous it all was.

When you guys fly out for graduation, please bring my boots, my grey sweater, my Batman belt, and phone. Mom, please try to have my phone activated by the time of my graduation so I can contact my friends when I am done with boot camp and so I can contact my friends while I am at SOI. Also, please bring to my graduation a pack of Marlboro Special Blend Reds. Just ask for Marlboro Special Blend Reds. If they ask short's or 100's, get shorts, but I don't think those ones come in 100's, and I'll need a lighter too. I don't know when I will be able to send this or when it will get to you, but Happy Mother's Day Mom, I love you.

On graduation day I want to go somewhere and get like 5 pizzas, a banana float, more ice cream for at the hotel, donuts, Doritos, chocolate chip cookies with milk, a blueberry pie, and a case of Miller High Life in glass bottles, not cans. I'm also going to need those cigarettes. I heard that Illinois passed a law that you have to be 21 to buy tobacco now. Is that true? When we get back home lets go to that Waffle House in Lawrence. I want a huge stack of pancakes with lots of bacon. And, more ice cream.

Lots of love,

Drew

For the bonfire or whatever we are going to have at the pond when I get back, I want these things!

- Pizza from that place in Hartford, lots of it.
- PBR
- Paw Paw Coconut Porter
- Paw Paw Citra Melon
- Founder's Dirty Bastard
- Founders All Day IPA
- Bells Two Hearted
- Bells Amber Ale
- Atwater Vanilla Java Porter
- Founders Breakfast Stout
- Dragons Milk
- Doritos - Taco, Cool Ranch, Sweet Spicy Chili, whatever the purple ones are

- *Cookies and donuts (sweetwaters)*
- *Gatorade*

I want all of that beer too, maybe more if I see it in the store and feel like I need it. I want to pick the donuts too.

So far in Phase II it is like week 1 all over again. The DI's turned it up and they fuck up our house a lot again. We get IT'ed a lot too. I think its because we don't have very much PT here so they IT us just to give us a workout. But the DI's turned it up big time. I think they want to get back at us because we have it so easy when we are with the PMI, and our SDI isn't around as much so he can't save us from the DI's. It fucking sucks. I can't wait to drink beer, eat chips, and watch some movies at home.

SEND
MORE
PICTURES
PLEASE

Drew

* * * * *

Today is 3 May 2016. How exciting of a letter and groups of notes. It has been weeks since we have heard from him and have obviously been very concerned on how he is doing. The news contained within Drew's letter could not have been better. We have been worrying about how he is doing and we see that he is great. What struck me most from the letter was Drew writing about how he has come to realize how loved he is and how fortunate he is to have all of the people in his life that care so much for him.

It struck me as very interesting given that several years ago I remember attending my little brother, Mike's wedding. Attending the wedding was a very close friend of my stepfather (Mike Barton), Brad Topp. I remember at the wedding just how proud I was of Drew and excited to introduce him to Brad Topp. Mr. Topp was always a favorite of ours as children growing up. We always had a lot of fun with him and he was someone that I looked up to greatly. It was nice to be able to introduce my son to him. I did that with such great pride and excitement.

Yet, the next day, Drew chastised me and indicated that it was upsetting for him to have me introduce him to Mr. Topp because it was so clear to him how disappointed in him I was and how much I dislike him. I was astonished. I do not know how we perceived the situation so differently. It is this type of thing that my mind jumps to regarding his last letter. Did a light switch just go on for him, having a realization of how much we love him.

The Marine Corps recruit is trained and taught so many different things at so many different levels in the process of becoming a Marine.

Something else that I loved in the letter was his plans to come home after completing graduation.

How ingenious and fiscally responsible of the United States Marine Corps to pay a new Marine and I think for that matter, any one in the Armed Services, their travel expenses from one destination to the next assigned destination. Every Marine Recruit that graduates from MCRD San Diego has, as their next destination, infantry training in San Diego. The expenditure for the Marine Corps to pay for these new Marines is to pay for them to get from San Diego to San Diego. Obviously, the burden and expense is on the Marine and his family to get him home and back. Very ingenious indeed.

Phase 2 is coming to a close. Recruits will travel back to MCRD on Mother's Day, 7 May 2016. Coincidentally falling on S-7.

Very interesting the dichotomy between the recruit, drill

instructors and the relationship with the instructor for the rifle training and shooting. The rifle instructor is not loud and in their face; but, is trying to teach the recruit something that is of the utmost importance to a Marine - operating their rifle. Given the significance of this endeavor, the drill instructors are not barking over their shoulders. As a result, the DI's await the recruit's return to the barracks and have to make up for their absence from one another for most of the day.

Every Marine is a Rifleman. The Drill Instructor's role and responsibility was most significant in Phase 1, continues to keep the recruits on their feet during Phase 2. That role yet remains to be seen through Phase 3.

* * * * *

Tuesday
May 3

I can't wait to see Buck when he first sees you!

Dad and I both have the week off while you will be home. That'll be so nice. I hope we have good weather. Unlike San Diego, Sunny every day.

Another long work day today. You've had a long day every day these past several weeks. Down time will be nice, huh?!

Love you bigger than space!

Mom

* * * * *

Dear Drew,

I have been picking some mushrooms. It is still a bit cold. I prefer going out to pick when it is hot and steamy and you are fighting off the black bugs. The mushrooms are as you well remember, in abundance.

I worked really hard to layer down some fresh top soil, grass seed and another layer of top soil and grass clippings in the big pee spot you made just outside the patio door. The grass has really come in well so you are going to have to remember that when you pee off the back deck, to get your shot into your mother's flower bed as opposed to the lawn.

Sgt. Butler, after he visited with us on the night of your departure and wanted the signed statement relating to whether or not you had ever suffered from tendinitis, said that the only issue he had with you, was your continuous peeing outdoors in public. I do not know how that became a habit for you. I imagine during week three of Phase II, you had quite a lot of opportunities to pee outdoors.

I am anxious to hear from you what the difference is between the weeks of Phase II when you are at Camp Pendleton. Obviously I believe the first week you are learning the rifle used in the Marine Corps and the techniques used to shoot it. Then week two, it appears to me is a lot of narrowing down your technique and actually taking the rifleman's test at the end of the week. Then week three appears to be a lot of field work and hiking. It looks like there are several extended − 5 mile, 8 mile and 3 mile hikes while you are at Camp Pendleton. Patrick had said there were a couple of overnight adventures in the woods while during that Phase.

I think that all of this is getting you pretty well primed for the Crucible. I do not think you will face anything that you have not already faced and accomplished during the Crucible except for the fact it is all crammed into two or three days and you have to perform different tasks that can only be accomplished as a team.

You will be getting this letter if they are delivering mail to you in Camp Pendleton. Towards the end of the last week in Phase II. The Sunday that ends Phase II is Mother's Day. Hopefully we will have received some mail from you by then with the Questionnaire that I had sent or the Mother's Day Card that I had sent to you for you to send back to your Mother. We understand if we do not get mail as I imagine going to Camp Pendleton created a whole new situation and there is probably not much time for you to send material back.

It was really nice to see the YouTube video with you in it. We could see your rack. You sent a questionnaire back indicating that you were on the top bed in the rack. It has been very nice to see the YouTube video and see your barracks and where you are living. I was able to show the video to Sgt. Butler and two other recruiters that were there that day. The recruiter that you and I had met with on one occasion pointed out how you could see in your face a cool and calmness, where as the recruit next to you clearly had signs of fear and anxiety in his expressions. All of this makes me very happy and proud to know you are doing well. That is how the parent gets through this – just hoping you are doing well and are okay.

You have a lot to be proud of and I hope that you are feeling it. Please know that we are very proud of you. Ride the wave of feeling of success and accomplishment. Keep humping.

Love,

Dad

P.S. Following the MCRD San Diego website and Facebook leads me to believe at times it can be a little cold there - given how parents and family dress for the graduations and family day events. I imagine it will warm up by your graduation.

I follow the weather on weather app and it looks like it is warm and sunny most days there.

Meeting Chuck Duncan tonight for his Men's Club. I think it would be nice to have Chuck and Patrick visit with us at the pond when you get home. Think on it.

Keep plugging away. Fight through what you must. It will all be worth it.

*   *   *   *   *

So the chow is better at MCRD than at Camp Pendleton. Perhaps that is a nice way of making the recruit look forward to going back to MCRD. We will have to get a count from Drew on how many recruits are no longer seen as a result of being unable to pass the rifle qualification test. How much do they allow them to work through the weekend after qualification day of T-34 of last and through this week?

What happens to these unfortunate ones who have been away from home for eight weeks. Eight weeks away from home and only a few more until graduation. What a tremendous amount of pressure to stay healthy and stay on track. Pressure, pressure, pressure. From Pick Up week through the first couple of weeks, there is constant pressure of a new environment and trying to see whether you are made for what it takes.

*   *   *   *   *

4 May 2016
T38
Wednesday

Dear Drew,

Hump day of last week of Phase 2, when you get this you will be back to MCRD.

Phase 3 - Keep humpin. Before you know it we will be drinking bottles of Miller High Life, smoking Marlboro Reds and Throwing another log on the bonfire and grabbing another slice of pizza. I see you send letters to us with a note pad. We received an awesome letter yesterday. Thank you. You should have a notepad where you just write a word or two, or notes if you can each day. I can't wait to hear all the details from you and a diary would be nice for reflection.

Dinner with Chuck last night. He loves hearing how great you are doing!!! He says I am not to bring you any clothes - phone is OK, but you are to wear your dress uniform until you get home. He says you have joined a brotherhood that only a few are allowed in and you should feel the pride. I get chills thinking about walking around with you in uniform. I will bring clothes because you asked, but I hope you listen to Chuck.

I know you have very limited time when you get home and I do not want to take all of it; but, please allow us to have you Sunday after the Saturday you get back to have Chuck and Patrick and pizza and beer at a midday bonfire and lunch with you. The following Saturday for family to come congratulate you and say goodbye as you probably leave that Sunday - that is where you should check into that deal Chuck suggested where you get to stay 30-60 days at home working the local recruiters office. You would enjoy being home through June and July.

Also keep your eyes and mind open to opportunities that may present themselves to you. See how you liked the rifle in-structor and how young he was. Stuff like that has you written all over it.

I recall how I used to always buy you so many things from the Military Surplus Store - meals, clothes, cooking utensils, pots, shovels, canteens - your altitech.

How you would dig trenches all day - of course this was your destiny. Love of outdoors - loyal and hard working to the core, and so of course to the Corps you are. How did someone come across Mucinex and Sudafed? I would have sent that to you if that were ok.

So glad you are feeling better. We knew you would love swimming. Glad it helped clean out the sinuses.

I am anxious to see what assignment you get during Team week/Interior Guard - Training week 8 - 1st week of Phase 3.

Study your Handbook. Stay fit. Stay strong, keep humpin. 1 day at a time. Home stretch - Don't fuck it up now. Miller

High Life - bottles and Marlboro Reds await you.

So VERY VERY proud of you!!! Love you. Miss you greatly, but I cannot wait to give my bear cub a big ole bear hug.

Love, Dad

* * * * *

The last few weeks are pressure-filled to see whether you are able to complete the mission. Everyone's mind is now gearing towards graduation. Passing the book work tests, Swim Certification and now becoming a Rifleman. Even the parents are thinking toward graduation.

* * * * *

Monday
May 2

Hi Mom. I was going to try to pick a flower that I saw at the rifle range and send it to you with the card, but I never had a chance to get it. At the rifle range there is a red firing line and if you cross it you get dropped, I didn't want to risk it.

The DIs never keep us informed as to what is going on in the outside world unless there is a terrorist attack, but they told us that Mother's Day is coming up. I was grateful for that. I already said Happy Mother's Day in a different letter, but now I have a card. Hopefully this means a little more.

I love you bigger than space.

Love, Drew

Thursday
5 May 2016
T39

Dear Drew,

Today Thursday T39 and T40 Friday on the Matrix are marked as "Table II". What did you guys do for Table II.

I hope you enjoy the bus ride back to MCRD. Enjoy the views. Before you know it you will be back on that bus on Sunday 10 and going back to Pendleton for the CRUCIBLE. Yikes. It is going to be hard; really hard. Very challenging, but hump through it. You know you can do it. Just do it!!!

Today is the 1 year anniversary of Uncle Dave's death. Wonderful, wonderful man.

Passing of time stinks - unless you are in a situation like you are right now and you cannot make it go fast enough. Fickle bitch it all is. Always setting goals and shooting towards things that require the passage of time, but then you think of loved ones that are no longer with us as a result of time flying by. Before you know it you will be home drinking some Miller High Life in bottles and Busch Light tall boys.

Jim Babin's funeral this weekend. Remember how you, Bennett and I made the Cooper pyramid in his pool. I had some very nice times with Jim. He was a very gregarious - fun - caring - nice kind of guy. It was awesome what we were able to do for Paw Paw Rocket Football and of course we could not have made that go anywhere without his son Jason. Jim died way too young. Bad heart genetics like our old buddy Chuck Muvrin. Jim also smoked a lot. Since you have quit through MCRD you should try and not start up again after graduation.

Weather is really foul here. Rainy - fine - but the bitter and biting cold is just getting old. I ran yesterday with long underwear, sweat pants, heavy shirts, winter jacket and full hat and gloves. Raining and cold.

I have paid for your plane ticket so be sure they do not take out any $ from your account for travel. Last week I mailed you your ticket. I sent travel information in two separate mailings so I am sure you are aware of flying out of San Diego Saturday morning after graduation. Chuck wants you wearing your uniform until you get home. I agree, please consider that.

I hope you get to eat all the protein/power bars I am sending you and getting all the cough drops. I never noticed the wide variety of cough drops on the market before this.

One foot in front of the other. Almost there. A journey of a thousand miles begins with one step.

Can't wait to see you. Love you.

Love Dad

*   *   *   *   *

Dearest Drew -

Thinking of you often, as always!

Today is 1 yr. Anniversary of Uncle Dave's death. Very sad to lose a special guy. Been a hard year for Aunt Elaine. She's had to learn to do a lot of things he always managed. She is lonely without him. Jason Babin's dad died this week. Mid 50's. How? Smoking. I know you are anxious for your cigarettes now, but please, eventually, be a non smoker. Your life is too precious and all that bad stuff runs in my family.

It has been the WORST weather here. Cold & rainy nearly every day.

Thank you for the Mother's Day Wishes.

The lilac tree to the side of the house looks so pretty. Those flowers are my favorite scent followed by lavender.

Enjoy the pictures. Fun looking through them. Life is flying by. When you all were little will be the best years of my life as I look back. I love being a mommy.

Love you bigger than space,

Mom

* * * * *

May 5

We just got done with table one of the rifle range. I shot expert, but I felt like I shot shit. I could have gotten a much better score. I got a 228. The day before we did a practice qualification day. I got four points higher on that one, and I shot like shit that day too. I was very disappointed in myself. At times aiming was hard for me though on Tuesday during the week of table one I woke up with some pretty bad pink eye in my shooting eye. It was only in my right eye.

Im writing this on Saturday, end of week of table one, and the pink eye is just now starting to feel a little bit better. I've never had pink eye before until now. It sucks. I've pretty much been waiting for it since the start of boot camp because everybody gets pink eye in boot camp. Back in phase one, I was talking with a third phase recruit and he said that its better to get pink eye before phase two so you can go to medical and get eye drops, because then you will already have eye drops in phase two.

In phase two if you go to medical you get dropped. Luckily the SDI saw that my eye was fucked up and he gave me eye drops so I wouldn't have to go to medical. The pink eye made it difficult to shoot. My vision would get blurry and I would have to adjust. The recruit from third phase I talked to said its very easy to get pink eye up north at Pendleton because of how dirty it is here. I probably got it at the worst time possible.

As far as hikes go, we have done a three mile and a five mile. The three mile was easy, and the five mile was easy too. I breezed right through the five mile.

During the hikes we wear our flaks, kevlars, and our main packs. Our main packs weight about 35-45 pounds. We do the eight mile hike the Saturday before we leave to MCRD.

Being at Pendleton we always see recruits getting ready for the Crucible and we see them patrolling while on the Crucible. Then on Thursdays we see them at chow with their eagle, globe and anchor, all standing at ease. Recruits are only allowed to stand at attention, that is heels together, feet at a 45-degree angle, and hands in tight fists with the thumbs along your trouser seams. I can't wait to stand however I want.

This is how I want it to go after graduation:

I will probably want to talk with some of the guys from my platoon, and a couple from other platoons as well. We might go to Starbucks on base for some coffee or something. You're all welcome to go to Starbucks with me too.

Then I'll go to the Marine PX to buy some stuff. I'll buy cigarettes if you guys don't bring me any. I'll smoke one, and then we will get the fuck out of there. I want to drive because its been a while and if you guys, (especially Bennett) can suck it up for me I want to have a cigarette on the way to the grocery store. One of the things I miss most is smoking and driving.

But, I want to go to the grocery store. I want to get one bag of Taco Doritos, one bag of Sweet and Spicy Chili Doritos, whatever the ones are that mom buys now. I also want to get a box of donuts (preferably Jelly filled) and some cookies too. I also really want some of those PB&J sandwiches that are round and sealed at the end with no crust (like the ones at school lunch). And, I want a six pack of Miller High Life and a six pack of PBR. Probably some cereal too. Then I want to go somewhere where I can get an ice-cream cone with a waffle cone.

And I want to order a pepperoni pizza and a pizza with pepperoni, sausage, and bacon. Then to the hotel to eat it. And I will most likely want to go out to eat somewhere for a late dinner. Somewhere where I can get a burger and jalapeno poppers.

So the tattoo, I don't care if I get it in San Diego or Kzoo, but I want us all to be together for it, and I would like to see some pictures soon of what the design is. I thought it was that knife from Anella's tattoo book. I liked that. I don't want anything loud or gaudy. Just something simple and easy. So send me pictures, and if you decide we are getting it in kzoo, I'm not going to Art and Soul, and I'm not going to Body Armor. I think it would be cool to do it in San Diego, though, as long as it doesn't fuck up us getting home ASAP.

Make sure you are letting Bennett and Anella read these letters too, as well as anyone else in our family who wants to read them. I'm writing these to all of you.

Here is something interesting. I've sort of forgotten that I have a first name. Its weird and my hands are really dark, it's a combination of the sun, dirt, and carbon getting on my hands when I clean my weapon. There is dirt and carbon permanently on my hands now. I named my weapon Alice, like Alice Cooper. Also Alice in Wonderland because I fell down the rabbit hole too.

There are a lot of guys here who have girlfriends back home, and a lot of those guys talk about how they want to get married when they get out of boot camp. All the DI's P.I.'s and all the other instructors say that their biggest piece of advice is to not get married. I think its funny, their reasons are that if their girls aren't back home fucking some other guy right now, they definitely will be once your deployed. They also say that you won't want to be tied down once you get your dress blues. They say that dress blues can make the ugliest dude sexy.

There's no way I would want a girlfriend while in boot camp, or when I'm wherever overseas. I'll probably get a lady friend in whatever countries I visit like Uncle Mark did in China.

It feels so weird to say that in one week I will be a third phase recruit and all of our mentalities will be in a different place. It's like going Freshman to Senior in High School. It feels like just yesterday we were the newbies on the depot. Soon we are the guys with our names on our chest, who other recruits see and can't believe.

I'm anxious to see the video I'm in. I remember a camera and I remember looking at it and hoping that somebody would get a kick out of a recruit staring at the camera. I don't remember what we were doing though. Were we in desert camis or woodland camis? Were we just in green T-shirts or did we have our blouses on? Not long after black Friday we changed from our deserts to the woodlands. We have been in woodlands ever since. We don't wear deserts again until phase three.

In phase three we get the patches on our chest, one has our name, the other says US Marines. We also will get our dog tags. My tags might be interesting. First of all, my DOB might be 10/26/95. They have been making that mistake a lot. The other thing about my tags, will be pretty hilarious if it actually happens. My DI might have fucked me on it though. I'll be pissed if he did. I don't want to say what it is and jinx it, but if it happens right I'm sure you will all get a laugh out of it.

I don't like the chow hall here at Pendleton, you get smaller portions and you're only allowed one peanut butter packet and one jelly. At MCRD I would get like five peanut butters, even though they make my farts really smelly. Also, I can't really eat my salad here because they put olives in it. Another thing about Pendleton is we are right by the ocean so its windy. It gets really cold at night, and it takes a while for it to warm up in the morning.

I really want to know more about the tattoo. Send me as much information as possible about the tattoo, and send me pictures too, and let me know where on the body everyone is getting it.

I have a scar on my forehead now. It pisses me off. I got it on the day of pugil sticks one. Way back in like week 2 or something. We had bayonet training right before the pugil sticks, so I think I accidentally got hit with a rifle because I first noticed it when I put the football helmet on for pugil sticks. I could feel it hurt when I put the helmet on. Its about the size of a dime or a penny above my right eye, and it hasn't really gotten any smaller. It got a little less visible because I got a little more tan, but you can still see it.

So, could you please read into ways to get rid of scars, because I really don't want to have a scar on my face. Its not even a cool looking scar. I would appreciate it if you would help me figure out how to get rid of it.

* * * * *

6 May 2016
T40
Friday

Dear Dear Drew

1 - 2 - 3 - 4 - I love the Marine Corp.

1 - 2 - 3 - 4 - Can't wait to fuck a pretty girl.

Came up with that in reference to your letter yesterday about recruits having girlfriends back home and DI's advice that would be very tough.

CONGRATULATIONS!!!!

Expert Rifleman. Awesome. Funny how you have a messed up eye. During hunting season my eye gets all messed up from always rubbing them in preparation for shooting. Damn hooded eyes.

I share your letters. I really like how you are so descriptive of some events. I can't wait to hear all the details.

After graduation we will do whatever you want; except please do not ditch us. We are excited to see you and hang out with you.

Can we get our tattoos during the week and schedule you for Friday or Saturday morning - probably have to do yours Friday. I do not know how long each takes; but we could get it all set up in San Diego and go with you Friday after graduation and just do yours - after some Marlboros and Miller High Life, in bottles of course, and some jelly donuts and PBJ's.

I heard there is a Mexican restaurant with the best fish tacos. Think about what you want for dinner - pizza - steak - chops - sea food??

Ha Ha - getting hungry?

Very proud of you Drew. Keep Humpin. Your training and progress is being followed by many many people. You are the only one in our family doing this - serving our Country. Even with all family and friends - you are on the minds of many. You are being an awesome role model for your brother and sister. This whole deal is just so incredible. You are in Phase III. Keep your eye on the prize. Do what it takes to get that emblem at the end of the Crucible and get to graduation. You are so close, stay healthy - study your handbook.

We will have Miller High Life in bottles on ice - lighters and Marlboro Reds. You just do what you gotta do to graduate.

Check out that deal Chuck suggested about working at the Recruiter's office in Kalamazoo before you have to go to Infantry School. You could enjoy some of the summer here.

I love your letter. Many many details are nice. I like how you looked at the YouTube camera and what you say about that in your letter. You were wearing button up shirts - tan/desert camo - long pants. I got a lot of nice photos from it. I still say I see you in the pool too. Stay strong, stay smart.

Love you Drew.

Love, Dad.

* * * * *

Friday a.m.
May 6

Dearest Drew-

Got a stack of letters Wednesday and another yesterday. You sound so good. Confident. Can you believe you are heading into phase 3. You must be so proud of yourself. Thinking back to the first couple of weeks - you've learned a lot about yourself.

Thank you for the Mother's Day card. Made me cry. A good cry. I appreciate it very much. Being your mom is a blessing. I loved our time together when you were little. You are a cuddly guy. I can picture you clearly in the sandbox, coming over to wipe your nose on my shirt. I never had a clean shirt.

Funny about the guys who are anxious to get married. Your DI is so right. BIG MISTAKE. Too young. Too much going on. If it was meant to be they will stick around. Those WWII vets went away for 3 years. Many of their women waited for them.

You are so handsome I can't imagine you in your dress blues.

Might as well bring the dish towel. I'm going to cry like a baby.

Aren't you grateful for a cool name like Cooper. Imagine the crap you would get from the DI's if your name was Niedzwiecki.

I cannot imagine the sense of pride you must have. You are the few, the proud. I saw a site on facebook that sells bracelets that have a charm that says "Marine mom". I'm going to order one to wear to your graduation. I am bursting with pride!

I am wondering if you are getting plenty to eat, why you are thinking of food all the time. Is it because you can't eat what you want when you want? Again, the ice cream references crack me up. You were never an ice cream guy. What happened? I agree with the Doritos - how can you beat those. You always loved crunchy chips.

You mentioned your tan. I dream about you a lot and you are tan in my dreams and your hair stubble is very blonde. I doubt that is true because you probably always have a hat on.

Bennett will work on the tattoo drawing this weekend and will mail Monday. We won't have time in San Diego before leaving, but I will make appointments for us all maybe on Monday or Tuesday when you're home. That is exam week for Bennett.

Dad is getting his on arm - biceps. I am leaning towards shoulder blade. Bennett is undecided. Don't know about Anella. There are fine lines involved so I will do some research on who is good at that.

Prince is now said to have died of drug overdose. He had addiction to opiates. He was scheduled for rehab treatment the day after he died. Apparently he is text book opiate addict. He originally took for back pain and led to long term use. Opiates not indicated for long term use. America has 5% of world's population and uses 80% of all opiates.

Trump has won the Republican Presidential race as nominee. Everyone in uproar.

What a relief you got those eye drops. Did you like the shooting part? You were obviously good at it.

Back to the tattoos. I know a lot of Marines get USMC tat

on arm. Let me know if you want appointment for that too.

How about an appointment to burn out your plantar warts?

I have been working long days. Last night home at 7:30. Finished charting at 9. Have most of today off. Have to make some phone calls. I am on call tonight : (

We actually have sun in forecast today. I am hoping to get some yard work done and a nap on the deck. The grass is really long having rain nearly every day the past few weeks.

Thank you for writing such nice letters to us. Dad photos them and shares them with family. Everyone so proud of you! Hope it's a good day for you.

Love you bigger than space!

Mom

Save the pics. Some I don't have copies.

* * * * *

I loved how Chuck said that Drew needs to wear his dress uniform home. I cannot imagine the feelings of pride and the chills running down my spine walking through an airport with my son, the Marine. Drew keeps asking for particular clothing. When I mentioned that to Chuck, his response was immediate, "do not send him any clothing."

I have heard stories of the new Marine immediately after graduation running across the parade deck to his bags and getting off the base as soon as possible. I enjoy listening to Chuck talk about how he immediately after running across the parade deck to his bag, got in a cab and went to the airport to go home. Literally, graduates will sprint from the parade deck to their bag.

Chuck told the story of how after he grabbed his hat after throwing it in the air, he went to his bag and hailed a taxi and went directly to the airport to fly home. Chuck did not have anyone attend his graduation ceremony. His mom and dad did, however, pick him up at the airport in Tulsa to take him home. Interestingly, Chuck said that he had no interest in talking with the drill instructors after graduation; they had made his life a shitty hell and he just wanted to get away from them as soon as possible.

From the parade deck to his bedroom at home, Chuck wore his dress uniform.

Table 1 and Table 2. What exactly does that mean on the Matrix. From Drew's letter that we received on 5 May 2016, he shot "expert." How very exciting. He is a Rifleman as all Marines are. I cannot imagine hitting a target at 500 yards. I am very curious as to the distinctions with rifleman and what is meant by him shooting "expert." Irregardless of the different definitions and the status of such, I could not be more proud than to hear he shot expert.

I am also very curious as to what it means to "drop." Does that just mean being pushed back or are you out. Surely I am glad that he did not try to cross a firing line to pick a flower for his mother.

I love how he is enjoying the hikes. Today is Friday, T-40 and he mentions a large hike. Tomorrow, Saturday, T-41 is followed by Mother's Day, S-7. They will be traveling back to MCRD.

What a way to end Phase 2. Knowing that he is doing great.

He has a good friend in Alice. Nice that he thought of Alice Cooper but Alice in Wonderland and him going down the rabbit hole could have so many different meanings.

Never has our society been so privileged. My generation and his, while we all have our struggles, society as a whole has never been so fortunate between the quality of life, supply of food, medical advancements and the development of technology in every field. By its very nature and existence, my generation and his is so spoiled.

With these incredible advancements and opportunities and our existence in a privileged manner, another whole set of difficulties, complexities, challenges and issues of trying to figure out who we are is presented. Does this result in the bully generation? Did Drew go down the rabbit hole at WMU, between semesters, trying to figure out who he is and where he is going, or did he fall down the rabbit hole at MCRD? His letters home clearly show a mature and proud individual.

The Marine Corps does not change a young man in terms of brain washing him into being someone or something that he was not before. It is a matter of bringing out characteristics and behavior that are within the person that have been tainted, obscured, or hidden, which has not allowed the individual to rise to a level of achievement and accomplishment that they have the potential to be. They come out having respect and honor for themselves and others, their teammates and others they work with and see the fat civilians and filthy animals among us - wondering how or why someone could live the way they do.

The Greatest Generation has been categorized as that because they lived with respect and honor for themselves and others. MCRD has given Drew the vision to pull from himself the respect and honor for himself and others that he should have and was instilled in him to a certain respect given the generation that his father comes from.

I tried to be a good father and also wanted to be a friend. Sometimes the two can be reconciled. What affect that has on raising Drew to being a young man and responsible, respectful man is quite complex. I do know that at this moment, I could not be more proud of Drew and do not know how I will hold it together at his graduation. I am simply ecstatic to what it has meant to all of us to have Drew go to MCRD San Diego. What a role model for his siblings and what a son to be proud of.

As much as I have fallen in love with the Marine Corps, I will let Drew's younger brother, Bennett, choose whatever branch of the military service he desires to join after he graduates from high school.

* * * * *

The Matrix has MCMAP (Marine Corp Martial Arts Program). I really enjoyed that. You come out of the Marine Corps recruit training with a brown belt. I really enjoyed this part of the program and believe that I will continue in this program.

I felt that it was a disappointment and that is why I want to continue forward with this. It seemed like anyone could pass it without even having to pay attention. It was quite a joke and I would like to learn more.

Drew poses with Grandpa Mike Barton during Family Day in San Diego.

PHASE 3
"ONCE A MARINE,
ALWAYS A MARINE"

CHAPTER 9
TEAM WEEK / INTERIOR GUARD
"ON GUARD – THE GUARDS"

* * * * *

The eighth week is interior guard. Interior guard is what the Marines call the guards who are on guard guarding things all the time, like fire watch. We all had to wear our Kevlar and Flak Jackets, we got rubber rifles, and we went outside and patrolled.

Team week is a lot of working parties, pretty much the entire week. I worked clothing supply. Clothing supply is a good place to work. In clothing supply, we hand out uniforms. A lot of people worked in the armory. We get issued our rifles with iron sites, and in Phase 2 we get RCO scopes on them. In the armory, we would take all the RCO scopes off and put iron sights on.

During interior guard, we were all assigned to different working parties and the assignments varied from day to day. From working in clothing supply to the armory, it was a nice break from drill and more drill. For example, at the armory, we would have RCO's and we would have to take those off and put those back on with the iron-sights.

When we are issued our rifles, they are with iron-sights. In Phase 2, they put RCO's on them. Once I was assigned to the armory, I had to take all of the RCO's off the weapons and put the iron-sights back on. We would have racks and racks of rifles. It was quite a cool week. We were able to put on our kevlars, flak jackets and go on patrols. I enjoyed working in the clothing distribution center because the civilian, who retired from the Navy, would give me news from the outside.

It was a big rumor among the recruits, that the age for using tobacco was being increased to 21, but the civilian in clothing distribution informed me that there were some nuances for those in the military. Very exciting news for someone wanting a dip or a smoke.

* * * * *

I went to a friend's funeral this weekend, James Babin – a gregarious, wonderful man. Jim died years before his time, sadly. While talking with a friend at the funeral visitation, he inquired as to what my son Drew is up to. I explained to him how he is finishing up his eighth training week at MCRD in San Diego with the Marine Corps. I bragged how Drew shot expert. The friend went on to describe how he shot expert at boot camp in the Army.

After he walked away, another friend from behind grabbed my shoulder and said, "Matt, please understand that what your son did, shooting expert in the Marine Corps, in no way compares to what that Army guy was expressing he did in the Army. The boot camps are in no way similar and the measurement for shooting expert are not comparable. This friend was Harold "Butch" Cirino. A Marine.

Butch went through Marine recruit training in 1968. He went into the Marines in July. In May, he had boots on the ground in Vietnam. During basic training, he was immediately transported upon graduation to machine gun school, then infantry training and after spending six months in Vietnam on Recon missions, they sent him to the Phillippines for jungle survival school. Butch's time in the Phillippines is highly secretive.

How cool is going to jungle survival school six months after you have been serving on Recon in Vietnam in the Marine Corps? Butch did not get the ten days off after boot camp. He had maybe seven days after machine gun school and infantry training before being sent to Vietnam. Whether you are at MCRD this year, last year, five years ago, 40 years ago, the torture is always watching the San Diego airport on the other side of the fence. People doing things, going places and you are stuck. To any Marine that went through MCRD San Diego, part of their story will include watching the planes at the San Diego International Airport. Torturous. Freedom and going home, so close, yet so far away.

An interesting point with my discussion with Cirino is the clear dichotomy between a fat civilian and a Marine. In the discussion I had with Butch about his helicopter being shot down in Vietnam and how he injured his shoulder after "his helicopter landed" (my words), Butch pointed out, while laughing, that the helicopter did not land, "it crashed!"

Butch was on a Recon mission where they were trying to plant hidden listening devices in the jungle when the helicopter sustained heavy fire and crashed to the ground, mangling Butch's body and leaving his shoulder in such destruction, he spent months and months having the shoulder repaired and reconstructed.

Today is Tuesday, 10 May 2016 or T-43. According to the Matrix is it is the day for initial uniform fitting. How exciting? The light at the end of the tunnel can be seen. This is the first week of Phase 3. It is Team Week, Interior Guard. Yesterday was the Practical Application. I am anxious to find out exactly what this week entails. I imagine MCRD is quite a complex and has numerous facilities conducting daily operations. Imagine that each week there is a group of Marine Recruits working their way through the Matrix.

Thus, every week there is a Team Week Interior Guard group that probably supplies a lot of the labor throughout the mess halls and building and grounds. Are the recruits performing kitchen duty and janitorial services this week? Are there recruits helping with security? I would imagine that there are 101 jobs that require attention. I am curious as to whether the recruits participate in that during this week.

Later in the week is the blood drive. With Drew's rare blood type (O-), he has always been very generous in donating his blood during different drives. In a few days, T-45 is the day for getting the Marine haircuts. The buzz cut from pick up week has grown out enough so that the Marine Corps style can be shaped among the stubble.

* * * * *

May 10
Tuesday

Dearest Drew -

You hang in there! End in sight!
Love you bigger than space!

Mom

* * * * *

10 May 2016
T43, Tuesday

Dear Drew,

What a week is training week 8. Uniform fitting, Marine haircut, Uniforms with your name, coming off of shooting expert. Service certified. Big hikes over.

Phases 1 and 2 are in the rear view mirror. Keep looking forward. Get to that finish line. I apologize if I am getting you in trouble with the things I have been mailing to you. Hopefully some of the treats make it through.

Yesterday I ran with long underwear, sweatshirts and winter jacket and hat. Still way too cold here. Bullshit Spring. It has been too cold and wet to stain the cabin, but hopefully it will be done before you come home.

Buck is doing great. He enjoys the cold. Sleeps all day on the couch. He enjoyed Mother's Day. Went on a couple hikes. He hikes well; but, I do not think he should run every day anymore. I love watching him swim.

Captured a very large raccoon the other day. It figured out how to get in the corn barrel by the chicken coop. It actually carried the bag of corn away. I found the bag 20 feet away. We are still getting a lot of eggs. This last flock of hens have been very productive.

Looks like you have more pugil sticks next week. Good luck. Another week or two and you are on the home stretch. Good luck. Stay strong - mentally and physically. I am very proud of you mister. Love you.

Love, Dad

* * * * *

I learned yesterday that the opportunity to have a longer leave between graduating from recruit training at MCRD and starting infantry school at Camp Pendleton is a matter of how backed up the schedule is at infantry school. I was wanting to find out how a new graduate such as Drew, could obtain the position at the recruiter's office that would allow him more time between graduation and infantry training. Sgt. Butler informed me that it is not necessarily about applying for the position, but more about the scheduling of infantry school.

Apparently towards the end of Drew's graduation, he will learn about the availability of this type of extended leave and position at his local recruiter's office if infantry school is backed up and requires new Marines to wait to attend.

* * * * *

Wednesday a.m.
May 11

Dearest Drew -

Are you enjoying the photos? It's amazing looking through them. It really wasn't that long ago but seems like a lifetime. We have really had a nice life. I think Dad and I provided as lovely a childhood as a kid could want. I feel very lucky. You were all healthy and smart. I got to be home. We had things to do. We got to travel. Your mom and dad love each other. No drug or alcohol issues. We laughed a lot.

We have so much to be thankful for and now we are so happy for you – almost done with boot camp. You will be a Marine. You will meet so many people. Travel to some places you've never been (I'm hoping for Hawaii). You are an outstanding young man. Your mommy loves you!

I think the mushroom season ended up being a bust. We got a few last week and just a few this past weekend. We have had terrible weather. Cold and rainy. Not many sunny days. Someone told me the Farmer's Almanac is predicting a dry and scorching summer.

Been seeing a lot of turtles. I've been finding tiny ones in the yard, size of a quarter. Painters. How did they get up here? Where are they going?

Bennett saw huge snake on two-track while running. He said he jumped and I say he screamed like a girl.

Had another long day at work. Have a child with brain cancer. Heartbreaking.

Anella put the picture I sent of the three of you in the wagon on facebook. She wrote "only a month until the three of us are together again." Sweet.

I got some vitamin E oil for you to use on your scar. I'll see if Dad can sneak it in your mail. Rub it in whenever you can. Be sure to respond to his tattoo questions so we can make plan.

Love you bigger than space!

Mom

Remember to save the pictures. We'll put them back in your photo box when home. Dad outside right now shooting HUGE raccoon stuck in critter trap by chickens.

* * * * *

11 May 2016
T44, Wednesday

Dear Drew,

Yesterday I went home for lunch. Still eating Bennett's turkey. Cold and rainy. When I went outside to pee off the deck - into flower bed - not the grass - I called Buck to come with me. He was all cozy on the couch. He wouldn't move; except to sit up and lay his head on the couch back and watch me. Cold and rainy vs warm and cozy. He wasn't going out!!

Before I mail you the photos that mom sends I snap a shot with my I-Phone and send some occasionally to Bennett, Anella and Mom - so we are looking at the photos when you are. I liked the one the other day of you ice skating at the pond. See-we did not always use the extension cords.

When we dropped you off back on March 13 - wow - some time ago now, Bennett took a picture of the Matrix at the recruiters office - hope you still have the one I sent you - mine sits on my office desk and I frequently examine it throughout the day. There was something I could not figure out and that was a couple of young men having their portraits over a couple of days.

When I stopped by the recruiter's office a couple of weeks ago, I learned that those are photos of Kalamazoo area recruits and each day the recruiters move their photos to reflect their progression through MCRD. On that visit I took a picture of you on the Matrix; but it did not show the entire Matrix. I have stopped by the recruiters office a couple of more times to get another photo; but, it is hit or miss trying to catch someone there. So I called Sgt. Butler yesterday and asked him to text me a complete Matrix with you on it.

Also, I asked him about how you could get a longer leave between graduating and Infantry School and working at the recruiter's office before Infantry training like Chuck suggested. Sgt. Butler said that is all dependant upon the Infantry School numbers. If they are backed up with Marines they place new graduates at recruiter's offices waiting for openings. Keep your eyes and ears open as to this issue perhaps coming up.

Make sure they know your flight home has been paid for.

I have not had a beer since I saw you last and will not have one until I see you again. Busch Light - tall boys. Miller High Life - in bottles and of course Pabst Blue Ribbon - bottles will be waiting us at the hotel after your graduation.

I think I previously told you about the raccoon terrorizing our chickens and how he was terminated this past weekend. I reset the trap near the coop and this morning I had the largest coon I have ever seen. Holy Cow, the chickens had to be scared as hell. After I dispatched the small bear the chickens were all sitting on their roosts outside in complete silence. Kinda eerie how they just sat there so quiet and still. It was like they were thinking what the hell just happened.

I am sending separately some vitamin E oil for your wound and scar treatment. Hope you get it.

Hang tough. Finish this - very very proud of you. Miss you. Love you.

Love Dad

* * * * *

Today, T-44 on the Matrix, says it is the Functional Obstacle Course. The photograph is quite inspiring, adventurous. I really believe that Drew will have a great time doing this obstacle course. The obvious concerns at this point is wrenching a knee or twisting an ankle. You have to stay healthy and finish this. Worry. Worry. Worry.

* * * * *

Tomorrow, T-45, the recruits get new haircuts to fashion style them as a Marine. I have scheduled an appointment for me to get a buzz cut on T-47. How exciting for them to get the Marine hairstyle and uniforms with their names on it with Marine as well. They have to be feeling strong and proud. The next three weeks, however, appear to be extremely challenging. Polishing what they have learned and thus far endured. Comprehensive examinations, confidence examination through the gas chamber and physical fitness final examinations. Not to mention, the Commander's inspection and crisp parade practice. What a few weeks to come. In some ways, Phase 3 can be worse than Phase 1.

* * * * *

Today is Thursday, 12 May and T-45 on the Matrix. Haircut day. Nine weeks ago, the recruits heads were shaved down as tight as electric clippers would take the stubble. The nine weeks of growth allows for the forming of the perfect Marine cut. Tight on the sides and a little on the top. Not much has changed with this hairstyle over the generations. It is fascinating how society changes from generation to generation.

I graduated high school in 1982 and had a very close relationship with my grandparents and great uncles that were teenagers in the 1920's. I remember writing a college paper about the roaring 20's and my grandma being a flapper in Chicago. From knowing folks with the cropped hairstyles from the 40's, 50's, 60's and the hippies from the 60's and 70's, surely a high school graduate from the 80's had seen it all. From Revolutionary War wigs to Civil War facial hair styling and the men's fur coats at the turn of the 20th Century to Peace-Sign necklaces and Vietnam POW bracelets of the 60's and 70's, what else could change or shock one's consciousness of style.

Tattoos have been around since man discovered fire. In the earliest days of the Navy, it was said that sailors would use ink and long needles to at least mark their name and date of birth in case they were lost at sea. I remember in high school, bad-ass kids were getting tats.

The millennials think nothing of a tattoo. Today's society, tattoos are quite common place. So how has the military changed and rolled with these practices and its steeply held tradition against tats that can be seen while in uniform. Today, the Navy loosened its restrictions about tattoos. The Marines issued new requirements a few weeks later.

Three weeks later the Marines announced their new tattoo policy put in place. There is a dichotomy amongst society as far as its views among the armed services and who are accepted into its ranks. Go to a Navy Recruiter, Army, Coast Guard, Marines, the mentality that the Armed Forces take whoever they can get, is well out of date.

Being accepted into the Marines is no small feat. Other than the obvious physical and professional demands, Marines are held to the highest standards for their appearance. The Marine Corps are much more low-key than the old rules (which is surprising, since the new rules are still pretty strict).

The Marine Corps Commandant said that "we've attempted to balance the individual desires of Marines with the need to maintain the disciplined appearance expected of our profession." The Commandant wanted the policy to allow Marines freedom and flexibility to express themselves, while also being clearly written and understandable for both Marines and their leadership.

The most important rule of all, he added, states that any tattoo a Marine receives cannot "express sexism, nudity, racism, vulgarity, or anything that is offensive and is of a nature to bring discredit to the Marine Corps or damage the nation's expectations of them."

These long-awaited updates were released in a 32-page booklet that explains the rules in painstaking detail. For example, here are just a few of the unauthorized locations for new tattoos; head, neck, the area two inches above the center of the elbow and one inch below, the area two inches above the wrist, hands (unless it's a single band tattoo on one finger that's smaller than 3/8 of an inch thick), and the area two inches above and below the center of the kneecap. So with such specific restrictions, where can you get a tattoo if you're in the Marine Corps?

Well, anywhere that fits the above standards, the booklet explains. Although these restrictions prevent Marines from getting a full sleeve tattoo, there have been a few positive changes to the old policy that will make getting a tattoo a bit more lenient.

First, band tattoos (the ones that circumvent a part of one's body) will now be allowed to reach up to three inches wide – a full inch wider than the previous rule. The ring-tattoo-on-one-hand is a completely new rule as well, allowing Marines to get a small band on a single finger. Another major rule change tackles the old policy requirement for tattoos that are visible in PT uniforms to be covered with a 5-inch diameter circle. Instead, the tattoos now simply must be able to be covered with the Marine's hand.

Every branch of the service is very selective. Expanding the regulations for allowing more tattoos and visible tattoos has nothing to do with expanding the pool of potential candidates. Rather, it is clearly a change based on the change of societal views and the usage of tattoos. Corporate America is doing the same thing with its employees for the exact same reasons. To the millennials, a tattoo is nothing more than what General George Armstrong Custer thought of his sideburns and mustache.

Criticism of those that join and support our Armed Services come from those that have not served. There is an honor and privilege that comes with having served that those who have not do not fully understand. Most people either are supportive of those that have, or compensate for their own inadequacy or insecurities by looking down their noses at those that do.

The United States of America has the most proficient, experienced and capable Armed Services on this planet for a reason. The most treasured asset of our Nation are those that make up the various branches of Armed Services. The United States Coast Guard is unmatched in the world for their unmatched role of safety and security of our shorelines and bodies of water. The U.S. Army has the greatest staying and securing power.

The United States Air Force has the greatest first strike capabilities and the Navy has the greatest transport capability and sustained protection and projection of power. The best striking power in land or sea is the United States Marine Corps. It is due to the selective process of acquiring and training programs that makes this the strongest military force in the world.

It is from the millennials that we are now drawing this fighting force. Never in the 1980's having thought of having seen all the different hairstyles that exist have occurred would one have ever thought of or anticipated seeing someone with purple, lime green or pink hair. The longer stylist mohawks or the various oddly-shaped and placed body piercings. It is our military force that is steep in tradition yet malleable enough to draw from the changes with society.

*   *   *   *   *

Thursday
May 12

Dearest Drew -

Think of you so often! Makes me go back in time and relive your childhood in my head. Boy you know just how to drive me crazy! We always pull through! You thought at one time you would have a bright future annoying people. I think you got the idea from a TV show that was a hidden camera prank kind of thing. The idea was to frustrate the poor unsuspecting victim. You thought you could irritate them much faster than it was done.

You're funny.

Have a vacation day today. Going to paint the upstairs hallway after I do some general cleaning. If all goes well and I can finish tomorrow then I may do the hallway downstairs over the weekend. Nothing going on this weekend and weather is suppose to be crummy.

I love you bigger than space!

Mom

P.S. I bought some vitamin E oil and Dad is sending. Suppose to be good for scars. Rub a little on your wound few times a day (a.m. and p.m.) Hope you get it.

* * * * *

12 May 2016
Thursday, T-45

Dear Drew,

It looks like you get your Marine Corps hair cut today. We need to sort out what we are doing about the Cooper tattoo. Bennett is supposed to be putting together a diagram that we will be sending to you shortly.

In the meantime, enclosed with this letter is a questionnaire that I ask that you fill out and send back in the self-addressed, postage paid envelope. Essentially, I am trying to figure out whether you want your mother and I, Anella and Bennet to get our tattoos in San Diego during your last week at MCRD and then schedule an appointment for you to go to the same parlor immediately after graduation or later that day. I do not believe there will be time Saturday morning as we will be flying out. That is if you are of the school of thought that we should do this in San Diego. I realize that you probably have had your stomach full of San Diego and do not have a problem if we all do it together in Kalamazoo. Obviously it does not matter to me, except to the extent that we do what you would prefer.

I am sure for you, thinking that Phase I and II are behind you and that you are well into Phase III now makes you feel quite good about yourself in that things are almost done. That is easy for me to say and I am sure it is quite a different story being in your shoes with still quite a road ahead. I have been attempting to commiserate with your situation by depriving myself of certain things and it is quite difficult and becomes quite emotionally draining. It allows me to feel some of your pain.

Although I am allowed to take a break and a respite from those deprivations where you are stuck there until June 10th. All I know is that when I am at my lowest, I just simply plow forward one step at a time. Like Patrick said, you will reach your breaking point, but just take one more step and just keep plowing forward. Eventually it will be over and you will be there.

Please know that you have those that love you, that are thinking of you daily and are praying and pulling for you in every which way we can. When you are at your lowest, just continue to take one step at a time and know that this will be over soon and the lasting effects will be positive for you for the rest of your life. The big picture is clearly a very big picture.

I hope that you are getting the little treats that I am sending and they are not causing you to get into too much trouble. I have tried to send the chewable protein, fruit bites, as I do not understand how that would be different from a power bar. It says "power protein" and I buy it from the same shelf as the protein bars. Clearly, I am not sending you anything worse than the can of Pepsi and two donuts you found under the bleachers.

Hang tough. Be proud. Keep forging forward. I am so so very proud of you.

Love, Dad

QUESTIONNAIRE

1. I Drew, am firm in my desire that the five of us go to the tattoo parlor and have our tats done at the same time. (Keep in mind that five people and one artist will take hours).

   _____ Yes   _____ No

Comments:_____

_____

2. I am fine with the four of you getting your tattoo's done and scheduling me to come in and have the same one done by the same artist some time Friday after graduation.

   _____ Yes   _____ No

Comments:_____

_____

3. See if you can find a parlor that has a number of artists and all five of us can be scheduled to have ours done on Friday after graduation.

   _____ Yes   _____ No

Comments:_____

_____

4. I think that we should have all five of us scheduled to do our tattoos in Kalamazoo, after we get home from graduation because I do not care if we do it in San Diego.

_____ Yes   _____ No

Comments:_____

_____

* * * * *

Going to MCRD San Diego would allow Drew to experience the trials and tribulations of and learn the art of letter writing. Of course whenever you send a letter to someone, you are curious as to whether or not it is being received. When you send responses to other letters, you are again curious whether they are hearing from you. Again, it is frustrating if the letters you receive from them do not indicate they are getting your letters, it is quite a learned art of communication.

This is part of why I have sent Questionnaires with postage paid return envelopes so that I could have answers to many of my questions and to see whether he was getting what I was sending. To further complicate things more on his end, he is not in the best position with time, energy or ability to exert the effort of writing letters upon the receipt of the letters that he is receiving from us. Hence, another reason for the Questionnaires.

Friday, T-46 is the blood drive. With Drew's rare blood type, he has always been very generous giving his blood. Frequently, the Red Cross calls the house to remind him that the time has past and he is again allowed to provide more blood. I have found it interesting that he was so giving in that endeavor. It is ironic to me that my father, Russell Cooper was very big with the Red Cross and very proud of the amounts of blood he gave over the years. Drew and he never really had much contact so it wasn't a learned generosity in that regard. Thus, the irony.

Each Friday, I like to color in the week number on the Matrix. I colored in number 8 today, Friday 13 May. I cannot believe Drew has been gone nine weeks and that there are only four remaining training weeks left on the Matrix to color in.

There are only 17 training days and three remaining Sundays before we get to the M-days on the Matrix. M-1 is the day after T-63, which is the end of the Crucible. M-1 is marked gear de-issue. I imagine the drudgery of that day is only overcome with the glory of giving back the equipment and getting ready to head back to MCRD and the final week. I can only imagine the elation felt by the recruits at that time.

* * * * *

May 9

Movement to MCRD. May 8th, Mother's Day.

It's funny that you say the guy next to me in the video looks scared. If we are at our racks, and it's the guy to my left at the same rack as me, then that's Stoltze. He is from Missouri. He says he is from Arkansas though because the part of Missouri he is from was taken from Arkansas in the Civil War. So people from that area consider themselves to be from Arkansas. Me and him have become pretty tight. In Pendleton we got different rack mates, and my new rack mate was the guy I sat next to on the plane here. Me and him always talk about all the good ass food we are going to eat when we get out. He always talks about a place called Pizza Ranch. There's one in Holland and one in Hudsonville. It's a pizza buffet. I always talk about Menas Joint and Sweet Waters. Nobody knows what those are though. I'm also consistantly thinking about Doritos and rice pudding from Saffron with almonds, and a mango slushie. PLEASE send some Snickers and Almond Joys.

Don't send the weird-shaped Snickers, just the regular-shaped ones. I don't want any Christmas trees or Easter eggs or whatever shape is in season now.

While we are in San Diego I want to go to In and Out, because everyone who is from here always talks about In and Out. So I'll get a burger there, and a pizza from a good pizza place. I would settle for Pizza Hut so we can get stuffed crust. And, you better not cause any friction when it comes to the beer I want. I want a six pack of Miller High Life for Friday night to celebrate because it is the Champagne of Beer, and a six pack for PBR for Saturday morning so I can sleep on the plane. I'm going through 13 weeks of hell, so I think I will have earned the right to do what I want for ten days. Even if that includes drinking six beers before we go to the airport.

I did not know that my recuriter was going to buy me dinner if I got a 242 on the range. He is not going to because I got 228, but that's because I was shooting with pink eye. Don't know what my overall score is with table 2 yet though. I felt like I shot like shit on that too.

We ate a lot of MRE's during field week. MRE's are pretty good. The chili macaroni was my favorite, followed by chili with beans, tuna and the BBQ shredded beef. The penne is really good too.

Thanks for the strawberry candies. They made my night. I should have a huge bag of those in my room that Gramma got me for Christmas.

When you come to San Diego, please bring my boots, my grey sweater and a T-shirt. Try to bring the T-shirt that has a girl on it with smoke coming out of her mouth. I like that one. My grey sweater is probably in the trailer or my room. You better know which sweater I'm talking about because I wore it almost every fucking day. It should have an American Red Cross pin in it. I found it at Meps when I went the first time and it's been on my grey sweater ever since. If it's not there, whatever, but bring me a black shirt, preferably the one I said earlier.

Also bring my phone and a charger and please please make sure my phone is activated again so I can use it the second I get out. And, if you can find it, please bring that blue hat I have that looks like the one George Bailey wears when he is a kid in "It's a Wonderful Life". Bring me the $80 that is in the middle drawer of my dresser.

So, things to bring to Drew:
-Boots-Grey Sweater-T-shirt (the one I said earlier) -Batman belt-George Bailey Hat-Activated phone.

If you can't find the George Bailey Hat, bring me a different hat that would look good on me. I like the red Kzoo Wings hat. In the letters you send me please acknowledge those things. Let me know when you get my letters, and let me know that you understand the things I am asking of you.

I love you all very much. Think about you guys all day long. Can't wait to be home.

Love, Drew

13 May 2016
Friday
T-46

Dear Drew,

It really lifts my spirits to hear how well you sound in your letter that we received today, 12 May. The postmark is San Diego on May 9th. May 9th would have been Monday, T-42, the first day of training week eight and the week marked Interior Guard on the Matrix. Today is Friday the 13th, T-46. The Matrix indicates that you are having a blood drive. I have been trying to get my dates military style and say 13 May, but obviously for Friday the 13th, there will be an exception to that rule.

I bet you are thinking about the plans relating to graduation day as I imagine there is not much more to think about than graduating and getting the hell out of there. Keep in mind that we are leaving to come to San Diego on Saturday, June 4th, M-2 on the Matrix. That will be two days after you have finished the Crucible. I imagine that what I send to you on training week 10 will not be delivered on the Tuesday, Wednesday, Thursday of the crucible. However, I will continue to send what I have been sending. I will attempt to get some Snickers and Almond Joy to you and will continue my daily shipment of power bars.

We are planning to leave with you on Saturday, June 11, after your Friday graduation. I imagine that I will stop sending that week as obviously we will be in San Diego and you will be in the Crucible. Obviously during the crucible you will not receive mail and we will not be sending anything to you after June 4th. June 4th is your final week and you should still be getting deliveries that final week. That will work out well as we will be in San Diego that last week and there will be no need to send things that week as you will be back home while they are delivered.

Everything you asked for we have taken care. This includes clothing, Miller High Life (bottles), PBR and Bush Tall Boys. I know you have not asked for Bush Tall Boys, but it is my intention that after graduation I will drink a Miller High Life, a bottle of PBR and a Bush Tall Boy. I have not had any beer since I last saw you and will not have any until I am again in your presence.

I think we will try to bring some In and Out burgers and some pizza to family day on Thursday, M-6. If you do not eat it then, I am sure we will eat it at the hotel later. I thought it may be nice to have a reunion with you on that Thursday, family day, and have a nice picnic. I plan on bringing In and Out burgers and pizza. If there is anything else specifically you want for Thursday, family day, please indicate so in a letter.

Do not worry about our providing responses as we will do what you request. I understand your concern about whether or not we are getting the letters. Rest assured, through rain, sleet, snow, hurricane, tornado and blizzard the United States Post Office will deliver your letters. It is the finest delivery system on this planet and you can have faith we are receiving your letters.

We will have ice cold Miller High Life in bottles, PBR, Bush Tall Boys at the hotel after graduation, as well as a couple of lighters and the specific Marlboro Red Blend that you have requested. The phone will be charged and activated. Asking your mother to do that now so if there is a delay, we will not have to deal with that issue. It will be fully charged and ready to roll.

Again, we will bring the clothing you have requested. However, Chuck and Patrick are very stern in their belief that you wear your uniform after graduation and until you get home. Obviously you can take it off to go swimming and bed, but I would be so proud and excited to walk with you through the airport in your uniform. It is a pride that you have earned and you should embrace it. Yes, Saturday morning before we leave before the airport, you can drink your PBRs.

I have sent to you Snickers, Reeses as well as strawberry hard candy in numerous packages. You indicate receiving some strawberry candies. I hope you have received them all. It seems this past week I have sent to you a package of black cherry cough drops. In that package, I included a number of different types of hard candies. I hope you discovered them. I do not know exactly what you are allowed to receive. I have simply tried to send things that were indicated as acceptable and hope I have not gotten into too much trouble with my slight deviations.

I hope you received the package of old fashion, hard lemon candies. These lemon drops are the type that my Grandma and Grandpa, Nelly and Stanley Thomas always kept in the glove compartment of their sedan. Every day I have sent a number of deliveries to you. I hope you are receiving most of them. You have my apologies if packages have been intercepted or you have received punishment for what I have sent. Please know that the thought and effort of trying to provide you with extra protein, nourishment and care has been there.

Love and miss you greatly. Hang tough. Be proud. Love you.

Love, Dad

Isn't the tat beautiful. Awesome work. Incredible hidden gems. Your and Anella's anchor. See the dual bladed sword. Our Twin Pines. Remember twin pines in our front yard - can see them from Serengetti. Superman with a "C" See any others?

CHAPTER 10
ONE MIND - ANY WEAPON
"CHESTY" PULLER

Training week 9, pugil sticks, combat fitness evaluation. We did PFT. It was MCMAP test to earn our belt. That was T49. It was a joke, anybody could pass it. You did not even have to pay attention in any of the training sessions. There was a lot of guys that missed most of the MCMAP things we did throughout the cycle, because they were on working parties or something.

So the pugel sticks half the people in the company did not do it because there was not enough time. That day was a MCMAP test. Combat fitness evaluation like PFT but for combat. Standing in line, they would have us stand there in place double time or they will make you sprint and sprint back.

"All right, they're on our left, they're on our right, they're in front of us, they're behind us ... they can't get away this time."
"Alright you bastards, try and shoot me!"
"Chesty" Puller

Monday
May 16

Dearest Drew,

Weekend is over. Dad said you had a long hike this weekend. I'm sure it went well for you.

It looks to be fairly cool there, highs in the 60s. I would have thought it would be much warmer at this time. I wonder if you are having typical San Diego weather or if its unusually cool.

Well yesterday May 15, we had SNOW. I went out looking for mushrooms and it started snowing.

Bennett met me down there. He was trying to take a picture of it. Its been a crummy mushroom season. Pretty much over now. I found about 8 big ones yesterday. Usually don't find them after the apple trees bloom and that was a few weeks ago.

I painted upstairs hallway Friday and good chunk of Saturday. Looks nice.

Bennett had golf tournament Saturday at Lake Cora. It was freezing. He got a medal for coming in 8th out of 58 kids. He was pretty happy.

Buck had a good weekend with lots of walks. Todd came over Friday and looked for mushrooms, and took Buck. Todd loves him.

I had coffee with Anella and Teja on Saturday. She seems very happy. He seems very kind. I'm glad for her and hope it works out for them. She's saying they are talking about future together. Not planning marriage for a few years.

I sure hope most of those guys you are with slow down about their desire to get married. I don't think they are mature enough to make such a decision. Need to be pretty sure and then absolutely sure before having children. You can be sure kids need their mom and dad!

Not much national news. Mostly Trump as Republican Presidential nominee.

Just a few weeks until we are all together again.

Be proud of yourself! I am proud of you!

Love you bigger than space!

Mom

* * * * *

16 May 2016
Monday
T-48

Dear Drew,

Today is Monday, 16 May 2016, T-48. Training week 9. Holy Cow! Just a couple of weeks left. Keep pushing buddy!

This weekend the weather was miserable. Each day I wore long underwear, sweatshirts, winter jacket and winter hat on my runs. Sunday, it actually snowed. That is unbelievable. May 15th and it is snowing. We have found some mushrooms, however it has been a very bad season. When it was wet, it was too cold. When it warmed up, it was too dry. This past week it has been unbelievably cold.

I have been doing a tremendous amount of work shredding my abs. Sunday I do not lift weights, but I continue with ab shredding. Yesterday I did three unaided, unassisted chin-ups all in one set. While I am a king on the dip rack, chin-ups have been a weakness. I was happy to do some unassisted. Bennett has been working hard on his abs for our contest. Where I believe he will have tightness, he will be missing the mass. I am predicting me 1, you 2, him 3.

Bennett and I set your new totem pole down at the beach house yesterday. We mixed up a couple bags of concrete and set it well. Now we just need to move the large boulder near the tree in your honor that we found and moved when you left on March 13.

I have set a coyote skull and cow skull at the bottom of the pole. I cannot believe how high it is. The photographs enclosed with this letter note how tall it is in comparison to the outhouse. You get through this week and there will just be one more week until the Crucible. Keep taking a step at a time and get through this.

I hope you are getting all the packages I am sending. I can't wait to drink a cold chilly one with you. I have not had, nor will I, any beer until you pop your first one open. Very proud of you Drew - keep humpin. Try and draw some pleasure from each day. Count your blessings.

Love you, Dad

* * * * *

Distinction without a difference. One of the small differences between Pariss Island and San Diego is the nightmare one encounters at Pariss Island with the sand fleas. Bugs become quite the irritant. The sand fleas digging into the skin as the recruit is not allowed to move is torture. The torturous desire to move the flea from eating you must be quite difficult. The environment in San Diego is much more hospitable. The climate is generally a lot more conducive to recruit training. It is not the swamps and humidity of South Carolina.

Most of the time the recruit encounters pleasant conditions of Southern California. HOWEVER, the torture in MCRD San Diego, that is not present at Pariss Island is equally difficult to deal with as the sand flea and is as torturous. Whether the Marine has gone through recruit training 30 years ago, 40 years ago, or last year, at MCRD in San Diego the report is the same, other than the roughest mountainous terrain and the humping up hills and mountains – it is complete torture sharing a boundary line with the San Diego Airport. Many recruits peer to their neighbor and watch the planes coming and going. It triggers one's imagination to far off places; any where other than MCRD San Diego.

Pariss Island is set deep in the swamps of South Carolina and no other person is ever seen, other than those in training. The imagination is left to its own devices, rather than having jelly donuts constantly staring you in the face from across the fence; and humping up mountains.

Training Week 9 comes after Team Week and Interior Guard break. Interior Guard and Team Week is not a respite, but it is a break. The developers of this Matrix and program for training new Marines understand just how far a person (a new Marine Recruit) can be pushed. A human can only be pushed so far without some type of break; not a respite.

Interior Guard and Team Week is action packed and filled. It is something different than what the recruit has thus far been going through. Training Week 9 throws them back into the frying pan.

Or, it is simply a matter of logistics. Aside from giving the recruit a respite or aside from having the man power to conduct and complete different requirements for the maintenance and running of the facility, Monday of Training Week 9, T-48, is the inventory and issuance of new uniforms with the recruit's name on it. Is it just a matter of how long it takes to get this new equipment produced and distributed that required the past week to be a little different? Plus the manpower needed for running the base is right there. How efficient.

* * * * *

17 May 2016
T49
Tuesday

Dear Drew,

I hope you still have the Matrix I sent to you and you indicated in a letter received. At the end of each week I color in the training week number. By the time you get this letter I will have colored in training week 9. Training week 10 you have the Comprehensive exam and week 11 is the Crucible.

Holy Crap Mister, you are almost there. Congratulations. Keep humping though. Have to get to the finish line now!!!

I cannot believe we will soon be getting on a plane to come see you.

Soon you will be drinking some ice cold Miller High Life and smoking a Marlboro - Yuck. How can you want to go back to smoking after you have kicked that filthy habit. Your lungs now are so pure and fresh. Imagine how healthy the tissue and membrane is. Smoking will be like a putrified assault - a killing of healthy fresh tissue. Dang, it sounds so gross and vile.

I think your next training will be so much nicer because we can have contact and your every moment will not be subject to scrutiny. You can eat what you want, sleep peacefully, watch TV, talk to family and friends - just get a break from it all. It certainly is a tough 13 weeks you have endured to graduate. When you are reading this 10 weeks are done. Be proud, be smart, be careful, and finish. An accomplishment that will last a lifetime.

AWESOME !!!!

So very proud of you Drew.

I was hoping to have *A Soldiers Home* released before your graduation. It is a close call. Either just before or after. I am comfortable having in my mind that it will be out before the 4th of July. What a great book for celebrating our country's Independence and good timing for summer reading enjoyment.

Brigadier General McDaniel is having a few words for the cover and Colonel Odom a drafter of the SCRA, is writing the Foreword.

Study your handbook. Work hard. Stay stubborn. Love you.

Love, Dad

* * * * *

Today is Tuesday, 17 May, 2016, T-49. The Matrix declares that today is Combat Fitness Evaluation Day. I imagine that today is quite a hectic day for Drew and his fellow recruits. Graduation is on their minds and of course, any injury may hold them back.

Tomorrow is another round of pugil sticks. I realize that Drew, in a previous letter indicated that he enjoys the pugil stick engagement. I, however, am overwhelmed today with the fear of injury or illness plaguing Drew. The end of this week will be ten weeks away and there are only two full weeks remaining. Then we move toward the final week and graduation.

If I am overwhelmed with these feelings, I cannot even imagine how the recruits are feeling with the finish line approaching. The pressure must be overwhelming. Having endured ten weeks of constant overview and activities, realizing the next few weeks entail such a hefty requirement towards completion.

There are combat fitness evaluations. Another round of pugil sticks. The warrior is brought out. One Mind, Any Weapon. The recruits are thrown right back into the frying pan as though the recruit training has started all over again. However, the recruits are different at this point. They are trained, disciplined and conditioned.

It is Black Friday revisited, but with a new understanding and most importantly the ability to be snap, quick, and appropriate in decision making and actions. It is the polishing and formulation of the recruit brought into being a new Marine. Training Week 9 will be very busy, physically demanding and stressful. The following week requires the comprehensive test, mental testing without the physical aspect, tests and demands. This week is all out warfare. Interestingly, after the past week the new recruit will welcome these tests and endeavors as physically and mentally demanding that they are, they are becoming Marines and desire the tests for their testosterone. What strapping young person does not love the concept of One Mind, Any Weapon?

*　*　*　*　*

Wednesday
May 18, 2016

Dearest Drew -

Yesterday was the first day since you've been gone that I was unable to write. It has been very busy at work. I didn't get home until 8 and charted until 9:30 and then needed to go to bed. It will be crazy busy for me until we leave for California. I will welcome the break! (So will you!)

On Facebook today they (MCRD) featured your company doing physical testing. There were about 8 pictures of guys running, doing crunches and pullups. Looked closely, did not see you.

You've always looked good in that olive green color :)

The sun is finally shining today, but still rather cool. I had to work this morning, then to grocery store, now home.

Dad is home for lunch and will take this with him to mail. Thinking about a nap on the deck.

Grandma posted funny picture of Buck, just his face and top of shoulders. It looks like he's smiling and looking right at camera. She put it on Facebook and added "Buck took a selfie"

I thought it was funny cuz that's what it looks like.

Couldn't stay up Sunday to watch "Game of Thrones" so also going to do that today (along with cleaning, etc).

Bought new charger for our phone. Couldn't find one in your room. Will have with us when we see you in just a few weeks.

Did you know Grandma's cats are 15? Running out of room here. Hope you have a good day. Be awesome!

Love you bigger than space!

Mom

* * * * *

T - 50
18 May 2016
Wednesday

Dear Drew,

Today, Wednesday, Hump Day, 18 May 2016, T-50 on the Matrix. You are probably receiving this letter either at the end of the second week in Phase III or the beginning of the third week of Phase III. Imagine that, you are in the third week of Phase III. After this week (the week that you are getting and reading this), there is only one more full week.

Next week is the Crucible. Hopefully you get this letter on Saturday as opposed to the beginning of the next week. If you get it on Monday, that will be cool too because I wanted to wish you good luck on your comprehensive exam set for Tuesday, T-55 on the Matrix.

You have always had a great mind and did well in your school work when you were interested and put your mind to it.

It always came quite easy to you and I hope you have had the opportunity to read your handbook and will do well on your exam. Good luck.

Also, it looks like on T-56, it says "museum visit and travel". I know at one point, Patrick said that he was able to go to a baseball game in San Diego towards the end of his thirteen week recruit training. Enjoy the museum or whatever travel you get to experience.

I am curious on the Matrix for T-51, there is not a photograph, but a drawing that says "one mind, any weapon" followed by "MCMAP Test." What is that? I know that it has been a difficult training mission, but I hope that you have been able to keep some notes so that we are able to have a good understanding of everything you have gone through and have an opportunity to drink some beers and catch up. Your letters have been very informative and we have greatly appreciated them.

I really hope that you are taking full advantage of your personal trainer there. Yesterday, I did two sets of four reps of unassisted chin-ups, two sets of three reps of unassisted pull-ups and two sets of six reps of aided chin-ups and two sets of six reps of aided pull-ups. This was in addition to my normal two-mile run, bench press like a first round NFL draft pick and extensive ab shredding. In my attempts to commiserate with your situation and to share in your pain, I have been working hard towards our contest. I am pretty excited about the chin-ups and pull-ups.

MCRD posted some Facebook postings related to your platoon and participation in the fitness evaluation. The Facebook posting indicates that there are three parts to the test: pull-ups, a three mile run and crunches. I think a perfect score is eighteen minutes in the three-mile run, I could not do a six minute pace for three miles.

We have actually seen pictures on Facebook of your platoon. I am writing to you on 18 May and it shows your platoon running an inventory physical fitness test on 16 May. 16 May on the Matrix is T-48 and the Matrix indicates an inventory PFT.

There are several photographs of their Facebook page showing you guys running, doing chin-ups and doing crunches. I see some guys doing chin-ups and some doing pull-ups. Which did you do? We are scouring the photos to find you.

Like I said previously, we have some good shots of you on black Friday on the YouTube video and also on the Marine Corps Recruit Depot Facebook page during swim week. I know one for sure is you near the pool and I am anxious to show a couple of other shots to you to determine whether it is you.

In the running, crunches and chin-ups, you are wearing green t-shirts and green shorts. Lucky that you get to wear shorts. I am still running in my sweatpants. Yesterday I even wore my winter jacket and hat.

It indicates to achieve a perfect score of 300, recruits must run 3 miles in 18 minutes, complete 100 crunches in two minutes and conduct 20 dead-hang pull ups. The Facebook page depicts a photograph of the drill instructors marking the recruit's scores on the top of their hands. Dang. 20 dead-hang pull-ups at one shot is impossible. I could kick out the 100 crunches in two minutes but there is no way I could do the three mile run in 18 minutes. Obviously, I am excited and anxious to hear your score, actually how you did in each event and I would most likely not understand the final score.

From the photographs, it appears quite cloudy during the day you had this final Inventory Physical Fitness Test. It looks like it would have been the perfect day with temperature and humidity for this day of physical feats of strength and endurance. Leaving hump day, I cannot help but to tell you to keep humping.

Love you. I am very proud of you. Hope all is well. I am so proud. Love you!!! Miss you greatly.

Love,

Dad

PS- Please be sure to open and see the treats inside any cough drop packages I sent. Cough drops and treats inside the cough drop bags. Hope candy makes it through. You need the extra calories.

* * * * *

Today is 18 May 2016, Wednesday. Hump-day. I hope that Drew is still humping. Today marks T-50 on the Matrix and is the second week of Phase 3. Today the Matrix indicates pugil sticks, IVB BAC. I do not know what these initials mean. The photograph and depiction of pugil stick combat on the Matrix at T-50 certainly looks more aggressive and violent than the photograph from T-7 and T-21. My concern and anxiety was alleviated as he indicated in correspondence that he enjoys pugil sticks.

* * * * *

Every time we went to chow – we ate, and we did pull ups and push ups; every meal. After breakfast, before we went back to the house, would do sit ups and pulls ups right outside the chow hall as soon as we got out. We would put our trays away, then step outside the chow hall, sprint to the pull up bars, do our three sets of 10, and then sprint over to where we formed up at. We would then go back to the house and put on PT gear and go to class in our PT gear.

After class we would go to PT. When PT was done we would go back to the house and take a PT shower. A PT shower is when you turn on all the shower heads and you get in line and you walk through the shower in a circle. Just to get wet and get the sweat off, then dry off and put your cami's back on, maybe have another class or do something else. We go to the PX once a week and get haircuts once a week. Go to noon chow, do pull ups after that. Go back, there was always stuff we were doing.

In Phase I and III we would get up at 5 am. In Phase II we would get up at 4 a.m., and Marine week we would get up at 4:30 a.m. The way they would wake us up was the last hour of fire watch, and some times the DI would do this too, flip the lights on and yell lights, lights, lights, lights, lights.

We would jump out of our racks as fast as we can, get your two sheets and blankets and hold them and get on line in front of your rack. But a lot of time the drill instructor, what they started doing to make the mornings go faster was the guide was on the last hour of fire watch every single night, so the 30 to 45 minutes before lights, they would have the guide come by and wake us all up.

Cause we did hygiene every night and our towels were wet after we showered and we hung them underneath the top rack to dry, and in the morning we would have to take them out and hang them on the front of the rack, and so he would wake us up and say fix your hygiene towel and go take a piss and get back in the rack. Most of the time if I woke up in the night to take a piss during the night I would fix my hygiene towel then so I would not have to get out of the rack when he said that.

5 a.m. Lights lights lights, lights. We get out of the rack with all our linen, put linen on our foot locker, quick head call, get back in line. Then make our racks and then get dressed. We would make our racks one sheet at a time. They would tell us first white sheet, bottom rack - ready move. Socks on line, ready move, socks on the body, ready move. Trousers on line, ready move, trousers on the body ready move, blouse on line, blouse on the body ready move, boots on line, boots on the body, ready move.

They never gave us enough time to lace up our boots and blouse our boots the right way, so we kind of just had to do that on our own when we got a second, before we stepped out of the house.

Sometimes we would have to get ready really fast and go to chow real quick. Sometimes we would clean the house for an hour before we went to chow. So we would get in formation outside the house and march to chow. We would normally have to stand in line at chow hall for anywhere from 10 to 30 minutes waiting for your turn to go inside. Every day was a race for who can get to chow first and be done first. But it did not even matter... a race with the other platoons....it did not even matter though because if you were the first ones to chow, and the first ones done, and the first ones back to the house, you would still have to wait for all the other platoons in the company to be done.

There were also other companies. Other companies from different weeks.

Bravo was right behind us, Delta behind them. Fox was the one that graduated just before we did.

In the chow hall the best thing they had in there was peanut butter and jelly. You got peanut butter in packets, and jelly like most restaurants have, plastic rectangle and you get it out with a knife. You could go get a couple pieces of bread too if you wanted. But they would yell at you for trying to make a PB & J sandwich, especially if you tried to spread the peanut butter and jelly around on the bread. One time they caught this kid trying to spread his peanut butter around on his bread. He ended up having to put his salad on his sand-

wich, a piece of cake, some noodles, jello, they made him put a watermelon rind on it. They made him put that on his sandwich, and they made him eat it.

The Matrix would only tell us one thing we were doing that day. Like one of the days on the Matrix says PX haircuts. That took probably 30 minutes to an hour out of that day, so the rest of the day we are doing a bunch of different things; like PT, classes and working parties. A lot of time was spent with them just fucking with us in the house, like war bags on line, ready move, war bags on requisite, ready move, war bags too slow, war bags on line, ready move, war bags back of house, war bags ready move, just do that 20 times in a row.

War bags dumped out, ready move, war bags or foot lockers on line, foot lockers ring room ready move, foot lockers back of the house ready move, do that a few times. Foot lockers dumped out ready move, do that a few times. Mattresses on line, ready move, mattresses back of the house, ready move, mattresses in the ring room ready move. They would have us make our racks and then have us tear the linen off like five times in a row. We would get our racks all made and they would say these racks look like trash, linen on line ready move.

We were busy with things all afternoon; until dinner chow. Breakfast, lunch and dinner were always at the same time. There was always drill. So normally after evening chow we would drill until square away time, and drill was out on the Grinder, the parade deck, and that was a lot of marching, and learning how to march. We probably drilled four to five hours out of the day. We would have our weapons with us during drill. You would get in trouble if you called your weapon a gun. It was either weapons or rifles. There was a lot of drill.

Every day, four or five hours there was drill.

Drill is marching and working with your weapon. Like how to do the different commands and stuff. That is why your feet hurt so much. We would just march. We would have to do inspection arms, every time we drilled. Like twice, once at the beginning and once at the end. You are at order arms with your weapons at your side. The butt stock on the deck. You bring it up 1 2 3 4 pull the charging handle back, 5 push it back in, 6 bring it up and look in the chamber to look for brass, 7 put it back down.

They would yell poooooorrrrt. Move to the button push, move to the cover close, move to the trigger freeze, arms then you would squeeze the trigger click bolt, then go back to port arms. You were holding it. That was a big one, we had the best inspection arms in the company. There were sling arms, where you put your weapon on your shoulder with the sling, and you adjust the sling and put it on with your forearm parallel to the deck, and your upper arm in line with the back with no more than half of your weapon covered with your upper arm.

There was stack arms where you would stack the weapons together. That is what we do when we went to class. We would stack them outside the classroom.

Then after evening drill we would go back for evening hygiene and then it was rack time. They would turn to Senior drill instructor square away time, and then during square away time that is when we would get to hygiene and do whatever they said we had to do. If we had time then we could read or write letters.

Normally we would not have enough time for that. Then we would have to stand in line in your skivvy drawers, and they would do BDR; basic health and hy-

giene inspections. They would inspect you every night. We would do hygiene during square away time. So if we were going to bed at 9 then we would get square away time at 7:30, so then we would be done with square away time by 8:30, so then we would do BDR, where the DI goes by with a flashlight to check everybody to make sure there was nothing medically wrong with them and give you a general overall inspection. Inside the squad bay it was completely dark.

He would say linen on foot locker, ready move, and then we would put our linen on the foot locker. Then either he would say first white sheet bottom rack, ready move. So we would just make our racks one sheet at a time. Then the top rack one sheet at a time. Sometimes he would make us get dressed before we did that, sometimes he wouldn't. We all hated it when he made us make our racks before we got dressed cause we were always so cold, just in our shorts and t-shirt.

Sometimes we would go to chow half an hour after we woke up, so 5 to 5:30, sometimes we would not go to chow till an hour to an hour and half later. Then we would just clean the house the whole time.

One of the DI's told me, because my beard grew in so fast, I should start waking up before lights and shave in the morning, so that night I did not shave because I planned to wake up and shave in the morning. But the DI during BDR which was a different DI gave me improper shave. That is the night he decided every time someone got improper shave they would get two hours of fire watch. That was bullshit that I got two hours of fire watch cause I was told by another DI to shave in the morning.

The recruit in the rack next to me, in phase 2, got these really nasty looking blisters on his lower back from his main pack. Every night the drill instructor would ask him - do you have to go to medical for those things on your back, and he would always say no. Cause you don't want to go to medical and get dropped.

Then there was a famous silver bullet, I guess two foot thermometer they shove up your ass if you pass out. So we were all afraid to pass out. You have to go to medical. It may or may not have been a thermometer it might have also been a means of hydrating through the rectum, they never told us.

If we woke up at 5 am, then lights would be at 9. If we woke up at 4 am, then it would be at 8 pm. They are pretty focused about getting you 8 hours. But no one ever got 8 hours of sleep. If you get up during the night to go pee there was a 50 pound dumbbell sitting there and you had to do 25 ammo can lifts before you went into the head and after you came out. That was a real bitch. You tried not to go to the head at night.

Every day you would get mail call, right before square away time. You knew we were going to have square away time when the DI came out of the duty hut with a big black garbage bag. It was full of mail. So when they passed that out you were inside your barracks or outside on line. Most of the time he would have us get in a school circle. You had to watch out cause he would throw the mail real hard and if it was thick like a card or something it could easily taken someone's eye out.

Every Friday there is a graduation; 42 graduations in a year.

Some guys are getting on the bus right now.

* * * * *

My anxiety at this point really relates to his physical well-being and mental preparedness for next week's comprehensive exam. Physically I know that he can complete the sustainability hike on T-53 and next week's final physical fitness test on T-57. I am also sure that he will enjoy the repelling on T-58. My concern for physical fitness is his health and his ability to not be dropped back. I am sure that he has been studying his handbook and is prepared for his written exam next week. Drew has always had a great mind and did well with his school work when he put his mind to it.

An additional point of concern relates to the packages that I have been sending to him. I have been sending 2-3 power bars daily in a 5 x 7 envelope. In addition, the envelope is perfect for a package of throat lozenges. In accordance with his letter, I have sent some Snickers, Almond Joy and Twix Candy Bars.

My anxiety relates to whether or not I am getting him in trouble for receiving these items. Matt Fasbender once related that towards the end of Phase 3, his son Alex had someone in his platoon receive a bunch of Snickers Bars. Alex reported that it was the best candy bar he had ever eaten. Hopefully, Drew is able to enjoy some of the treats that I am sending.

It is very exciting to look at the Marine Corps Recruit Depot's Facebook and website. The Facebook postings of course allows for comments and obviously you will read when older Marines in recruit training years ago did their three mile hike they were wearing full gear, carried numerous canteens and their rifle. Well, there are sustainability hikes where these recruits do that.

However, there is always going to be the type of story about when I went to school I walked five miles uphill to and from school in four feet of snow. Not much changes through the course of time sometimes. However, I do think it is a point of pride for Marines that Marine Recruit Training does not allow Marines to smoke cigarettes, chew tobacco or play on their computer devices and have telephone contact. There is no contact outside of their platoon. Just little points such as this would take away from the severity and strictness of the thirteen week period.

* * * * *

19 May 2016
T51
Thursday

Dear Drew,

You are so close!!! Dude, keep humpin

I recently finished Ronnie Cox's audio book on the making of Deliverance. Very very nicely done. He is such a great story teller. Gives some great stories about the making of one of the greatest of all times movies. Remember before our Tennessee trip a few years ago I introduced you to the movie?

Yesterday I moved the rock we declared to be your Marine rock over to the base of the new totem pole we raised in your honor. This boulder is so cool. It has a lot of fossilization throughout it and is a green of the type found now, around Lake Superior. You just know this rock was delivered to this area by the glaciers as they cut down thousands of years ago forming the land we now refer to as Michigan. The rock is so heavy I had to—through great effort, roll it over. One person cannot lift it. I can't wait to drink some PBRs with you and add some to the totem pole.

In the Facebook photos I mentioned yesterday I noticed the

sneakers you guys are wearing are of the type I like, find comfortable and wear. I think they are New Balance brand. I find they give good support.

The chin up photos are interesting. I note those waiting in line are standing at attention,. Like you said a recruit always has to stand at attention.

The course schedule for Western Michigan University classes through the Oshea Lifelong Learning Institute came out yesterday. The class I am developing and teaching on the Servicemembers Civil Relief Act is on the schedule. Hopefully, *A Soldier's Home* will be available. That will be fun discussing in a classroom setting.

This morning someone asked me if I have big plans for Memorial Weekend. Holy Cow!! That is next weekend. Just a few days away from when you are reading this. My response was just hanging around home - getting things ready for our departure to San Diego the week after. Everyone is so excited to see you and be able to call you a Marine. WOW, what an incredible accomplishment. We are so very proud of you!!!

"One Mind any Weapon" is today. Later in the week is your final uniform fitting. You guys have to be feeling good about yourselves. Savor the good feelings and moments.

Around the time you get this you will be completing your written test and final physical fitness test and the Crucible is on your mind. Just remember you have done everything that you will face in the Crucible except this final test is one of endurance and teamwork. Good luck. I am thinking of you every day and will keep my fingers crossed these last few weeks as you cross the finish line. The worst is behind you. Your are now fine tuning to having the honor and privilege of being a Marine.

Chuck said he has written to you about wearing your uniform home. I imagine it just did not occur to you that that is what you do. Would Superman fly across the sky without his uniform? Would Batman jump in the Bat Mobile without his uniform? How could you not wear your uniform home. We have to get a picture of you in uniform with Buck. He needs to understand where you have been.

Attached is an ad I pulled from Sports Illustrated. Thought it was pretty nice.

Very proud of you Mister!!! Love you, Take care. Keep your head out of your ass.

Love, Dad

May 19
Thursday a.m.

Dearest Drew -

Hoping this finds you well. So many things through the day remind me of you and make me smile. Yesterday I was taking a moment to put my thoughts together and it reminded me of the thinking chair. Remember that red Blues Clues chair? Then as a teen you put that chair on the roof of the barn. I think thinking chairs are a great idea.

I feel I spend a lot of time working things out in my head. I've never had a best friend girl to unload my inner most thoughts. My high school/middle school years were pretty crappy and I kept to myself. No one knew what was going on. When I told my dad he came and got us. Husband's don't want to hear what is going on in their wive's head. Now the past few years Dad will sometimes get upset with me because I am quiet.

Honestly, I've spent so many years thinking to myself it is difficult to open up. Having a hard time in my head lately, work has been really difficult. Difficult patient situations. Too busy. Too many new technology crap thrown at us. I am not good at self care. I take care of everyone else. Dad comes home every day and works out.

No matter what. I get home and its late. I have charting, dinner to prepare, things to clean up. I need to just have the mind set of putting myself before all of that and walk for an hour. Again, this would give me head time to process my day with added benefit of exercise.

I can't tell you how Dad and Bennett's new found diet focus irritates me. Hoping to finish painting side of garage this weekend. Dad and Bennett will complain about it. Of course I'm being ridiculous. You were so sweet before you left wanting to finish that for me, but the weather wasn't cooperative. I want it done before you come home.

It is a beautiful day today. Figures, I've got one of those long days ahead. I did not mow this weekend. Wasn't feeling great and now it looks horrible in our yard. Anxious to do yard work tomorrow. I have to work 1st half of day, but supposed to be nice again and I will enjoy soaking up the sun!

Anella is making our tattoo appointment for the 5 of us. She is checking into who is good at fine lines as there is some delicate lines in the design.

Today is the conference golf tournament. Bennett gets to miss the whole day of school. It's in Dowagiac. I will drive right by there today on my way to Niles. I have a boy that has brain cancer. Heavy stuff.

As I write this morning the birds are so loud. Wonder if you hear many birds there.

You are so close to the finish line. Can you believe it?

I love you bigger than space!

Mom

* * * * *

T-51 on the Matrix has an M-16 and a long dagger followed by the words "One Mind, Any Weapon." What goes through one's mind with this statement? Chesty Puller.

Tomorrow, T-52, is the second fitting for uniforms. How exciting. They have to be feeling like they are once again human beings. Even more importantly, they are that much closer to being called a Marine. This week is coming to a close and I am sure they are contemplating next week's written exam and final physical fitness test.

With the Crucible and its excruciating 54-hour test of endurance moving through their mind. The end of the Crucible and the days remaining at Marine Corps Recruit Depot commence with M-1. The beginning of Marine Week. The Marines are no longer just recruits. On M-2, Drew's Grandpa, Mother, Father, Brother and Sister will depart from Kalamazoo, Michigan to San Diego to our Marine.

*   *   *   *   *

May 10

BEST Protein Bars
Gatorade Bars
Quest Bars (Apple Pie, cookies & cream, and cinnamon roll. I have had)
Cliff bars (chocolate chip and white chocolate macadamia nut are the best I've had so far)
Colossal bars (I think it's the big cookie & cream one)
Snickers Bars (I received a Snickers last night and it was the best thing that happened to me in the past two months.)
Whenever Bars
Fiber One Blueberry Strudel

Receiving a protein bar makes any night better. But as good as the protein bars are, I would prefer a letter over a protein bar any day. Don't let that deter you from sending protein bars though. I just thought of this, a Pay Day would be KILLER. Some days I don't get any letters, then the next day I will get a shit ton and I won't have time to read them all. So I'm in suspense the whole time as to what the letters say. I heard Honorable Mr. Obama was in Flint.

During team week, at least the first two days I went to supply to pass out uniforms to recruits from other platoons. One of the guys running supply was a retired Navy guy. He was fun to shoot the shit with. He said that in California you now must be 21 to buy tobacco products. Where else is that law in place? He also said that Obama was in Flint recently.

Third phase is not much better than first phase so far. Second phase was good because for the first two weeks we spent most our time with the PMI's.

The theme in third phase is that we are third phase recruits, but we are acting like first phase or receiving recruits. I wrote a letter to my recruiter, Sgt. Butler, way back in 1st phase and I have not gotten any letters from him yet, so please contact him again for me to ask about Recruiters Assistance. I heard there's a good chance that infantry guy will get RA because SO1 is backed up right now.

Another thing I need to add to the list of things I want you to bring for me are my sunglasses. Either the Aviators with the circle between the lenses, or the black ones in the cloth case, which I think I left in the center console of the Explorer. The other Aviators I think I left on the shelf in the living room.

8 mile hike sucked. It was raining and some of the

puddles almost went up to our knees. The days for the 8 mile and the McMap review were flip-flopped, so we hiked the same day as Bravo Company. They are one week behind us. We passed by each other in the 8 mile, and they weren't even wearing their flaks or kevlars, (that's helmets and heavy-ass vests, both very uncomfortable, especially with our main packs).

To add on to that we all heard that Bravo got two Cliff Bars each after the hike and they got a two hour nap. That's First Battalion for you. I don't even remember what a nap feels like.

FOR GRADUATION DAY: Do not buy any of the stuff I asked for before I graduate. I want to go to the store and pick it all out myself. Except cigarettes. Please have Marlboro special blend Reds and a lighter on deck for me right after I graduate. A can of Copenhagen mint too please for the airport.

It's hard to handle my nicotine cravings when I'm always seeing DI's with a dip in. All of the PMI's and coaches at the range had dip, and sometimes I can smell it when the DI's are screaming right in my face, and the guide in our platoon says he brought a can of dip on the plane ride here, so I want to try that. Everyone that dips here talks about Copenhagen Mint because apparently it came out the day boot camp started.

I can't wait to be out of this place. I'm so close to graduating, but it feels like its still so far away. Boot camp sucks because I don't even feel any stronger. I can do a few more pull-ups and my running condition is better, but other than that I feel like I got weaker. I bet I will lose the Ab contest. I will win after SOI though. SOI is a lot more physical.

GOOD NEWS, the new legal age to buy tobacco in California is 21, but I can still buy them with my mili-

tary ID. My ID picture sucks. I'm pale and my face is all chopped up from shaving in a hurry. We took the pictures during Receiving Week. (Please don't let this news deter you from having a pack of Marlboro Special Blend Red ready for me, and a six pack of Miller High Life for Friday night, and a sixer of PBR for Saturday morning.

IMPORTANT Do not send cough drops anymore. Repeat: Do not send cough drops anymore. Only send one protein bar at a time. Again, only one protein bar at a time. I highly appreciate all the other care packages, but things have changed here.

Our DI's always tell us that we are the booger platoon or we are the butt crack of LIMA company. They fuck with us a lot because of that. The thing is we always hear other DI's in the company saying the same exact things to their platoons.

* * * * *

Hooray- Hooray! NO. OORAH!! We are two and a half weeks into May. We received a letter from Drew today. Drew's letter references "RA". Which stands for Recruit Assistance and SOI is School of Infantry. He is referencing what was addressed earlier relating to the ten day leave that he has between MCRD graduation and infantry school.

As Sgt. Butler had previously addressed, that period fluctuates depending on whether infantry school is back-logged. It is nice to see that Drew would like to stay home longer than the ten days that he is given and is questioning whether he is eligible for RA.

Modern technology is such a wonder. I took a photograph

of the portion of Drew's letter relating to his questions for Sgt. Butler and requesting that I make contact with him. I sent the photograph via text to Sgt. Butler. He promptly responded indicating that this is an issue that Drew needs to address at MCRD in San Diego. Drew will receive his next assignment there and the leave assignment from which he is to report. Therefore, I am going to send him a letter letting him know that I did as he wished and contacted Sgt. Butler and that he now needs to follow-up on his request in San Diego.

Interestingly, Drew finds himself feeling weaker even though he is doing more pull-ups than when he went in. I think that he was doing around 10 pull-ups going in. Obviously, he is above the minimum of 4. I imagine that being exhausted causes one to feel weaker.

I am concerned about how he feels at times. However, I also recognize that his letters to his mom and dad are also an opportunity for him to vent and get the negative feelings off his mind and chest. Today, Drew's mother received a telephone call from Drew's grandmother in Virginia. She was crying and said that she had never received a sweeter letter than she received from Drew today. He is very sweet and kind to the core. Drew's dedication will be beyond reproach to the Corps.

It is interesting, my assumptions relating to Team Week and Interior Guard ring true to a certain extent given Drew's assignment to the supply depot. Imagine every week that retired Navy employee (gave outside world news) has the assistance of some recruit during week 8, 9th week in, first week of Phase 3 and their Team Week / Interior Guard Week. It is an incredible operation at MCRD in San Diego and it runs efficiently and proficiently.

* * * * *

20 May 2016
Friday

T-52

Dear Drew,

Got your letter yesterday May 19 - T51 (Thursday) when I got home from work. Don't worry about the ab contest. If you are doing more pull-ups now than when you first got there, you are getting stronger. Don't worry about it. I am sure that you are getting very well conditioned. I bet you feel weaker because of exhaustion - tired.

I imagine your feelings of being weaker are associated with how exhausted you are. Your mood does not sound good. I hope that you can remember how much Chuck draws upon his days of recruit training. For the rest of your life, the difficult times you are going through right now will be something that you can wear as a badge of honor forever. In just a few more weeks it will be over and the worse will be behind you as you will be a Marine and you do not have to deal with recruit training and the bullshit that you are enduring with your DI's.

Your letter indicates no more cough drops. I will not send any more cough drops. Please be aware that I have sent nothing else to you since getting this letter relating to cough drops. I will continue sending power bars. However, please be aware that I have sent two or three care packages with bars every day. I have written letters to you every day. I am sorry if the system there does not allow you to see and receive packages every day, but I have been on it from this end.

We will let you go to the grocery store after your graduation. I thought you would be happy just having what we will get for you. We can discuss all of these particulars on family day. It is my plan to bring to you on family day some In and Out burgers and a pizza, unless you write and direct otherwise. It is very important that you understand that we will not be receiving letters the week leading up to your graduation. We will be in San Diego. Therefore, if there is anything that you want to tell us, you need to do that now.

I imagine that next week when you get this letter, that weekend, if you send a letter out, it will be the last letter that we receive. Keep humping. We are leaving for San Diego Saturday June 4, M2.

Your mother received a telephone call from your grandma in Virginia yesterday. She was completely pleased and crying with joy due to the wonderful letter she received from you. You are such a wonderful and kind person to the core. I imagine the Corps will have no other more dedicated than you.

We will bring everything you have asked in your previous letter and more. For example, we will have sunglasses, your sweater, your shoes, belt, shirt, phone, phone charger, etc., etc., etc. We know that it really doesn't matter what you have at that time as you will have Miller High Life, cold and in bottles, and the cigarettes that you want. I will get the specific blend of Marlboro Reds and a lighter. Before you know it, you will be home and in your uniform so that I can get a picture of you with Buck.

So very proud. Love you.

Love,

Dad

P.S. I just cannot believe that when you are reading this letter the CRUCIBLE is next week. The Saturday after the Crucible - M2 on the Matrix we are flying to San Diego. Very nice that all of us - including Grandpa are coming. That Monday - M3 - the week after the Crucible, I am going to see if I can get on the base at MCRD and see if I can wander around. I doubt it but it is worth checking out. I wonder if on Family Day they will let us see where you did pull ups.

So very proud of you!!! Miss you!!! Love you buddy. Love Dad

Drew's Marine Corps Rock and Totem Pole - coming along well.

* * * * *

May 20
Friday a.m.

Dearest Drew -

TGIF!
It's been a brutal week for me. How about you?
I'm a bit dehydrated. Going to drink a lot today (water).
Looks like pretty morning. I am going to clean and do yard work. It'll be nice feeling to put everything back together.
Todd is out in honey hole right now turkey hunting. He came last Friday too. He saw a hen. Bennett was so lucky to get that turkey like he did.
Omi left me message yesterday that she got letter from you and was sweetest thing she ever got. You are such a sweet guy. I love how kind you are! You've always been that way. You are a good person! I love you so much!
As I am writing, Buck is curled up on the couch purring. He's got the life!
Yesterday was conference golf. Bennett got to miss school. It was a beautiful day. Their team came in 2nd yesterday, but then they average scores for season and they came in 5th. Bennett shot 84, pretty good. He said Zolp was thrilled with their 2nd place finish. He's never had a good golf team. One of the boys cheats and it drives Bennett crazy. He pads his score. All the boys know it. I'm surprised they don't give him more crap about it.
The air outside by our house smells really good right now. It's the honeysuckle bushes in the woods. It's glorious!

Hope you are enjoying the pictures. Where did the time go?

Love you bigger than space!

Mom

* * * * *

I have an over-riding anxiety as to whether or not I have caused trouble for Drew concerning some of the items I have sent to him. Surely I have done nothing worse than what I know some grandmothers have done, trying to send through Ginger-snap cookies.

Matt and Drew in front of the Ralph's store in San Diego, just after graduation. Drew's favorite movie is, "The Big Lebowski," featuring the main character, The Dude, whose only ID was a Ralph's card.

253

CHAPTER 11
A WEEK OF FINALS
"Test Week – Running Out Of Time"

Training week 10 is your final drill, comprehensive exam, museum visit, travel, final PFT, that is Test Week.

*   *   *   *   *

$\mathbf{T}$raining week 10, which starts on Monday, T-54 involves the final drill. Unless you have a Matrix, you do not know what happens from day to day. It has been one thing following me throughout this book, referring to the Matrix. Imagine, during the last eleven weeks, not knowing what will happen in the next five minutes, hour or day.

The recruit has some idea as to the week they are entering into; graduation being the final week and the Crucible before that. By this time the recruit is realizing that they are nearing the Crucible. Therefore, while the Matrix, final drill, final comprehensive exam, final physical fitness test and the commander's inspection happen all in this week, the recruit is not aware of the details as the Crucible is weighing heavily on their mind. It has been a long road and they are just wanting to get to the finish line and receive their Eagle, Globe and Anchor Pin, EGA. Get to Marine week and graduation.

Historically known as a great literary master, Leo Tolstoy had joined the military service so that he could see the world and live life. Those that are encouraging a writer always declare to write what you know about. Leo Tolstoy came from wealth and was living in a time where privilege was given to those in his station in life. To help him with his desires and youthful fancies, he joined the military service and traveled the world living life; so one day he could know something to write about.

There have been so many stories of people who have declared the military is what gave them the life they now live. A successful and happy life that can only have been obtained through their start in the United States Military Service. There are those who have told stories of being seven years old and doing nothing but picking cotton until the age of 18. Their life would be nothing more than continuing to pick cotton. Joining the U.S. Military allowed them the opportunity to see the world and to meet people that they would never have the opportunity to meet. To learn skills and become able to function as a citizen of our country and to help serve humanity.

Of course Drew did not want to join the Coast Guard or the Navy, Air Force or Army. With his parents' lack of understanding of the different branches of the service, they did have an understanding that the Marine Corps is quite a different branch than the others. Of course, their son, who wanted to join the military, chose the Marine Corps.

Now that he is in the Marine Corps, he is not considering what type of trade or education he could obtain for life after the Corps – he wants to go all the way. He chose the few and the proud and the one branch of service that is the most difficult to become a member. Why not go all the way and choose to go into infantry. If he is in for a penny, he is in for a pound.

I love the Leo Tolstoy story because in college and high school, Drew had discussed a desire to write. He has always kept journals and sits down and writes out his thoughts. Is he Leo Tolstoy?

It is interesting for me to see one of Drew's initial letters and a mention of regret on whether or not he should have ever joined. Through my reading, as well as discussions with other Marines, I have found that it is quite common for most, in the first week or two, regret their decision. Of course you would. It is a situation unlike anything you have experienced before. You are exhausted, hungry and driven beyond what you have ever been driven before. It would be only natural for you to have feelings of regret.

At the end of it all, the Marine Corps is not about learning how to be a mechanic or a computer operator. The Marine

Corps provides a staple for having an overall sense of dealing with whatever situation is presented. The Marine infantry division's greatest skill is problem solving. Whatever organization, military or civilian, the situation of blaming others always presents itself – whether below or above you. A Marine learns how to contribute to solving the problem and learns how to develop the skills necessary to make the situation better. My friend, Mike Griffin once told me that if one were to ever join the service, it would be the Marine Corps as he had an uncle that once said "who else would you want serving to your left and right? Join the Marines and you will know that the person to your left or right will treat you as a loved one."

There is the story of those who have run for political office and who have had great exposure to meeting large numbers of people in society in an open and friendly situation. However, most always express that the situation allowed them exposure to so many people that told them they would be nothing today if they had not served in the military. It is a concept discussed in "Gates of Fire", which is the unofficial bible of the Marine Corps Infantry. Marines view themselves as modern day Spartans. It is a principle of sacrificing yourself - your time, comfort, individual-ness and even your life for others around you. It has the concept that the "opposite of fear is not courage, but love."

Throughout corporate America, leaders of an organization will tell you that Marines are like super-human, not with just physical strength but also their sense of honor and duty. They are among the best employees in the civilian economy. How comforting must it be in a bad predicament and scary situation to be comforted, knowing that your fear is over-powered by the love for your fellow Marine and Corps, and knowing those around you are of the same faith. The old expression safety in numbers has a heightened application.

Keeping the faith. There have been those that say the Marine Corps is like a religion. The culture of the Army and Navy are pretty much like any other modern military force. The Air

Force is run more like a corporation. The analogy to a religion is due to the fact a Marine is committed to Country and the Corps. Semper Fidelis and the expression once a Marine, always a Marine exemplifies those commitments. A Marine can join any other branch of service and not undergo the rigors of boot camp. The Marine Corps does not offer reciprocity to recruits coming from the other branches.

Unstoppable resolve, commitment, determination and a mind toward problem solving. What better way of becoming a well-rounded person. These are the characteristics that a person who gets it, will have coming out of the Corps. Marine Corps principles are what lead one into living a productive life for the rest of their life. That is why once a Marine, always a Marine.

* * * * *

23 May 2016
T-54
Monday
Holy Cow T54
T's end at 63

Dear Drew,

As I write this letter, there are only two and a half weeks left. We fly out in two weeks. When you get this letter, there will actually be one and a half weeks left for you. You will be getting this letter just before or after the Crucible. Good luck. My prayers and thoughts are constantly with you and certainly during the three days of the Crucible.

This week, the weather service is indicating that it will be in the 80's in Paw Paw. It indicates that it will be in the 70's in San Diego. For the near three months that you have been gone, it is incredible that the weather in Michigan will be nicer than in Southern California. It is unbelievable that we actually had snow, not yesterday, but last Sunday. How in the world can you go from having a snow fall to 80 degrees within a week.

I love your Marine rock under your totem pole. I cannot believe the size of this rock. The fossilization is really nice, color is a green that you only see in rocks in Lake Superior. Clearly this rock was moved by the glaciers thousands of years ago when Michigan was formed. Cleaning up around the beach house, I found your first life preserver. It is just a tiny little foam life jacket and I was able to strap it around the totem pole.

This weekend I made a nice shelf and placed it on totem pole and coyote skulls from the coyote's that we skinned out this winter. At the base of the totem pole near your rock, I placed that big cow's head skull that we have had for some years.

Things are coming down to the wire with *A Soldier's Home*. It will be out either before I leave for San Diego or when we get back. I have placed the NFL book into the pipeline so that it can be released at the beginning of this season. I am so excited to see you for many reasons. I miss you greatly and cannot wait to see you. There is a project that I would like to blow by you that I think will be very exciting for both of us.

This past weekend, we got a lot done around the house. Putting a fresh coat of asphalt seal on the driveway and finished painting the west end of the garage. I moved the antique boat to the garden I used to plow that your mother never used. The two Martin homes that we set up have not been used. It is nice that the sparrows have not taken it over, but it would be exciting to have some Martins move in. I placed Martin decoys on each house. Perhaps that is being effective in keeping the sparrows away.

Everyone is excited to fly out to see you. It will be a lot of fun to walk the shores of the Pacific Ocean and check out the different piers. I am willing to bet that some of the piers that we will see, were put into place by our old friend, the Canonies. Back in the day when Mr. Canonie was active in the operations of Canonie enterprises, they built seawalls and piers all around the world.

Next week, your Uncle Mark Niedzwiecki closes on his house on West Lake. How very exciting.

When you get this letter you will have finished quite a productive week. On Monday, T-54 you have final drill. On T-55 you will have done the comprehensive written exam. On T-57 you will have undergone the final physical fitness test. I noticed that on T-56 and T-57, it indicates that you will travel. I am anxious to know where you go. I remember Patrick saying that they went to a San Diego Padres baseball game. What an incredibly busy and productive week.

Keep humping.

Love,

Dad

Next week - Gas mask on Monday, Crucible Tues, Wed, Thurs. Warriors Feast and then MI on Friday. Feel the pride. So proud, you deserve it.

Just be cool in the Gas Mask test - You chase snakes while swimming, swim though patches of lily pads, sleep in the woods with coyotes. A little gas is no big deal for my Cool Hand Drew.

I miss you greatly. I have been watching past movies we enjoyed together. I drive the Explorer once a week - makes me feel closer to you - and keeps it in good working order. Bennett and I are hoping to be able to see where you did your pull up test. We are going to see who can do more chin ups there, him or I. I am sure you can do more than us.

So very proud of you Drew!!! Miss you. Love you. I can't wait to see you.

Love Dad.

Monday a.m.
May 23

Dearest Drew -

Geez buddy. We will be leaving in less than 2 weeks!
You are doing final things this week. Dad thinks you may
be going to a baseball game or something fun this week. That
would be something. Dad thinks we keep writing until we leave.
Before you know it you will be at the Crucible. Wondering if
you are feeling anxious about it or confident. You will be great,
cuz you're you. Be a leader. You are smart, kind, brave, strong.

We've had 3 days of beautiful weather. I was asked to work
Friday, but declined. Work has been so hard lately and I'm not
done until late. I really am trying to take care of myself. When
I work so late I am dehydrated. I don't eat right. No time for
walking or taking care of the house. So, I had a glorious day
Friday doing yard work all day. It was so nice. The yard looks
good. Saturday I spent the entire day morning to night sealing
the driveway. It took a long time, but it looks good.

Yesterday I cleaned, balanced checkbook, went to pond,
grocery store, made great dinner and washed my car. Can you
believe last Sunday we had snow flakes and yesterday I was float-
ing around pond in my plastic boat soaking up the sun? It felt
glorious. There are thousands of tadpoles along the shoreline.

Dad came to pond too. The raft had drifted around the bend
over the winter. Dad got in rowboat to drag it back. Buck stood
at the front of the boat the whole time. It was a cute site. Buck
had a wonderful afternoon swimming, digging holes.

Another beautiful day today but alas need to go to work.
Boo-hoo.

Austin's grad party is Saturday and I'm going to miss it. I
am taking Bennett to Tom Petty concert in Chicago. We need

to leave by noon to get there, park. It is a general admission so we want to get in line early.

Anyhoo - Austin seems like a nice kid, I'm sorry to miss his party.

Today is 2nd day of French Open Tennis, would love to watch tennis all day!

Big fire in California in Monterey. I checked it and its quite a distance from San Diego, 7 hours to drive.

There was a plane crash this weekend on plane going from Paris to Egypt. Looks like it blew up from bomb. Scary world.

I grilled chicken yesterday and made a good salad. It'll be interesting to see what you want to eat while home. It'll go fast :(

Mindy and Dan going to come over that next day after we are home, a Sunday, because the next weekend they will be in West Virginia to family gathering there. Hope it's nice weather and we can have bon fire. Remember when beach house 1st done and you and Anella decorated your bed areas? So cute!

Slept late today and Dad about ready to leave. Will write more tomorrow.

Love you bigger than space!

Mom

* * * * *

T-55. 24 May 2016. My heart and my mind relating to Drew are in two separate and distinct feelings and concerns. My heart wonders whether or not he has been able to develop friendships. I know their time with others is rather limited, given how Patrick told me that he did not get to learn the first name of the fellow recruits he became friendly with until after family day. Of course you would not learn the first name of someone because it is always "Recruit Last Name".

That does not affect the bond that one develops and it is my hope that Drew has developed some bonds through this period away from home. In one of his letters, he has indicated that he has developed friendships.

I am curious as to when he goes to the PX. He referenced it in a letter, so I do not have any idea as to how each minute, hour and day is accounted for and when the recruit will have an opportunity to go to the PX.

In opposition to this, is my mind, in knowing that contrary to what my heart feels, is on the technical aspects of what is occurring. He has the comprehensive examination today. It is my understanding that throughout recruit training there is class time. The drill instructors are always pounding away different lessons. Is this something that if you are paying attention during class and are aware of what is going on around you while the drill instructors are pounding away and have spent time reading your hand book, you will fly through the written examination.

Is it about Marine Corps history and all the abbreviations such as PFT for physical fitness test or the one that I didn't even know until Drew got to MCRD Marine Corps Recruit Depot. Does he go through these abbreviations RTB, Recruit Training Battalion; PLT, Platoon; DI, Drill Instructor; SDI, Senior Drill Instructor; CO, Commanding Officer; CG, Commanding General; CMS, Commandant Marine Corps.

Does he have to have a knowledge of this chain of command? There is a whole new definition of words. For example meal time - chow; drinking water - hydrate; shower - hygiene; marching - drill; uniform head gear - cover; blouse - any shirt that is part of the Marine Corps uniform; pants - trousers; shoes - go fasters; underwear - skivies; water bottle - bowl / canteen; flashlight - moonbeam. A Marine never refers to their gun; it is a weapon - M-16A2. What is the MCT or Marine Combat Training? AYE, AYE to carry on.

We must always remember that the Marine Corps is a department of the Navy as Senator John McCain's son referred to as the Men's Department. There are always those types of

Naval references such as port holes, the quarter deck, the bulk head, hatch, port, starboard, bow and aft, the ladder well and the foot locker. Of course everyone knows that you sleep in a rack located in the squad bay and the DI's are in the duty hut. Hopefully you don't have to hit the head too much and get through the T-day's to make it through H-days. You are, after all, a fresh blood and hopefully your Susie is not hooking up with a Jody – that is your girlfriend back home cheating on you with some guy.

So today, Drew is taking probably not an ink stick, pen, but using a lead stick, pencil, to get through the final written exam. It seems for most that the written exam is a lot easier to get through than the PFTs.

Throughout the twelve-week training period, there has been quite a lot of classroom instruction. Obviously a break from PFT. However, the mind is put at work in the classroom that includes general military subject such as Marine Corps principles, first aid, and the M-16 A-4 service rifle. The Marine Corps values of honor, courage and commitment come through in practical applications and discussions and are throughout the written examination.

This final written academic test is the second of two written tests that the recruits take during their twelve week training. Recruits must pass both the practical application test and the written test in order to graduate. Mentioned items, the test also includes leadership, Marine Corps policy and organization and BWT (Basic Warrior Training). This includes subjects like land navigation and hand and arm signals. Of course, it includes marksmanship. This is what Drew will be doing today, on T-55; or not.

But for his final written academic test, the final practical application test is done through a series of tests and events and knowledge and mastery of first aid skills, customs and courtesies like saluting or boarding a ship and Marine Corps uniform and rank identification. Assembly and disassembly.

Essentially, the classroom is broken into two different areas. The final practical application test and the final written academic test.

24 May 2016
T55
Tuesday

Dear Drew,

Holy Cow, when you get this letter you will be at the end of T days. Most likely you will be done with the Crucible (If you get this before good luck, you will do great), and entering M days. I am so very proud of you and cannot wait to see you. No one knows more than you how long the road has been and how excited you are to be done with these past 13 weeks, and see Buck again.

How incredible to think how miserable, tortuous, and disgusting the past 13 weeks have been yet how honorable and serious of a badge of honor it will be for you for the rest of your life.

Recall how Chuck recounted those days for him - over 20 years ago; but like they were yesterday. Horrible things may become funny over time and just imagine wanting to go back. Remember how Chuck wished he could go with you. I bet that sounds like complete bullshit to you now. How fucked up - or can you see it now.

Is life not fun and exhilarating. Imagine how cold and crisp those beers will be after graduating. Achieving goals is what makes life worth living. Meeting challenges causes overwhelming feelings. Be proud of what you have accomplished. I do not think I could have done what you have. It is an awesome accomplishment. I am jealous of you on so many levels - but SO VERY VERY PROUD. Keep humpin, See you soon. Love you.

Love, Dad

Tuesday
May 24

Dearest Drew -

Dad said today is your written test. I am not anxious about that for you. You are so smart. I do feel sorry for some of the guys that aren't as sharp as you, who may struggle with the test. By this time I can't imagine the DI's have to be helpful to get them through. You guys are almost done. Almost there!!

Another long work day yesterday and looking at another today. The long days are hard for me as I am dehydrated by the end, and have a headache. It's hard to explain to anyone else what it's like managing care visit after visit to people who are approaching death. Not only is this emotionally draining, it takes a lot of time, experience, and know how to do it well.

I do need to find better coping mechanisms for myself. Bennett's really been on my case and told Dad he's worried I will be dead before I'm 60, which is true. It's always easier telling someone else what to do, right ?

We have another beautiful day though looking at the 10 day forecast we have nothing but clouds and rain.

My brother Mark is closing on a house that he bought on Friday. Dad is the POA and will be signing the papers for him. Movers are bringing his stuff from Detroit to Portage on Saturday. He has a cat that the girls will take care of while he's gone. I guess the cat is very sweet. Paige will enjoy that.

I don't know if he's told his boys yet that he bought a house on West Lake. I guess he will be back end of June through the July 4th holiday and will have his boys then. He hasn't even seen the house yet, bought it with Todd's recommendation.

Dad's ready to go to office. Will write more tomorrow.

Love you bigger than space!

Mom

* * * * *

I keep looking at the Matrix and I cannot get my stomach to stop rolling over thinking that the Crucible is next week. I have a real estate closing on Tuesday when Drew will be undergoing the Crucible. How can I sit in a title office and enjoy the day, knowing that he is starting the first day of a three-day torturous journey?

I just cannot imagine what these recruits go through. I recall my days in high school going to football or wrestling camp. I hated being away from home for one week. I hated the dormitory living, I hated the dorm food. Good golly, that was for one week. I just really do not think I could have done this when I was 18, 19 or 20 years old.

It really takes a special kind of animal to endure the rigors of recruit training at MCRD in San Diego. I believe the honor, courage and commitment that is instilled in these young people make for the well-rounded and courageous person willing to serve humanity and allows for the complete person to go on to the rest of their life knowing that once a Marine, always a Marine.

In Drew's last letter, he talked about how there are several letters that he hasn't read yet. Do I even write a letter for T-56 and T-57 through T-63? Obviously, during the Crucible of T-61, T-62 and T-63 he will not be receiving mail. He will not even be at MCRD on S-10, this coming Sunday, they transport back to Camp Pendleton. My only solace and hope is that training week 10 and 11 is so busy and hectic that time will just be flying by for my Drew.

Today I confirmed the hotel reservations in San Diego. I was happy to find that we have two swimming pools and two jacuzzis. Gosh. What a diametrically opposed set of accommodations that Drew's family will have in San Diego for one week, compared to what he endured for the past thirteen weeks. The Marine recruit sustained the torture of watching people come and go from the San Diego International Airport and I am worried about whether or not Drew's mother will be satisfied with her water-front view.

25 May 2016

T56, Wednesday

Dear Drew,

Funny how I just realized how I begin each letter - Dear Drew - calling you by your first name - something you have probably not heard since leaving home. Probably forgot what it sounds like. Fortunately you have a pretty nice sounding last name or in the case of some like Cooper Klett, who got blessed to have it as a first. The great Peyton Manning has a brother named Cooper. Cooper is German - for a barrel maker - that's why I like having wooden barrels around.

My friend, Matt Fasbender has pointed out our connection as Fasbender is German for the occupational name for a Cooper.

Museum visit and travel today, what museum? And what travel?

Soon you get that as a Marine. Semper Fi. How f-ing cool!!!!

Tomorrow you have final physical fitness test. It will be interesting to see how your initial scores/ reps midway and final scores compare.

I have such anxiety over the gas chamber. You are too cool and brave for it to be a problem.

I am betting you had fun at the Crucible. I cannot believe we leave next week.

I can't wait to drink some Busch Light tall boys at the pond with a big bonfire. I am not drinking a beer until I can pop one open with you.

Love you. Keep tearing the shit up.

Love, Dad

Wednesday
May 25

Dearest Drew -

Oh boy am I getting excited to see you! I am missing you big time! You are such a special guy. I am so proud of you.

I have saved the fruit stickers on the trim in the kitchen. I have now decided I will leave it alone forever. Sometimes I'll look up at them and shake my head and smile. What's a mom to do? You are the king of putting your garbage in odd places. Will being a Marine change that?

Today is Omi's birthday. She was so happy about your note she said she's going to frame it.

My step mom, Deb, sent me a picture of my dad's head-stone. In front of it is a picture of my grandpa's stone. I guess it's his old stone. When my grandma died a new stone was purchased with both of their names on it. Dad has kept his Dad's old stone. My grandpa died at 54. Just a few years older than me. He had lung cancer. My mom's dad also died of lung cancer and my dad's sister died in her 40s from lung cancer.

My grandpa's full name is - was - Edward Theodore Niedzwiecki. A great name. I have nice memories of him. Everyone says he and my grandma were very good people. I am overly jealous of people who get to adulthood and still have grandparents. I just have childhood memories of all of mine. Longevity does not run in my family.

I have today off. Much needed. Going to clean and go get some flowers for my pots. Also putting together some fairy gardens. I've been looking for an old red rusty radio flyer wagon to make a fairy garden. I have an old bird bath I'm gong to make one there, too. Dad said on graduation day you are done about noon.

Been thinking about what you want to do? Do you want to go to San Diego's famous Mission Beach and swim in ocean?

At least briefly? Do you want to zone out at our hotel's 2 exotic pools?

I need to go cuz dad is ready to go to office.

I hope good things happen to you today.

Love you bigger than space!

Mom

* * * * *

My anxiety now relates to the upcoming gas chamber. I imagine this environment is much like any other environment where people are talking about things and trying to help one another. I imagine there are occasions where they see people who have gone through it before. I recall Drew talking about his recruiters talking about the gas chamber. Be calm, cool and collective and you will get through it.

I would imagine that there is a lot of talk about and helping one another when it comes to upcoming events that are causing stress and anxiety. What a week to deal with, to get through all of the final tests. Then, next week is the Crucible. The anxiety and difficulty that I am having right now relates to the inability to talk with Drew and try to give him pointers or advice. But who in the hell am I to give someone advice about getting through the gas chamber. Dang. I am just so proud of him and cannot wait to see him.

Throughout this entire period, Drew's siblings only see parents that are exuding pride and admiration for their child and their sibling. How do they not some time in the future, join the military service. What an incredible way to not just honor thyself, but to give honor, respect and commitment to our country. Honor, respect, being a Marine – it develops an incredibly well-rounded person and provides them with a badge of honor that they can then carry for the rest of their lives.

My cellphone is ringing just as I am heading into a meeting.

I can see that it is a San Diego telephone number – identified as such on my phone. My stomach drops to the floor as I take the call. It's Drew! Oh my God. Is he injured? Is he hurt? Does he have problems? What is the situation? I find out that they are given an opportunity to call so as to make sure that all of their travel arrangements have been made.

How exciting! I just finished writing him a letter and posing questions in the letter. Obviously, I am having anxiety over the Crucible and the Gas Chamber, how Drew is feeling, and whether he is prepared. How incredible to have received a call from him.

He is feeling great. He is ready for the Crucible and he is completely ready for the gas chamber. The reason that he was allowed to call me today was because they are making sure that his travel arrangements are taken care. I reminded Drew that I sent him a letter with his airplane ticket. Drew indicated that he was aware of the ticket and had received it. However, he was taking advantage of the opportunity to call me. How awesome. My heart is racing and I feel so good. Drew is feeling good and is all excited and ready to be done.

* * * * *

26 May 2016
T57
Thursday

Dear Drew,

It was so exciting for me to get a telephone call from you yesterday. The highlight of the month for sure. You sounded great. Strong. Confident. You spoke so clearly and were so easily understood. Now we just need to have Anella learn how to speak. I cannot understand 85% of what she says on the phone.

About ½ hour before you called I was telling your mother I am just beside myself worrying about the gas chamber and the Crucible. I know you will do great, but, I wanted to know how you are feeling and whether you are hampered with any injuries. Awesome to hear you feel good - feel strong and are not worried about Crucible or gas chamber.

I am sorry I got you in trouble for sending some candy. I have not sent anything I am not supposed to since you told me to stop.

When you called it was 5:30 a.m. your time. I bet you have enjoyed becoming accustomed to a new time schedule. I told so many people about hearing from you - so exciting. The timing just could not have been better. Such a big relief for me and my concerns about gas chamber and the Crucible.

Words cannot express the pride I am feeling. Thank you for being such a fuckin STUD. Love you.

Love, Dad

* * * * *

Thursday
May 26

Dearest Drew -

Man did you freak out your dad yesterday with the phone call. He said it was so nice to hear your voice. He said you sounded really good. We will get your letter about your thoughts on tattoo and work on it. It will all be OK.

The French Open Tennis is on now, the next 2 weeks. Since they are 6 hours ahead I can catch matches in the morning though bummer to have to go to work. I could watch tennis all day. I had day off yesterday and enjoyed very much. Took Buck to pond for hour and half. He's so cute now he just goes in and swims around.

He's sleeping on his back on the couch with his legs sticking up in air. Remember when Uncle Todd thought you named him Fuck.

Suppose to have rain today. We are warmer here than in San Diego. That surprises me.

Bennett has district golf today He gets to miss full day of school.

Dad's been into wearing tie clips. His new thing. He's so weird.

Teja gave Anella a nice necklace for her birthday. He couldn't wait. She said he's never given a gift before.

Gotta go Dad's ready to leave.

Love you bigger than space!

Mom

Can't wait to see you very soon!

* * * * *

I still have exhilaration from having the opportunity to talk with Drew as I was not expecting that phone call. Talk about highs and lows. Seeing the call coming in—the worry and immediate anxiety of receiving a call from San Diego when I have been, for the last several weeks, worried about getting a bad phone call; to having such an exhilarating conversation. It is just so incredible.

Regardless, I still have anxiety over the gas chamber. My understanding is that you go into the chamber with your gas mask on and the room fills with gas. The point is to not hold your breath, but take your mask off, breath in the gas and then you are allowed to leave. I understand that they are asking you to experience the gas. The thing you do not want to do is to hold your breath because when you remove your mask, you will be sucking in more gas, which will become a problem.

I am not sure about this and am anxious to have Drew clarify the situation.

I have really enjoyed Drew's statement about how I have to stop sending him the candy; it is getting him in trouble. However, he did comment that he loved the candy bars.

Upon conveying my discussion with Chuck, Chuck shared the story about how mamas would send cookies and the drill instructors would have the recruit take one bite so they could be sure it was not poisoned. Once they knew it was good to eat, the drill instructors all enjoyed mama's cookies.

* * * * *

A couple times I have ran into a guy who is from South Haven. He is also in LIMA company, Platoon 3245. I think there are six platoons in LIMA. Isn't that weird though? We just got to talking once and found out we came from the same place. He must have been dropped to LIMA because he wasn't on the plane ride here with me. But, it gets even more crazy. He recognized the name Cooper because apparently Casey Cooper is always over at his house to hang out with his little brother. His name was Rooker, or maybe its spelled Ruker. I don't know, but that's his name in case you mention it to Uncle Dick or something.

I don't think that the tat design sent is really my style. It looks like it came out of Lord of the Rings, and I love Lord of the Rings, but not on my body forever. The anchor sword was a good idea, but now that I see it, the mash up looks kind of weird. Too much stuff in one thing. I thought we were getting the one from Anella's book. I like that one. Let's not get it in San Diego if it will take up most of our time that Friday. If we get

it in Kzoo, let's NOT go to Body Armor, Art & Soul, or
Crazy Monkey.

Crazy Monkey is good for spur of the moment
things like my forearm tattoos, but not if we schedule
it. I don't know, maybe Crazy Monkey would be fine.
Let's get the tattoo together.

Probably in Kzoo, but it would be cool to get it in
San Diego. A simple design. Old school style, like from
Anella's book, the one I was sent is too much.

ANSWERS TO QUESTIONNAIRE

1. I Drew, am firm in my desire that the five of us go to the
tattoo parlor and have our tats done at the same time. (Keep in
mind that five people and one artist will take hours).

__X__ Yes _____ No

Or, we can find a parlor with 5 artists.

__X__ Yes _____ No

In San Diego?

_____ Yes _____ No

Comments:_____

_____

2. I am fine with the four of you getting your tattoo's done
and scheduling me to come in and have the same one done by
the same artist some time Friday after graduation.

_____ Yes __X__ No

Comments:_____

_____

3. See if you can find a parlor that has a number of artists
and all five of us can be scheduled to have ours done on Friday

after graduation.

_____ Yes   _____ No

Comments: Sure

4. I think that we should have all five of us scheduled to do our tattoos in Kalamazoo, after we get home from graduation because I do not care if we do it in San Diego.

_____ Yes   _____ No

Comments: Sure. I think we should get the dagger from Anella's tattoo book. The one I was sent might be too complicated for the size we are thinking. And it's not really my style. It seems a little too fantasy for me. I wanted an old school style tattoo. I don't really like anything new school. I just think its too loud with the whole anchor-sword mash up with the complicated blade. I really liked the one from Anella's book. I just want something simple. Nothing complicated or gaudy. Just really simple and old school style.

*   *   *   *   *

The relief I felt after receiving the telephone call on 25 May is only accentuated by the letter I received from Drew today (26 May 2016). The letter is really generic. To me, this is an indication that he is doing okay and is just moving through the Matrix and recruit training. He is speaking in just a normal tone and dealing with the issue at hand in a manner that is calm, cool and collected. There is not a sense of urgency, nor an expression of needing help or complaint or distress.

It is nice to know that he is not concerned about getting through the gas chamber test, nor is he all that worried about the Crucible. He is healthy and feeling good. He is probably as happy as one could be under the circumstances. There is probably not much more one could ask at this stage of the process.

As training week 10 comes to an end, Drew will have his final repel down a fast rope and have the commander's inspection on Saturday. On Sunday, S-10, they move back to Camp Pendleton for the final week of training. Given the telephone call and his last letter, my feelings are of confidence and pride. What a wonderful feeling to have going into Memorial Day weekend. We are looking forward to the upcoming memorial dedications and Monday's parade. At the same time, Drew and his fellow recruits will undergo the gas chamber test.

* * * * *

Friday
May 27
T58
Dear Drew,

Holy cow - you only have 1 training week left. By the time you get this letter the Crucible is over. Congratulations!!! I can't wait to hear all about it.

Cold beer here - cold beer here. I can smell it and taste it. I cannot wait to pop some chilly ones with you.

At the Memorial Day Parade and service this year, I will be thinking of you and the gas chamber test. On the Matrix - Monday - Memorial Day is T60 and the gas chamber.

I saw Joe Muvrin this morning - I was telling him all about you and my great pride for you. Taylor started Tuesday with the Navy boot camp in Chicago. I told him the joke Senator John McCain likes to tell. Senator McCain is a war hero. He was in the Navy. A POW for years in Vietnam. He likes to say "I wanted to join the Marines; but, my parents were still married". The joke being that Marines come from broken homes. Senator McCain's son - a Marine - responds by saying "yea - you know how the Marine Corps is a department of the Navy? –Yes - the Mens Department".

I am looking forward to sitting at the pond with a bonfire and hearing from you some Marine history stories. I am trying to study some of the incredible historical events - different battles and war stories. I bet you have learned so much. The Marine Corps is rich with history.

Very soon you will be a Marine. Before you know it you will be home running off the dock with Buck nipping at your ass.

Stay strong. Good luck finishing this out. Be proud. You have so much to feel great about.

Love you Drew.

Love, Dad

* * * * *

Friday
May 27

Dearest Drew-

Man oh man, buddy boy. Not long now. Holiday weekend coming up. So proud of you!

We will work on tattoo. Yes, all 5 of us together.

Everyone says you need to wear your dress blues home. We get back to Kalamazoo at decent time. Have to drop off Grandpa and it will be so cool for Grandma to see you in your uniform. She will be so proud and that will mean a lot to her.

So many people say that San Diego is their favorite city ever. Wonder while you're at Pendleton will you have time off to see stuff.

Bennett had district golf yesterday. He did really well. Was only few strokes shy of a medal. He and Nick are moving on to regionals next Thursday. He had one shot, a par 5 near clubhouse, all coaches watching. He had 3 shots down fairway to green. He was about 20-30 yards away and hit the ball with his chipping club and it bounced a few times and then bounced right into the hole. The spectators all started clapping.

The movers are bringing my brother Mark's things to the house on West Lake today. He is still in China until end of June. Todd went to Detroit yesterday to pick up the cat. He's bringing the cat here this morning for me to watch until Tuesday when the house officially closes. The sellers are graciously allowing his things to go into house now as his lease is up end of month which is this week.

Apparently the Cubs are off to great start. Just FYI.

I'm going to do yard work this morning and then do some shopping. Have list of errands and grocery list.

Tomorrow is Austin's open house 12-4. We are going to stop there on way to Chicago. Bennett can't believe he's going to see Tom Petty.

Think of you always!

Love you bigger than space!

Mom

Drew, center, marches with his platoon on Family Day.

CHAPTER 12
TOLSTOY AND THE CRUCIBLE
"GAS MASKS, THEN WORKING TOWARDS OUR EAGLE, GLOBE AND ANCHOR"

Training week 11 is gas mask and Crucible.

I have been trying to study some of the historic Marine battles that have recognizable names in society. For example, Iwo Jima, Guadalcanal, Okinawa and Tarawa. There are of course, numerous World War II events such as D-Day and the Battle of the Bulge.

Someone like me will never understand what a soldier experiences and endures of the likes that were at the Beaches of Normandy, fought in the Argonne Forest; endured in the Battle of Bladensburg; the Battle of New Orleans; the Battle of Belleau Wood; the Battle of Wake Island; the Battle of Guadalcanal; the Battle of Tarawa; the Battle of Mariana Islands; the Battle of Iwo Jima; the Battle of Okinawa; the Battle of the Chosin Reservoir; the Second Battle of Khe Sanh; the Battle of Hue City; or those who went to Korea, Vietnam, or fought in the middle East in places like the Bloody Triangle in Iraq and the Mountain Terrain of Afghanistan.

Never will I understand what Steve Haddad endured in Vietnam. Steve left MCRD San Diego in 1967 and endured two years in Vietnam. Steve is the recipient of three Purple Hearts and the Navy Cross. The highest award bestowed upon a person is the Medal of Honor. Keep in mind that this is most often given to someone who was killed in combat performing heroic measures.

The next highest is the Navy Cross. Steve received it due to his life-saving heroic decisions and actions in a bunker under heavy attack by ground fire and grenades in the jungles of Vietnam. Steve is a true hero and someone that I had known for years as the front desk clerk at the local branch of the United States Post Office and one that I have developed a very nice friendship with.

I had never learned of his heroic awards until years into

our friendship and not until after I became part of the Marine Corps family; through my son, Drew. Not until I was part of the Marine Corps family did Steve tell me he was a Marine.

During World War II, people would think there was something wrong with you if you were not in the service. Some where along the lines, society looked down upon those that joined the service. Now, people like me who did not have the honor, privilege or the true understanding of what servicemembers have sacrificed and have given, an incredible honor for their children joining the service. This honor is only tempered by the worry given that the situation is a dramatic and drastic unknown.

Today is 30 May 2016 – Memorial Day. The family went to the Memorial Day Parade and service in Veteran's Park in Paw Paw, Michigan.

Matt poses with Marine Steve Haddad, who wrote the foreword for this book. Steve received numerous medals for his service during the Vietnam War.

* * * * *

We were prepared for the gas chamber through instruction in the bleachers right outside of the gas chamber. We were first handed our gas masks and put them on as we were led into the gas chamber, which was large enough to hold the entire platoon. We lined up against the far wall. Then they mixed the chemicals in the middle of the room and the gas came out.

You were told to keep your eyes open and breathe through the gas mask. Then you were told to pull the gas mask away from your face and you held it there 15 seconds; but, they do not start the time until they see and confirm that everyone has the gas mask away from their face. So it is actually longer than 15 seconds. You were under the impression you were going to just breathe slowly and not hold your breath.

The way it works when you go in is you are in one line. They open the door and from the time they tell you to get in the gas chamber until you are in the gas chamber you have 7 to 9 seconds to get your gas mask on. Because it is in the gas mask bag like a carrier around your waist and on your side. So they give the word and you pull it out and get it on and you have 7 to 9 seconds to get it on your face.

I got it on my face fine, but then as I was walking in the DI yanked it off my face. Then after you held it away from your face they told you to put it back on your face and you blew out hard to clear the filter. You have to put your hands over the thing in the front so the gas could clear out. So the gas would clear out and you would blow out. Then you were told again to completely remove the gas mask.

You were going to slowly breathe through your

mouth and through your nose, and it felt like shredded crystallized glass and burning, crystallized glass that was on fire. You were coughing through your mouth so you tried to breathe through your nose, and coughing caused you to empty your lungs. It was hard to keep your eyes open because it felt like they were swelling up. You need to keep your eyes open, so you could see them.

We were not instructed to keep our eyes open, but you had to keep them open to see them to know when to put your gas mask back on. It felt like forever when we were breathing in the gas. We had to keep the gas mask out in front of us much longer and hold it away from our face. Then after you were allowed to put the gas mask back on you were told to clear it. Some of the people threw up in their gas masks, it was like they actually threw up all in their face. Then when you take it off and come back out you rinse it in a chlorine solution, soapy solution and then clear water.

Then they take you back to your squad bay, and you are allowed to shower. That is gas chamber round 2. The idea is to take a cold shower because the hot shower will open your pores up and you relive the whole gas chamber over again. The gas sticks to your skin and burns your skin. We went in with buttoned down sleeves around our wrists to minimize the exposure to the skin.

You cannot wear contact lenses because they will scratch the cornea of your eyes and blind you. They said if you wear contacts they melt to your eyeball, but that is not true, it is something they say to scare you, but it hardens the contact and they shatter and scratch your retina.

So the key is to limit the exposure of your skin and

to breathe slowly through your nose and mouth so you are not trying to hold your breath because if you hold your breath they will make you have your mask off for a longer period of time than you can hold your breath and you are going to end up sucking in a lot of gas when you gasp for air.

A lot of guys did the power breathing that we learned in swim week when we had to float. We had our cami's and our boots on in the pool and we had to float on our backs for as long as they made us. You have to fill your lungs up with air as much as you can so you can float in the pool. You are trying to keep your lungs filled with air and just taking it in and out in little bursts.

So after the shower we had all our clothes that were exposed to gas laundered. We took them out to the wash racks behind every squad bay, it was just like a big cement sink basically and faucets all down the line. We took our scuds brushes which we use to sweep the floor on our hands and knees a few times a day. The soap runner would run by with laundry detergent and pour it on top of our cami's and we would scrub them and rinse them off and there were some things we hung them on to dry.

*   *   *   *   *

Drew went to his gas chamber test. We went to a parade. At the parade, I ran into an old friend who asked about Drew. His son graduated high school the same year as Drew. Throughout Drew's thirteen weeks at MCRD, this particular friend and I ran into each other several times. On each occasion he has asked with interest about Drew and his recruit training. This friend is a Veteran of the United States Army.

I can just feel the envy from this gentleman, wishing that his son too, would join a branch of the military service. I saw him before the parade and after the celebration at Veteran's park. On both occasions, he asked that when Drew is on leave between recruit training and infantry school that he be allowed to buy us dinner and have Drew meet with his son.

While Drew went to high school with this young man, the two were not necessarily close friends. However, they obviously know one another. I do not think a father can be more proud of their child than having them succeed in their service to our Nation. I can just feel the envy gushing from this friend and desire to have Drew meet with his son and perhaps have some of that need for fulfilling military service rub off.

I honestly believe that Drew has started down a path that will allow him to wear a badge of honor for the rest of his life.

*   *   *   *   *

31 May 2016
T-61
Tuesday

Dear Drew,

Yesterday you completed the gas chamber test. It really helped me having the opportunity to talk with you about it and you were not concerned. Hopefully it went as you planned. Today is T-61 and you start the Crucible. I really think that you are going to enjoy it. It is my understanding that you are only given three MREs for the entire event. I hope that you do not eat them all at once.

Matt Fasbender's son, Alex, told him that someone in his platoon ate all three MREs on the first day and the DI's would not let anyone share with him throughout the rest because he was such an idiot for having eaten them all at once and that if he passed out from exhaustion and starvation that was his problem and he would be dropped and allowed to try it again – this time without being so stupid.

We are leaving this week. I cannot believe that it is Tuesday. We need to start packing and getting everything in order for our departure on Saturday morning. It is incredible to look at the Matrix and see that we are leaving this Saturday. I have marked that next Saturday you will be home. Can you believe that? Look at how much you will accomplish this week and next! It is simply incredible to think that you will be home next week.

This is the last letter that I am writing to you. You have indicated in your last letter that you have a number of letters that you have not even been able to read yet. I doubt you will be able to read any letters this week. In fact, you are probably not getting this letter until the beginning of next week. I cannot believe that I am able to say that this is my last letter to you.

I am so very proud of you. I cannot wait to see you.

Love,

Dad

Love you Mister !! So very very proud. Love, Dad

* * * * *

Today is Memorial Day 2016. How many people actually understand the difference between our Country's celebration of Memorial Day and Veteran's Day? Worrying, worrying, worrying. Now I am worried about when Drew comes home, how he is going to feel about what he has gotten himself into. Is he going to feel the pride of being a part of the few and the proud? I think it is time to let the worry go because the road ahead is long and he is going to travel the world. You cannot continue to worry and worry.

Someone like me will never know the price paid by soldiers that experienced going to Normandy, and Iwo Jima. While those of my generation that did not serve may never know the price paid, we certainly can be allowed to worry for our children. On Memorial Day, Drew endured the gas chamber test. Tuesday, 31 May (T-61), Drew starts on his three-day journey of the Crucible. It is my understanding at this point, the recruits for the last few weeks have been talking about nothing else. I have come to understand through my discussions with Chuck that it actually becomes anti-climatic.

Everything they do in the Crucible is something that they have already done. This however, tests their ability to endure exhaustion, hunger and everything that they have done in the past is done under the test of a different endurance level. They must endure the hunger, the lack of sleep and the complete exhaustion of their musculature. There are a number of things that must be accomplished and can only be accomplished as a team. Ammunition cans can get across the ditch or over the wall only if they work together as a team.

At the end of the third day, they come across their finish line and back into Camp where they are awarded their Marine Emblem (the Eagle, Globe and Anchor (EGA), that they will accept as a sign of their acceptance into the few and proud—the United States Marine Corps. That evening, they will receive the Warrior's Meal, which ends their training days on T-63.

* * * * *

So we got a full eight hours of sleep the night before the Crucible. If you had fire watch, which I had fire watch that night, you only got seven, maybe six cause they woke us up pretty early. We were not very comfortable because we were sleeping on Isomats, which are basically yoga mats. We were in a pole barn-type building, sleeping on Isomats on a concrete floor and were allowed to use sleeping bags.

We usually would keep them in our main packs, but

we would use them during field week and Crucible. So we were in there. During field week and Crucible we had to sleep in our sleeping bags on our Isomats with our weapon. The M-16 was inside our sleeping bag with us the whole time. It was not that uncomfortable actually.

They woke us up the same as always, lights, lights, lights, lights. We stood up on our mats with our weapons in our hand. We got dressed really fast. My platoon was the last platoon to leave to start doing the Crucible stations, so while we were waiting for all the other platoons to go, we just sat down on the floor in the hooches (that is what we called the pole barns), we sat down and cleaned our weapons for maybe 45 minutes before we stepped off. All the other platoons were gone so we stepped off.

Each station had a paragraph, we called them citations. It was a paragraph about a Marine, who had won a Silver Star or Medal of Honor or Navy Cross—most of whom had died while earning them. The DI would read it, and we would be standing at attention, about the marine and what he did to earn whatever award he got.

We would take out our canteens. If it was a station about Smedly Butler, and he would state here is a toast to Smedly Butler, and we would all say toast to Smedly Butler and we would lift our canteens and take a drink of water. Then whatever station we were on they would try to base it on what the Marine had done to earn it.

So the first one, the Marine carried a bunch of wounded Marines away from danger so they could be evacuated from the combat zone and fixed up, so we just buddy dragged back and forth and back and forth.

Then we got to do some shooting, and we each got to

shoot 10 rounds. They were unknown distances too, so like at the rifle range when we would shoot we would know the distances, but this one there would be targets that popped up and if you shoot them they would go down. They were unknown distances so we would have to figure it out ourselves.

On our Acogs (scope) there is a line going down for distances, like there is a vertical line with hash marks on it. The way you figure out distance, how far away a target is, is the hash marks on the vertical lines, like the length of them equals the average width of a man's shoulder is whatever distance it is, the target is, so you would have to line it up with the target shoulders and whichever one was closest that is the line we would aim with. I did pretty good on that.

After that we got searched. Every time we shot we would get searched thoroughly for any brass. We all got three MRE's for the entire crucible. A lot of people ate a snack after the shooting, but I ate a pack of peanut butter, a cracker and tootsie rolls the first day, so I had a lot of food left for the second day.

After the shooting we did boxing, body boxing. They would yell at you for hitting in the face, but as the fights progressed they were getting excited when people were hitting each other in the face. While two people were boxing the rest of the platoon were in a circle outside of the octagon we were fighting in. There were signs up for different exercises, like one for pushups, jumping jacks, squats, and some for elite hand punch and rear hand punch, different MCMAP moves and so we would do that and when the fight ended we would switch stations.

After that we did the chillest station of the entire Crucible, which was the IED station, where they had different fake IED's set up on a table so we could see what they looked like. Then we just walked down like a gravel road trying to spot IED's they had set up. The whole time we were in full gear with our weapons, Kevlar, and not our full gear, just our day gear, which is like a back pack. If you stepped on an IED it would make a buzzing sound, and then the instructor would gather you around and teach you about the IED.

Then after that, shit basically just hit the fan. Stations were just really hard things you had to do. It was in the morning still. We did this one obstacle where there were three different platforms and we had to swing from one platform to the other and then the other platform on a rope. I was really surprised because there were only two people in my platoon actually made it across. It was me and one of the squad leaders. For some reason everyone else just could not make it across. There was another one next to that one, it was like a 12 to 15 foot wall and we had to get everyone over it.

There was a rope swing that only me and the other squad leader could do. There was a rope hanging in the middle, and there is one platform, and you get on it with a rope, and there are two more platforms, like in a triangle. You have to swing to the one on the left and then swing to the last one. The other guys couldn't do it because they would swing, but they would not swing towards the platform. It is kind of a weird angle. I did my first swing and did not swing near the other platforms. I swung back and I was still on the first platform, then I just kind of figured it out.

Then there was the John Basilone challenge. There were four man fire teams. There is one person who was doing covering fire the whole time, providing secu-

rity. Two people were carrying two ammo cans, one in each hand, and the fourth person was carrying a really large ammo can. We had to go up this really steep hill. If we got too far apart from each other they would tell us to go back down, so we stayed really tight. So we would not have to go back down, and it was really easy. When we got to the top of the hill we got in security positions on the top of hill to provide security. When they blew the whistle we had to run to where we left the ammo cans at when we got to the top and bring them over to the people running ammo cans.

There was one station that was pretty fun, just different obstacles.

The telephone pole station really sucked, probably the worst one. It was the second day. It was a bitch. The telephone poles are really heavy, and you get four people per pole, and they do not organize them according to equal height. We had like a real tall person. We had to carry them 20 to 40 yards and then do an exercise. Like they would have to squat, and they would say down, and you had to stay down until everyone got down and they would say up, and we would get up. Then you would like have to push it up over your head and stuff, and then we would do curls where you would have to curl it down and up.

The first evening we got back to the hooches. They made us field hygiene, we had our field hygiene kits, which was toothbrush, toothpaste, razor and baby wipes. I did not have toothpaste because mine exploded, so I threw it away it was all nasty, so I borrowed some to brush my teeth, and I borrowed shave cream to shave my face.

We take our shirts off and go back behind the hooches. They said take one baby wipe out and wipe your armpits. *Take one baby wipe out and wipe your chest. Take one baby wipe out and wipe your junk and ass crack. Then we would throw away our baby wipes. We went to bed fully dressed the second night. We were wearing our full cami's blouse trousers, and socks, but we did not have our boots on. The night before the Crucible we went to bed normal, and the first night of the Crucible we went to bed like that, got four hours of sleep.*

So the second morning, the second day, we got up just like the first day. There was an assault course. We did more stations and telephone poles. There is one station that was really fun, they had probably like 12 different scenarios set up. There were wooden walls separating them all. This is the second day. We spent two to three hours at this station. There was one scenario that had two beams and a pipe going over the beams to simulate a middle part of a bridge that was broken, there was one pipe on the side we were on and one on the far side, and a rope and a barrel. Our job in the scenario was to get the barrel onto the other side of the bridge. We couldn't touch underneath the bridge.

There were rules for each scenario and places we could not touch. If they caught us touching it or breaking any of the rules they would make us sprint with ammo cans. So we had to prop the first pipe up on the middle part of the bridge and shimmy up it, and then move it to the other side to get the other pipe, so we had a pipe leaning against the middle of the bridge on both sides.

Then we had to get the barrel across, we had one person push it up and the other person in the middle grab it. Then we had to get everyone in our group across the bridge. There was another one with a big drainage pipe we had to crawl through and rescue some dummies that were injured and get them out and to safety. There were a bunch of different stations like that.

With 287 people it takes a long time to work through all of these stations. We did not all do them in the same order. While we were doing one station another platoon was doing a different one we had already done or we still had to do. Your platoon had 54 people. We did pugel sticks in the Crucible too, that was fun. The second night of the Crucible we went to sleep and we got maybe a little more than two hours of sleep.

All night we did not get any sleep as we were cleaning weapons and doing a bunch of hiking. We would have to hike so far to get from one station to the next station. That is how we walked or ran, so it was like 73-75 miles. So that is what was taking up a lot of time is doing 73 miles. The first night we went on a night hike. We did not have to bring any packs with us, but we had our weapons. It was a 4 mile hike. The first lead series each person had two ammo cans and the way back each person had to carry two ammo cans.

The first night we got about 4 hours of sleep. The second night we got 2 hours of sleep. The morning of the Reaper hike we got up at 2:30 a.m. and left at 3 to hike to the Reaper, I think 6 miles. We got there as the sun was rising. We climbed the Reaper and then did the Eagle Globe and Anchor ceremony and then we got to hike all the way back, not to the hooches but to the actual squad bay and we did the Warrior's Breakfast.

The Warrior's Breakfast, at the show hall at Camp Pendleton, was the same as usual breakfast layout, except they had steak, and some really good cake. We were allowed to go up for seconds too. A lot of people puked. There were a bunch of civilians there and we could sit and talk with them as well. Our drill instructors sat with us too, so we were able to talk to our drill instructors. I talked with my Senior DI about the new tattoo policy.

* * * * *

The next day is M-1 and they are back to the reality of the mundane and turning in all of their gear. M-2 is Saturday and they transport back to MCRD in San Diego.

S-11 marks their last Sunday worship service. They have to be feeling so proud and fulfilled in what they have achieved. Does it seem like the time has flown by, or are they ready to get the hell out of there?

I will have sent my last letters to him at the beginning of this week. I figured that my last letter to him would be on the day of the beginning of the Crucible. He had indicated that there were letters that he has yet to have read and I doubt he will read any this week and I will let him get caught up on his reading throughout the week.

CHAPTER 13
GETTING THROUGH THE M'S / MARINE WEEK
"CHILLING BUT SUCKED. MOVE MOVE MOVE – FAST. MOVE FAST, FAST, FAST, FAST...THEN WAIT... WAIT... WAIT... WAIT... WAIT..."

Matt, Laurie, Bennett and Anella at Family Day.

Training week 12 is your M week. Just when you think things will calm down a little, training week 12 is very hectic. We have to move fast that week for some reason. They would always tell us you better be the first ones there, but what happens if you are the first ones there then you are just waiting around for the rest of the company to get done, with chow or something and get there.

* * * * *

These new recruits have gone through so much so fast. Beyond the physical and mental exhaustion, there has to be an additional overload—an overwhelming experience of what they have done and where they are going. Do they get a feeling of being expendable after graduation? They don't even go back into the barracks.

Every Thursday is a family day and every Friday a group is graduating and they get their bags outside the barracks because there is a need for another group coming in. Every Monday there is a recruit standing at the yellow footprints. Every Friday, there is a Black Friday for those recruits just getting started and a Friday graduation for those finishing. How many started pick up week with Drew and are now looking like Marines and looking forward to graduation?

Attending Family Day and graduation at MCRD San Diego was a highlight of my life. Family Day was exceptional and the graduation ceremony was compelling. Thank you USMC.

Quite an accomplishment: and just the beginning.
Semper Fi.

During Family Day (the day before graduation) Drew and Matt embrace after weeks of Marine training.

65530684R00179

Made in the USA
Lexington, KY
15 July 2017